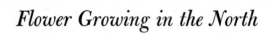

Flower Growing in the North

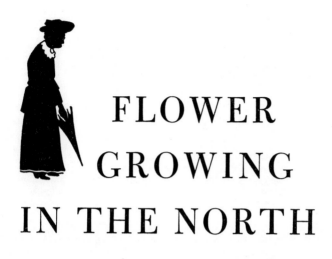

FLOWER GROWING IN THE NORTH

A Month-by-Month Guide

by George E. Luxton

University of Minnesota Press, Minneapolis

PRINTED AT THE LUND PRESS, INC., MINNEAPOLIS

Library of Congress Catalog Card Number: 56-11613

PUBLISHED IN GREAT BRITAIN, INDIA, AND PAKISTAN BY GEOFFREY CUMBERLEGE:
OXFORD UNIVERSITY PRESS, LONDON, BOMBAY, AND KARACHI

SECOND PRINTING 1957

To my wife

ADA

whose help and constant interest
through the years have made
this book possible

❧ PREFACE ❧

My love for the earth and the things that grow in it began many years ago in Grandma's garden and on her little farm near London, Ontario. And with the love for the earth came the knowledge gained from the rich store of Grandma's gardening experience. Her eyes were keen and her wit was sound; what I learned from her was fundamentally true and has stood me in good stead over the years.

To Grandma's knowledge I have added gleanings from other amateur gardeners and hints from useful books and magazines. I have profited from lectures at our University of Minnesota and from memberships in garden clubs and societies. Perhaps by far the most important experience was gained in my own garden.

The other amateurs who have aided me are numberless. Many of them have written to me after reading my column in the Minneapolis Sunday *Tribune* to add their own ideas to mine. Their suggestions I have found very valuable, and my heart has been warmed by their interest and their eagerness to share.

Many professional gardeners — including nurserymen, florists, and seed experts who have hastened to inform me of new discoveries in the horticultural world—have also been of immense help. Among them are Dr. Leon C. Snyder, head of the Department of Horticulture at the University of Minnesota, and members of the department, including O. C. Turnquist, J. D. Winter, R. E. Widmer, R. J. Stadtherr, C. G. Hard, and A. E. Hutchins. Carl Holst, rosarian of the Minneapolis municipal rose garden at Lyndale Park, has shared with me his priceless knowledge of roses.

I am most grateful, too, to Dr. A. Orville Dahl, chairman of the

PREFACE

Department of Botany at the University of Minnesota, who, at the publisher's request, checked the final manuscript of this book for accuracy. I gladly express my thanks too to the staff of the University of Minnesota Press, whose cooperation and patience have helped to produce this book.

And finally, I here acknowledge my appreciation and gratitude to the Minneapolis Star and Tribune Company for generously granting me and the publisher permission to incorporate in this book much material that originally appeared in print in the Minneapolis Sunday *Tribune,* including the silhouette of Grandma which has been a feature of my weekly columns in that paper for many years.

GEORGE E. LUXTON

☙ CONTENTS ☙

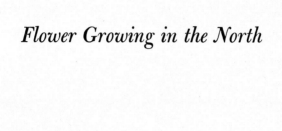

Flower Growing in the North

☙ JANUARY ☙

HERE in the North, January is usually the coldest winter month. Heavy snows and subzero cold keep us indoors most of the time, yet an ardent gardener can already see signs that spring is not too far away. The shortest day of winter is past and very gradually the days grow longer. Every day the sun is brighter and warmer as it climbs higher in the sky. Christmas and the winter holidays are over, and in a few weeks the seed and nursery catalogs will be arriving.

WINTER CHORES OUTDOORS

With Christmas over, the discarded Christmas tree can still bring pleasure and be of use outdoors. As soon as the needles seem dry and begin to drop, get the tree outside quickly. Indoors it can be a fire hazard and burn with almost explosive force. Outdoors you can set it up on the most sheltered side of the house as a bird feeding station.

Another use for your discarded Christmas tree — or you might ask your neighbor to give you his — is for completing the winter protection of your roses.

Last fall you should have hilled a mound of earth around the base of each rosebush to protect the roots. When this hilled earth is solidly frozen — but preferably before the snow covers the ground — it is time for the next step in their winter protection: covering the hilled mounds and the space between them with an insulating mulch, not to keep the roses warm but to keep them cold and at as even a temperature as possible. It is the alternate thawing and freezing of late winter and early spring that damages the roots.

3

JANUARY

A heavy blanket of marsh hay, straw, or excelsior is fine for this purpose, or a good covering of dry leaves if you happen to have some cached away. Oak leaves are best because they don't mat readily. Whatever material you use, the covering should be from 6 to 10 inches deep and should be held in place by chicken wire or light branches. It is well to include some mothballs to discourage rodents. Evergreen boughs make a good cover because they not only hold in the frost but also permit ventilation, thus preventing mildew.

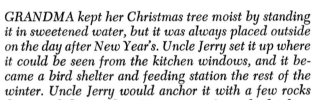

GRANDMA kept her Christmas tree moist by standing it in sweetened water, but it was always placed outside on the day after New Year's. Uncle Jerry set it up where it could be seen from the kitchen windows, and it became a bird shelter and feeding station the rest of the winter. Uncle Jerry would anchor it with a few rocks around the base, and during the winter scraps from the kitchen were placed in the branches for the birds. There was also a big piece of suet tied to the trunk high up. Blue jays and magpies would quarrel over this. Often while they were quarreling, a big crow would come flopping in and gobble it up or carry it away.

If a heavy snowfall comes before you have covered the hilled roses, don't worry. Keep your mulching material stored and ready for use, and when a period of mild, thawing weather arrives you can apply the protective layer of mulch.

A deep blanket of snow can be a wonderful protective cover, though unlike leaves or hay, it can't be counted on to stay put. But deep snow may bring other problems. Rabbits, squirrels, and mice may become very destructive because their usual food is almost unobtainable, and raise havoc with your woody plants. During very severe winter weather, with deep snow, the rodents sometimes will burrow down and girdle or completely sever woody plants at the earth line.

It will pay you to protect shrubbery, young fruit trees, berry canes, grapevines, ornamentals, and evergreens, especially those that were planted in the last few years. This can be done by one or both of two methods. At a seed store you can buy rodent repellents — and deer repellents if needed — that can be painted or sprayed on woody plants where they might be eaten. The lime-sulphur spray used to control scale on trees also acts as a deterrent to rabbits.

The other method is to wrap the trees or shrubs with protective metal collars. During the next mild spell, when the snow has melted, wrap the threatened trees with aluminum foil, the kind used in the kitchen, or with a loose collar of wire netting or hardware cloth, extending from an inch below the soil line (if possible) to a foot above the estimated snow line.

If the snow around your trees, especially the fruit trees, is deep enough so that rabbits can reach the branches, they will eat them also. In fact they seem to prefer the branches. In this case a chicken-wire fence around each tree or group of trees is practical if you can dig far enough down in the snow so the rabbits will not tunnel under it.

If rabbits have already damaged an ornamental tree, you may or may not be able to save it. If the bark has been eaten around the trunk, destroying the inner cambium tissue, the tree will die unless the careful operation of bridge grafting is performed. This work should be done by a tree expert and, unless the tree is valuable, it is perhaps better to plant a new one in the spring and protect it at once from rodents.

If the damage is not severe, the loose bark should be trimmed off neatly and the exposed wood painted with tree paint, obtainable in most seed stores and nurseries. Shellac can be used if tree paint is not obtainable.

Be careful to paint only the exposed wood, not the outer bark — often called the gray bark — nor the thin cambium tissue just under the outer bark, or you may hinder or destroy the growth over the wound. It is from this inner tissue that the new covering is generated.

If shrubbery and vines close to the house are being crushed in a

5

mound of ice from water dripping off the roof, protect them with a temporary eave trough, or a lean-to over the shrubs. A few wide boards may do the trick.

Many deciduous shrubs and trees can be pruned and trimmed now, while they are dormant, if a pleasant January day should arrive and tempt you to spend some time outdoors. But do not prune the spring-blooming shrubs at this time or you will destroy most of next spring's blossoms.

WINTER GARDENING INDOORS

During our long, cold winter, the northern gardener can find much pleasure in growing flowers and foliage plants indoors. At Christmas time such flowering plants as poinsettias, cyclamens, azaleas, hydrangeas, and cinerarias arrive as gifts to make our houses gay with color, and old favorites like African violets, fibrous-rooted begonias, geraniums, ivies, and philodendrons go on giving pleasure year after year. Later on, in the months when different house plants need special attention, I will say more about the special requirements of each plant. Right now let's consider the general needs of your indoor garden.

With longer days and the increasing warmth of the sun, house plants that have been dozing for several months are showing signs of activity. New leaves are beginning to appear on some and tiny buds are forming on others.

These plants will appreciate some special attention. First of all, take the smooth-leaved house plants and the African violets to the kitchen sink. Roll each pot on its side along the edge of the sink and spray the entire plant thoroughly on both sides of the leaves and in the center with tepid water. This will wash off a considerable accumulation of dust and grime and dead leaves.

A special rubber sprayer designed for this work can be purchased in garden stores. The sprinkler used for spraying clothes before ironing will also do the job fairly well. Fill the sprayer from a large pot of water that feels just slightly warm. The water will cool a little before it comes in contact with the leaves.

Never trust water that comes directly from a mixing faucet. The temperature might change and the plants could be hopelessly chilled or cooked. Shake the plants well after sprinkling. If drops of water remain, remove them with cleansing tissue or allow them to dry before placing the plants in the sun.

These shower baths will invigorate the plants, and frequently will rid them of plant lice and other pests. Some home gardeners give their house plants this treatment every two weeks.

GRANDMA knew what to do to keep shrubbery, fruit trees, and evergreens from being crushed by heavy snow. She had Uncle Jerry gently raise and lower the loaded branches from underneath with the back of a snow shovel or broom, thus shaking off the snow without damaging the brittle branches. When the snow was frozen, Uncle had to wait until it had melted a bit. If the branches were bowed out of shape they were propped up with boxes or notched boards for a few weeks.

As plants begin to grow new leaves and flower buds they will require more water and more food, unless the soil in which you potted them last fall was quite rich. However, use judgment in watering. Inspect your plants every day, but do not water unless they really need it. More house plants are killed by overwatering than ever die from thirst.

Most plants should not be watered until the surface of the soil feels dry. Then they should be watered thoroughly — either by watering from above until the water runs out the drainage hole, or from below, by standing the pot in a pan of tepid water until the surface soil is no longer dry. When watering from above, do not get water into the center or crown of the plant, as this might encourage rot. Either method of watering is satisfactory, but never allow a plant to stand in water after its soil is thoroughly soaked. On the other hand, never allow the earth in the pots to get so dry it becomes hard and packed.

7

JANUARY

Small pots need watering more often than large ones, and pots in warm or sunny places more often than those in dark, cool, or humid locations.

There are a few house plants, however, for which dry soil is a greater hazard than overwatering. These include the azalea, cyclamen, and the poinsettia when in leaf. They require the earth they are growing in to be constantly moist and very well drained. Cyclamens should be watered by placing them for half an hour every day in a pail of tepid water reaching halfway up the pot.

Light, temperature, humidity, and some plant food are also important to your house plants. While some plants, such as philodendron, ivy, and ferns, can live in subdued light, sunshine is essential to develop blossoms on geraniums, begonias, and many other flowering plants. During the winter, sunlight is good for African violets, but before long the sun will be too strong and warm.

Flowering plants require an even temperature to produce their most beautiful blooms. In general, a daytime reading of 65 to 70 degrees is best, while at night it must be cooler, just as it is outdoors after the sun goes down. Ideal nighttime temperature is around 55 degrees. If your house plants are growing on window sills, the chances are that the temperature is about right for most of them.

GRANDMA finally surrendered to tobacco. Little bugs were to blame. These bugs were making merry on Grandma's house plants and they refused to die, although doused with soapsuds and other home remedies. Grandma had heard that in faraway New York State tobacco smoke was used to kill plant pests. But she just couldn't allow Uncle Jerry to smoke his awful pipe in the living room. So off she went to the village and bought twelve cigars for thirty cents for poor Jerry. He had to sit beside the plants and blow the smoke at them. The bugs just up and died. Uncle said he didn't blame them. If I remember right the brand of the cigars was either the Freckled Girl or the Speckled Trout.

There it is usually 10 to 15 degrees cooler than in the room. In very cold weather a newspaper should be used to protect plants from the intense cold of the window glass.

Providing proper humidity for house plants is often difficult. A too-dry atmosphere is the cause of most of our troubles with house plants during the winter — such as drying and curling buds, blasting, and an almost invisible insect infestation.

There are, however, methods that will help to maintain the humid atmosphere most house plants need. You can place a bowl of water on the radiator nearest the plants. Growing bulbs in pebbles and water among the potted plants will help, and grouping plants together will increase the humidity around them. Spraying your plants once a week with a sprayer full of tepid water will increase the humidity and discourage pests. Wiping broad-leaved specimens like philodendrons and rubber plants with a damp cloth prevents dust from clogging any pores and provides extra moisture.

One fairly simple method of providing enough humidity is to half fill the saucers in which your flowerpots stand with gravel or pebbles. Keep water poured over these pebbles and evaporation will take place. The bottoms of the pots must always rest on top of the pebbles above the water level maintained. Otherwise the plant roots will be constantly flooded, a condition that leads to rot.

Perhaps the best method of all, however, is to buy or have a tinsmith make watertight metal trays about one and a half inches deep and the length and width of your window sills. Cover the bottom of the tray with a half-inch of coarse gravel and charcoal and set the pots on this layer.

When watering your plants, you water directly into the trays instead of into the pots so that at first the water comes up the sides of the pots about half an inch. Usually the plants will soak up this surplus water in an hour. The pots should stand on, not in, the flooded gravel, which will constantly evaporate moisture into the foliage. You will quickly learn how much water to pour into the trays. Be sure your plants are thoroughly watered but do not allow them to stand in water more than an hour.

Galvanized chicken-feeding trays are admirable for this pur-

9

pose. The standard length is twenty-five inches, and they are wide enough to take four-inch pots. These trays are sold by poultry supply companies and some seed dealers. Aluminum baking pans might also be used.

Give your plants adequate ventilation. During the winter you should open a window in an adjoining room just a trifle for two short periods a day, except during near-zero weather. Be sure your plants are never exposed to a direct draft, however.

Get the habit of giving your plants about a quarter-turn every two days so that all sides will be exposed to the sunlight regularly.

Do not allow plants to become tall and leggy. Prune off to the desired height. This top pruning will encourage a sturdy bushy side growth.

All plants that are showing signs of fresh growth should be fed plant food in liquid or tablet form. There are several good commercial plant foods that will supply house plants with all the elements they need for best growth. But do not feed a plant that is resting or dormant.

A tonic for ivies and ferns that are showing spring life is one teaspoonful of ordinary household ammonia in a quart of tepid soft water — that is, rain or water from clean snow. This is a quickly available nitrogen fertilizer. This solution also is useful in routing springtails, little insects seen on the surface of the soil and in the saucers soon after watering. So far as is known, springtails in small numbers are harmless to plants, but their presence usually indicates too much watering. If they are very numerous, damage to the roots of plants may result.

Every week or so cultivate the surface of the soil in your flowerpots with a little rake fashioned from a two-tined kitchen fork, with half an inch of the tines bent at right angles. The surface of the soil should be so loose that water disappears almost instantly if you water your plants from above.

If the earth in your flowerpots is moldy, mossy, or hard-packed and the plants are doing poorly, knock one of the ailing plants completely out of its pot for root inspection. Open up the drain hole in the pot. Lay a curved bit of broken pot over the hole, and replace the old earth with a fresh, porous potting mixture over a layer of charcoal and coarse gravel. Often after such drastic treatment it is best to prune off about half the top growth of the plant to compensate for the root loss and disturbance.

For repotting plants or potting new ones, use a loamy, water-retaining mixture. Probably you can buy a bushel of good potting mixture from a greenhouse or your nurseryman. Next summer you can mix up your own and put away a few pails in the basement for your future indoor potting. To make a bushel of good potting mixture you should combine approximately two parts of loamy garden soil, one part rather coarse sharp builder's sand, one part humus from thoroughly decayed leaves or material from your compost heap, a half part dried cow manure, and a cupful of steamed bone meal. Foliage plants can use as much as 50 per cent organic matter, while succulents and cacti like more sand.

GRANDMA'S house plants bloomed so beautifully in the dead of winter, I think, because she watered them in the evening with soft, warm water — water warmer than tepid. She said it offset the night chill. On real cold nights she slipped newspapers between the plants and the window glass. She always had melted ice or snow water heating in the "reservoir," a horizontal tank attached to the kitchen stove. This soft water also was dandy for washing our hair.

When potting, place half an inch of pea-size charcoal in the bottom of all pots for drainage. Use only clay flowerpots; scrub and scald old ones, and soak new ones first in hot then in cold water. Avoid metal pots and containers that have no drainage provision. In such containers, a layer of charcoal will help for a while to prevent the soil from becoming foul. Better yet, drill some drainage holes in the bottom and place the container on a large planter, saucer, or flower boat.

For cactus, use one part of the above mixture and one part sharp builder's sand, mixed with one level teaspoon each of hardwood ashes and inorganic plant food for a four-inch pot. This rule does not apply to Christmas cactus, however, which needs a rich potting mixture like other flowering plants.

One of the best ways to have the freshness and beauty of spring in your indoor window garden while winter is storming a few inches away is to plant bulbs. The fancy-leaf caladium tubers will be on sale in a few weeks, as well as tuberous begonias to start indoors for outdoor bloom this summer. Hyacinth and narcissus bulbs are usually started in October and November, but it is still not too late to start another bowl of white or yellow narcissuses. Tulips also are usually started in pots in the fall if they are wanted for indoor bloom, but with luck even these can still be planted and flower in the house before March.

Calla Lily. The beautiful calla lily is now obtainable in white, yellow, and pink varieties. The calla root, or tuber, should be planted with the top one inch above the soil in a loose, loamy mixture of one part peatmoss, two parts good garden earth, one part decayed cow or sheep manure, and one half part coarse sand. Use a six-inch pot, not the shallow type. Keep the soil mixture two inches below the pot rim to allow for future additions of rich top dressing around the top of the tuber as the plant grows. This top dressing is one third each manure, sand, and loamy earth.

The calla will root well in a cool, light place, but as soon as the top growth starts, move it to a sunny, warm window. Keep well watered, and when buds appear give the plant an application of liquid manure or a solution consisting of one teaspoonful of ammonium sulphate dissolved in a quart of water.

When roots and leaves are well started use more water, and when in good growth, keep the soil very moist. Never let the plant become dry while in flower; it is almost a swamp plant, but likes sunshine. After the blossoms have faded and the weather is warm, lay the plant, in its pot, outside on its side in a shady, sheltered spot to rest and ripen for next season's blooming. Next autumn take it in and repot in a larger container, repeating the procedure of this season.

Amaryllis. The amaryllis is one of the most satisfactory of indoor plants. The new Dutch hybrid amaryllis is very fine, and produces the largest flowers it is possible to grow in the house. The gorgeous fire-red, crimson, rose, and white flowers appear in clusters of two to four at the top of the stem, often striped in two or more colors and up to ten inches across.

Amaryllis bulbs usually are started in January, February, or March in good loamy soil. Use a deep flowerpot that is only one inch larger in circumference than the bulb. These plants enjoy being cramped — in fact it is necessary to cramp them if you want good bloom. Cover only half the bulb with soil, leaving the neck and shoulders exposed. Put plenty of broken crock in the bottom of the pot to allow for proper drainage. After potting, place in a cool (60 to 70 degrees), shady place until the bulb takes root.

When a flower bud appears, move the plant to a curtained window and water sparingly until leaves begin to develop. Once leaves appear, put it in a sunny window and water freely. Every month to six weeks dissolve a pinch of complete plant food in the water used to provide moisture.

When flowering is past, cut off the flower stalks. Keep the plants in the sun, water them regularly, and feed every four to six weeks with a small amount of complete plant food in the water. After all danger of frost is past, set the pot, bulb and all, deep in the ground in a shaded part of the garden, sheltered from the wind. Put ashes under the bottom of the pot to keep out worms and slugs and water during dry spells.

About the last of August, dig up the pot and lay it on its side in the shade near the house where it will get no water. The leaves will then gradually die. Before frost comes, put plant, still in its pot, in the basement in a cool place, remove the dried leaves, and forget about it.

In December or January watch for signs of growth, for if the growing season is reached and the plant is neglected, injury follows. When leaves begin to reappear, scrape away as much of the old earth surface as you can without disturbing the roots. Replace it with fresh soil, water sparingly, but keep in a cool, dark place

13

until the stalk appears and reaches a height of about four inches. And so another cycle of growth and bloom will begin.

Bethlehem Star. The Bethlehem star is perhaps not so well known, but with its cluster of star-like blossoms, it is an outstanding house flower. Plant one to four in a pot.

GRANDMA had one of the most beautiful amaryllis plants I ever saw. Its blossoms were a deep rose, the petals were tipped with white, and deep in its throat it was almost black. Uncle Jerry had brought it from the Netherlands. He had been a sailor in his younger days and had brought Grandma many unusual plants. Some didn't last very long but this amaryllis lived for at least twenty years. It became so large that Grandma grew it in a wooden pail. Some years it had offshoots of little bulbs. Uncle called them "little pups." They were always spoken for by the neighbors.

Anemone. Anemones should be planted three to six tubers to a pot in good garden soil with the tops of the tubers about half an inch below the surface. Keep moderately damp, and after they are through blooming transplant the entire cluster to your garden in the spring. When dormant they may be potted again, although *Anemone coronaria* is not long-lived. Neither is it reliably hardy out-of-doors in this climate.

Oxalis. The oxalis is very easy to grow. There are many species, but the three most often seen are pink, white, and yellow. Plant three or more bulbs of the same color together in a five-inch pot. Don't mix the colors because each color has different growing habits. Keep the soil moist until the bulbs sprout, then place in a sunny window. When the flower buds appear, give the plants an application of plant food once a week.

In the late spring, the oxalis can be set out in a semishaded spot in your garden and they will go on growing until frost. A good healthy pot of oxalis may last for several years, and they are pest-proof.

Narcissus. Narcissus bulbs are usually started in the late fall for December and January bloom indoors; but many seed stores still have bulbs available. Either the Paper White or the yellow variety, Soleil d'Or, can still be started to add a fragrant breath of spring to your indoor window sill.

Buy large bulbs of good quality. Arrange them close together in a shallow bowl and add an inch or so of small pebbles or gravel to hold them upright and in place. Add water, keeping the water level just at the bottom of the bulbs. A little charcoal will help to keep the water fresh. Set the bowl in a dark, cool place for two weeks to a month or until roots are well formed among the pebbles. Add water when necessary to maintain the level.

When roots are formed, put the bowl in a sunny, cool window and you will soon have fragrant flowers that bloom for several weeks. When flowering is over discard the bulbs, as they cannot be forced into bloom again.

Tulip. Tulip bulbs for indoor bloom are usually planted in pots in the fall, but if you received some bulbs as Christmas gifts or still have some you failed to plant in October, try starting them now. You may be able to bring them into bloom before spring arrives outdoors.

If possible use the low, wide pots called bulb pans, but ordinary flowerpots can be used. In the bottom place a shallow layer of charcoal. Use a good but not too rich potting mixture, consisting of two parts of good garden earth, one part sand, and one part peatmoss.

Plant the tulips five or six in a five-inch pan or six to nine in a six-inch pan. Place each bulb so that its point is half an inch below the soil surface. The pot must now be kept in a dark and cool place where it cannot freeze or dry out too much. A cool basement or porch with a temperature of from 40 to 50 degrees is suitable. The pot should remain there for two or three months, or until a good root growth is established.

When placed in storage this way, the pot should be thoroughly soaked. No further watering should be necessary, but the soil should be prevented from drying out excessively. Root action will follow. When top growth begins, the pot may be brought into a warmer room or kept in the storage place to retard bloom until wanted.

GRANDMA could never find enough flowerpots. She needed them for her indoor winter garden, and for the gift plants she gave away by the score to sick folks and friends. Metal cans were scarce in Grandma's day, and when she obtained a few they were heated, and while still warm, heavily coated with beeswax to prevent rusting. In the bottom she put an inch of mixed gravel and charcoal for drainage and sanitation. Uncle Jerry covered the outside with a thin layer of birchbark, stuck on with clear shellac. These containers were really quite attractive and would last for several years. Plants in them required much less watering than containers with drainage holes; in fact, you had to be careful not to overwater.

When roots are well developed and bloom is desired quickly, the pot must be given as much sun as possible and kept in a temperature that averages 60 degrees until stems, leaves, and flower buds are formed. After the buds are formed, a temperature of 70 degrees will bring out the flowers. The soil should be kept moist but no fertilizer applied. When bloom is finished, the tulips should be kept watered and given some plant food. When the leaves turn yellow, watering should cease and the bulbs allowed to dry. In the fall you can plant them outdoors in the garden and after one spring of rest, they should bloom again.

Gloxinia. Gloxinias are our most beautiful and most nearly perfect house plants. There is no other plant that has such a wide color range in its blossoms and such subtle variations and blending of shades.

There are four methods of obtaining gloxinias. You can buy them from the florist as potted plants in full bloom and with numerous promising buds. Then there is the fascinating pastime of raising them yourself from tubers, commonly called bulbs, obtainable in most seed stores and nurseries. You can also raise gloxinias from seed or grow them from leaf cuttings. These last two methods are more difficult, however.

A fully matured blossoming plant from the store or greenhouse should be placed in a semishaded window. An east exposure is good provided the sun's rays are filtered through a thin curtain of cloth or plastic. The direct rays of the sun are almost sure to burn the plant. Do not overwater — usually once or twice a week is sufficient. This is governed to some extent by the humidity of your house, but try to keep the plant slightly on the dry side. Always use tepid water, about 85 to 90 degrees. To avoid overwatering, water from the top and discard any drainage in the saucer unless the plant is standing on pebbles. Fertilize sparingly with a commercial plant food or a weak solution of cow or sheep manure.

Don't be disturbed if all buds do not open. A really sturdy plant often has more buds than it has strength to develop. Bud blast also can be caused by too much or too little moisture — usually too much. Keep plants out of drafts, either hot or cold, and keep water off the foliage. At the end of the flowering period gloxinias should be dried off gradually, unless the plant is a new variety that prefers to be kept in constant growth. When the foliage has ripened, the tubers should be stored in dry vermiculite at a temperature of not less than 50 degrees, or the tubers may be stored in the dry soil in the pots in which they were grown.

To gardeners who wish to try raising their own gloxinias from tubers, seeds, or cuttings, I recommend *Gloxinias and How to Grow Them* by Peggie Schulz.

To start gloxinia tubers, place them in a layer of two or three inches of fine sphagnum moss or vermiculite in a shallow tray or box. Place them, indented side up, so that the tops of the bulbs are level with the surface, being careful not to pack the moss. Set the pots in a warm place and keep them uniformly moist with tepid water. Keep water off the top of the tubers.

17

JANUARY

When the tubers have sprouted two or three leaves they are ready to be transplanted into soil in six-inch pots. The soil should be the same mixture that is used for African violets, containing loam, leafmold, peatmoss, manure, and sand. You can get such potting mixtures ready-prepared from a dealer, but it is cheaper to prepare your own and keep a supply in the basement.

Keep the gloxinias only moderately wet for the first four weeks. As growth increases, water more frequently, taking care to keep it off the foliage and especially out of the crown of the plant. One or two feedings of a complete commercial fertilizer (one level teaspoonful per pot) is generally sufficient. Liquid and soluble fertilizers work very well also. From this point on your growing tubers should have the same care discussed above for gloxinia plants bought from the florist. It usually takes about four months for a started tuber to come into bloom.

To raise gloxinias from seed takes from eight to ten months and is a tedious but fascinating procedure. Sprinkle the very small seeds on a dampened mixture of sand and fine sifted peatmoss or sphagnum moss, but don't cover the seed. Just press it into the growing medium and cover the container with plastic or glass to prevent drying out.

Place the container in a warm, shaded place and keep moist until the seedling leaves are about a quarter of an inch across. Then transplant them, using a pair of tweezers to pick out the plants. Put about two dozen, each in a tiny hole made in the rich earth, in a four-inch pot, and firm the earth around them. In about a month to six weeks transplant each plant into a two-and-a-half-inch pot, and in another two months repot them again in five-inch pots where they will remain until they blossom. After blooming, discontinue watering and store the dry tubers in peatmoss or dry vermiculite for their dormant period.

To grow gloxinias from leaf cuttings, make cuttings from a mature plant in lusty growth. Root them by thrusting the leaf stalks (petioles) about an inch into damp sand, peatmoss, or vermiculite. Cover the cuttings with glass or plastic to retain moisture until a new plant forms on the leaf stalk. When the parent leaf begins to turn yellow, the new little plants can be potted and given the same care as other gloxinia plants.

African Violet. This is the time of year when most African violets are coming out of their winter siesta and beginning to bloom again. The African violet is a first cousin of the gloxinia and one of our most popular house plants. It comes in every shade from white through pink and blue to deep purple, and is becoming increasingly easy to grow.

GRANDMA had no prepared plant foods. She fed her plants once a week with a solution of half a cup of dried cow manure dissolved in a gallon of warm water. Uncle Jerry prepared it for her. And how her plants did blossom! Today you can purchase dried cow manure in seed stores and mix your own solution. There were some strange beliefs many years ago, and even today some people think that chopped raw beef, turkey gizzards, and fresh poultry blood are excellent food for house plants. Perhaps they do have some merit but Grandma did not hold to them at all. She said her plants were just plain old-fashioned vegetation, not meat-hungry animals, and if some plants lived when given such treatment they did so in spite of it, not because of it.

African violets need a warm temperature, moist soil, and lots of light, but not strong direct sunshine. They will flourish in an east or north window, but a south or west exposure will also do. They enjoy the weak sunlight of November, December, January, and the first half of February, but when the sun's rays become stronger, violets should be protected from direct sunshine with thin curtains. Thin frosted plastic or large sheets of thin white paper between the plants and the window glass will also do the trick. Too much sun often will turn the foliage light green or yellow and blast the flower buds. However, the weak sunshine early in the morning and late in the day is beneficial.

19

JANUARY

Now that the January sun is growing warmer, the African violets in your window will require more moisture and a moderate increase in balanced plant food. Bring this about very gradually, however. Most expert growers water their violets with warm or tepid water until warm spring days are really here. Never use water cooler than room temperature. African violets require ample moisture, but they should be watered only when the soil feels dry. Don't water regularly, but inspect regularly and water when needed.

The idea that African violets must be watered from the bottom is now practically obsolete. Time has proved that top-of-soil watering is all right, provided the water is tepid, the soil is sufficiently loose to absorb the water quickly, and care is taken not to damage the foliage. But watering in the saucers is still satisfactory. If all water is not absorbed within half an hour, however, discard the surplus. Check the drainage hole in the bottom of the pot frequently. It will help if you place the pots on three flat pebbles or bottle caps in their saucers. Don't use pots that have no drainage hole. Clay pots are best — metal cans soon form root-destroying rust.

Potted violets fresh from the florist are not likely to require fertilizer for several weeks, and newly potted plants will not require it until new roots begin forming. Older plants should be fed about every two or three weeks. I prefer a reliable liquid plant food diluted even more than the directions advise. Many violets are burned and ruined by overfertilizing, which is usually indicated by discolored leaves, falling blossoms, and rot in the crown.

Contrary to many people's belief, African violets benefit from an occasional tepid shower bath just as other house plants do. For years it was believed that water on the soft downy leaves would make spots and cause rotting. This has been proved erroneous, but certain precautions must be observed. The water used must be lukewarm or warmer than room temperature; the plants should be shaken gently after their shower to remove clinging water; drops that remain should be removed with cleansing tissue or soft cloth folded to a point; and the plants should not be put in the sun until the water has evaporated completely from the foliage.

20

Violets can be taken to the kitchen sink for a shower bath every two weeks, along with your other house plants.

What are some of the troubles encountered in growing African violets? Perhaps the most frequent complaint is that the violets fail to bloom although the foliage is healthy. Remember, no plant blooms all the time. They must have periods of rest, so don't force them with excessive feeding and watering. Reduce the feeding to almost nothing during these rest periods.

In general, however, the most important requirement for bloom is plenty of light. Keep your plants no farther than one foot from the window, where light can reach the entire plant. Most African violets bloom more freely when the plants form open rosettes. When the leaves grow almost upright and are so thick that they crowd and shade the center of the plant, the tiny flower buds often can't develop properly. Clipping off some of these center leaves with their stems often will help the plant to bloom. Nip off a few of the stems half an inch above the crown, using curved scissors, so that the plant is more of a rosette. Usually it will respond very soon by bursting into bloom. However, there are a few varieties, such as Blue Chard, to which dense, upright growth is natural, and these should not be pruned.

When African violet foliage looks unhealthy, there may be several causes. If the lower leaves have a dark, sodden appearance, fungus infection may be the cause. This sometimes takes the form of crown rot, which may result from overwatering. Another possible cause is mechanical injury to the stems. Examine the edge of the pot. A rough edge may have injured the leaf stems where they hang over. Always examine pots, both new and old, when potting and remedy imperfections. Sandpaper the edges smooth and rub with paraffin or floor wax to make a protective coating.

A drying or yellowing of the lower leaves does not always indicate trouble. These leaves are usually the oldest, and it is nature's way to discard them when they are no longer useful. They should be carefully removed to keep the plant looking attractive. Never jerk off either flower or leaf stems, because they usually break or pull off from the plant crown leaving a wound where fungus organisms may enter. Cut off the leaf stems about half an inch from the crown, and the remaining stem will dry up naturally. A little garden lime, ordinary chalk, or a mild fungicide such as Semesan, dusted on wounds is a good precaution.

Diseases and insect pests are not usually a problem with African violets, but it is a good idea to isolate a new plant from other plants for a couple of weeks until you are sure it is absolutely healthy. Isolation should be the rule for any diseased or infested plant. If insect infestation is the trouble, try a bath at the kitchen sink before using powerful insecticides and fungicides. If this does not solve the problem, there are special spray preparations for African violets which are effective when used as directed. If these do not cure an ailing plant fairly quickly, wrap it in paper and consign it to the garbage can or incinerator before the trouble spreads to your other plants.

GRANDMA had no African violets; they were not known in her day. But she did have several pots of the sweet-smelling English violets on the foot-wide sill of the kitchen window in her Ontario farmhouse. They multiplied and blossomed amazingly, perhaps due to the steam of the teakettle. She was always giving divisions to her neighbors. The original plant was said to have been brought from England by Greatgrandmother. I have seen this variety flourishing outdoors in Victoria, Canada, without winter protection. Wouldn't Grandma have enjoyed our African violets?

When African violets grow too large for their containers, or when a new crown starts to grow and crowds the plant, then it is time to repot. African violets are much prettier and better bloomers when only one crown is allowed in a pot. If a crown has little plantlets growing out from its sides, soak the crowded plant well, remove it from the pot, and gently separate the sections. Some plantlets will be twins, but don't separate them. Plant them in three-inch or larger pots. Some gardeners recommend planting the sections in a half-inch layer of peatmoss spread on top of the potting soil.

When potting little plants or repotting old ones, put a bit of broken pot over the drain hole for good drainage and put an inch of small stones or washed cinders and charcoal in the bottom of the pot to keep the soil sweet. A fairly good potting mixture for African violets is one part each of good garden soil, coarse builder's sand, sifted material from the compost heap, and leafmold. It is likely your plants will be in the pots a long time, however, and a little extra care and expense in preparing a good lasting potting mixture will pay big dividends in lusty plants with a maximum of bloom. An excellent mixture is four quarts loam, two quarts coarse builder's sand, one quart dry cow manure, a half cup bone meal, and two cups granulated (commonly called hen-size) charcoal. Many greenhouses will sell a few pounds of their own African violet potting mixture. Always use builder's sand, not fine or white sand, and never use dirty pots.

Another way to increase your collection of African violets is to start new plants from rooted leaf cuttings. To do this, cut several mature leaves from vigorous plants. Allow about one inch of leaf stalk (petiole) to remain on the cutting. The leaf stalks can then be rooted in various ways. One good method is to start them in a large glass container, such as an old aquarium or round glass bowl, which can be partially covered to maintain a humid atmosphere without restricting light. In the bottom of the vessel put a one-inch layer of pebbles for drainage and then two or three inches of a well-moistened rooting medium such as vermiculite or sand. Insert the stalks about a third of an inch into the rooting medium. Do not allow the leaves to touch each other.

A sheet of glass or clear plastic may be laid over the propagating container and raised slightly if too much heat or condensation develops. Keep the container in a light but not sunny window. Keep the rooting medium constantly moist but not sloppy. Use soft water if possible or boil and cool city or hard well water.

Another method for starting violet leaf stalks is to use a shallow bowl with some small stones to hold the leaves above water. Keep adding just enough tepid water to keep the stalk ends wet. Some amateurs also have success starting leaves in soft or rain water, with the stalk end poked through a hole in cardboard on a drinking glass. Both these methods are simpler than the covered container method but may not be so consistently successful.

Some leaves will form roots and plantlets in a few weeks, but others may take months. When the tiny new plantlets appear on the old leaf stalks, they can be gently removed and planted in potting mixture in individual small pots, or a number of new plantlets may be planted together in a large container for later transplanting. Usually there is rooting material clinging to the rootlets. That is good; disturb it as little as possible.

Indoor Garden Pests. The warm sun and longer days that quicken our window gardens into new life also bring into evidence some garden pests. Mealy bugs may appear on your African violets or foliage plants. The little cottony masses adhering to the leaves and stems are protecting the mealy bugs that harm and frequently kill plants. A bit of cotton on a toothpick moistened with alcohol, lemon extract, or perfume will almost instantly dissolve the bugs and their homes.

The same treatment is also effective for scale on ivies and ferns. Scale is a sucking insect. It is usually discovered as small, hard, oblong, brown or gray masses — sometimes mistaken for seed spores — sticking tightly to stems and leaves. Often the leaves become sticky and shiny.

Soapy water is beneficial for washing when red spiders, scales, and certain other insects are present on ivies. Mix one teaspoon of kerosene in a gallon of warm, strong suds. For ferns reduce kerosene to one-half teaspoon. Hold the plant upside down and plunge the green growth into the mixture, but do not allow any of the solution to touch the earth or pot. Hold the earth in the pot with your fingers and swish the plant around in the well-mixed solution for several minutes. Then lay the pot on its side for about six hours to drain. After it has drained, rinse it thoroughly in tepid, clear water. Repeat the process if scales appear again.

If the infestation is not severe, it often can be overcome with a nicotine sulphate treatment. This treatment is also effective for plant lice or aphids. Spray the plant, especially on the underside of the leaves, with nicotine sulphate available at your dealers. Mix the sulphate with soapsuds as advised on the container and follow directions carefully. Malathion, a newer insecticide, can also be used to control aphids, mealy bugs, early scale infestation, and red spiders, or spider mites. Follow the directions given by the manufacturer.

GRANDMA examined her stored bulbs and roots in midwinter. She would rout all mildewed or decayed ones and then dry and dust the wooden box containers with mixed air-slaked lime and sulphur. She called the sulphur "brimstone" — guess she picked the word up from a fiery minister who visited the village once a year. The healthy bulbs and roots were treated to a mixture of dry wood ashes, sulphur, red pepper, and shaved camphor. Grandma didn't have modern insecticides and fungicides in her day, but bad bugs certainly "vamoosed," as Uncle Jerry said, when Grandma treated them.

Spider mites or red spiders are one of the worst pests on house plants. They attack all types of plants, making small white speckles on the leaves and forming a fine webbing over the foliage. Dusting sulphur, Aramite, Dimite, or Malathion may be used according to directions to control them. Cyclamen mites also do much damage, attacking all kinds of plants and causing curled and deformed leaves. Infested plants can seldom be cured, although Malathion may help. Badly infested plants should be discarded.

Earth in flowerpots often becomes infested with maggots or worms that probably will mature into the gnats sometimes seen fluttering in and above the foliage. Watering the plants once a week with a solution of lime water usually will remedy the trouble. Dusting the soil with 5 per cent chlordane dust is even better.

Sometimes earthworms or angleworms are present in the soil. They do no damage other than loosening the soil and causing the roots to become dry. If they become so numerous they have to be removed, just upset the earth out of the pots and remove the worms. Again, however, lightly dusting the soil with a chlordane dust, 5 per cent strength, will remedy most trouble caused by worms, springtails, and other insects in the soil.

GRANDMA had little trouble with rabbits on her farm. On bright, sunny days all during the winter she had Uncle Jerry do the necessary pruning of fruit and ornamental trees, berry bushes, and grape vines. The cuttings then were carried about a hundred feet away from the trees and placed in piles. There the rabbits found shelter. They ate the cuttings and did not harm the growing trees and shrubs. This plan just suited Uncle Jerry because he did not have to hurry. He was not permitted to shoot the rabbits because, as Grandma explained, "In a way they are our guests and they now trust us."

You can now purchase house plant sprays such as Malathion and DDT in aerosol pressurized containers or in straight liquid form for you to dilute and use in a hand sprayer. Both are effective for many plant insect troubles, including red spider mites, cyclamen mites, and thrips. Be sure to read and follow directions on the containers.

REMINDERS

Now is a good time to examine the gladiolus corms, cannas, dahlias, and other bulbs and roots stored in your basement cold room. Try to keep the temperature rather cool — between 40 and 50 degrees. If too warm, the bulbs may sprout. If the dahlias seem to be shrinking, try sprinkling them with water. Packing them in damp sand or moss helps too. Examine them again in a week or two, and if mildew is evident, try for a cooler temperature and dust them with sulphur. Do not lay them on an earth or cement floor. Store them in clean flats. A dusting of 5 to 10 per cent DDT or chlordane usually will discourage insects on gladiolus corms and canna tubers.

Better not use salt on your icy walks. The same goes for sand mixtures that contain salt. Grass and flowers are easily killed by a saline solution. Keep a pail of dry sand next to your heating plant. A good sprinkling of this warm sand on icy walks or steps will create a gritty foothold almost instantly, and it is easier on rugs than salt if tracked into the house.

If no spot in your garden can be thawed enough for planting those tulip bulbs you received for Christmas now, try storing them in your refrigerator until planting time next fall. Ordinary storage is not practical, as the bulbs are likely to sprout and shrink. But I have stored tulip bulbs in air-tight plastic bags for a whole year on the bottom shelf of my refrigerator (at 34 degrees), planted them in the fall, and had fine blossoms the next spring. The bulbs must be in good condition, however, not sprouted, and air-tight bags must be used to prevent dehydration.

If a really mild day should come along this January, get out the garden hose and treat your evergreens to a shower bath. You will be surprised at the amount of soot and dirt that washes off them, and how it brightens their color. They will also absorb considerable much-needed moisture.

⚱ FEBRUARY ⚱

By FEBRUARY the northern gardener feels he is over the hump of winter. The sun is much warmer through the south windows and the daylight lingers longer each afternoon. Best of all, perhaps, from the gardener's point of view, many of the new seed and nursery catalogs have arrived. These beautiful and optimistic works of art remind us that it is time to plan now for the busy garden days ahead. Every year as we pore over the new catalogs and plan our new purchases, we are positive that this year's garden will be the most beautiful ever. Last summer's disappointments are forgotten in the excitement and challenge of a new garden year.

Most catalogs offer to sell by mail not only seeds and bulbs of annual and perennial flowers but also field-grown plants of perennials, shrubs, and ornamental trees. These plants are shipped to you during their dormant period, and careful handling usually ensures success when they are replanted in your garden.

If there is a good nursery near your home, however, it may be wiser to buy your perennial plants and shrubs in person. In this way plants can be moved with a minimum of danger to their survival, for they can be freshly dug, carried home in your car with earth about their roots, and replanted within a few hours. With dormant shrubs and trees the advantages of buying from a local nursery are not so great as for annual and perennial plants, however.

Many catalogs are divided into different sections devoted to vegetables, annual and perennial flowers, roses and other shrubs, fruit trees and berry bushes, shade trees, and various garden supplies. The first few pages of each division usually describe the latest developments of the nation's best horticultural hybridizers. Here we find new varieties of flowers and vegetables that after years of research and breeding have proven their worth in twenty-one different trial gardens in this country and Canada, to the satisfaction of the All America Selections judges.

All America Selections is a nonprofit organization, voluntarily supported. It coordinates research and pre-introductory testing of new varieties of flowers and vegetable seeds. It is governed and operated by a council of expert judges.

The familiar "AAS" or "All America Selections" certification mark on seed packets or in catalogs designates varieties that have merited All America's recommendation. This is the only accredited and generally accepted guide to the very best of new flower and vegetable varieties for North America. The Gold Medal award is the highest AAS award that a plant can win, and it is not awarded every year. Bronze Medal awards are usually given to several outstanding new flower and vegetable varieties each year, but sometimes only one new variety can meet the rigid standards demanded of an AAS winner.

New varieties are judged during a long and rigorous period of testing. For more than twenty years plant breeders from all over the world have been sending their promising new varieties to W. Ray Hastings, founder and executive secretary of the All America trials. Hastings in turn sends the seeds or plants to judges who plant them in trial grounds. Sample plants and seeds are identified only by registration number.

Testing and comparing the many proposed new varieties with leading similar kinds already in commercial production is the annual work of twenty-six judges in as many different climatic sections of the United States and southern Canada. Selected trial gardens are used so the new flower varieties may be grown in different soil, climate, and geographic locations. Two years are allowed for each judge to make a fair trial of each entry.

Appearance is not the only concern of plant breeders. Insect and disease resistance, earlier and longer blooming seasons, and more abundant blooms are very necessary qualifications. Awards are given to the varieties meriting such distinction and all seedsmen have equal opportunity to obtain seeds of the winners for introduction during the first season of distribution. Thus gardeners and planters may order the new award-winning seeds from their sources of seed supply. However, these new AAS seeds usually are sold out early because of big demand and limited supply the first year, so it is quite important to order early.

GRANDMA used to sit at the kitchen table, excitedly studying the new seed catalogs by the light of a kerosene lamp — she called it a coal-oil lamp. Uncle Jerry had brought them from the post office four miles away, for there was no rural delivery. The post office was in Johnstone's harness shop. Uncle was sure Johnstone held up the catalogs at least a week while he looked them over. These catalogs contained not more than twenty pages, each illustrated with a few woodcuts that were used year after year. Only one page was given to flower seeds and from it Grandma got her list.

Very similar to the All America Selections organization is the All America Rose Selections (AARS), which tests and judges new rose varieties. The catalogs that specialize in roses — and to my mind these are the most beautiful catalogs of all — feature both the new All America award roses and the roses that have been chosen for these honors in past years. The older All America prizewinners are sometimes your best buy, for not only have they withstood the test of time but they are also usually less expensive than the newest selections. Every catalog lists a dozen or more outstanding ones.

When you have digested well the catalogs' contents, study your garden from the window or, if the weather and snow permit, pull on your overshoes and tramp around the yard. It will do you good to study the shrubbery in its winter garb. This close-up will enable you to make a better plan of your requirements before writing out your selections.

Perhaps the most permanent and important assets for a beautiful yard are well-grown shade trees. These are a lasting source of pleasure as well as a real addition to the value of your property. Their shade and cool, green foliage form a needed contrast and background to sunny flower borders, and their falling leaves in autumn can make rich compost to add fertility to the flower beds.

While walking about your yard this wintry day, try to visualize where shade will be most needed in the summer, where you want screening from your neighbors, and where new trees will not shadow your flower borders or compete with them for nutriment from the soil. Notice the orientation of the trees and shrubs you already have and plan to place any new flower borders where they will not be too shaded and will get a maximum of sunlight.

Along with trees and shrubs a healthy green lawn is another vitally important asset to your grounds. Here in the North, where winter snow is plentiful and rainfall is usually adequate, we can grow fine lawns with a minimum of hard work. A beautiful growth of grass can never be taken for granted, however, and when spring and summer arrive, we will be spending almost as much time on lawn care as on our flower borders.

Trees, shrubs, and green lawns form a perfect setting, but the flower borders are the jewels of the home garden. Even the handsomest lawn and trees seem incomplete and lifeless without the colorful accent of blooming flowers. Whether you are planning to start a brand-new flower border or to improve an old one, your most important aim should be to provide a continuous procession of color from early spring to late fall. This can be done by using all the different forms of flowering plants — perennials, biennials, annuals, and bulbs.

Hardy perennials are the real backbone of a garden, for they establish the garden's permanent character. Along with the spring-blooming bulbs — scillas, crocuses, hyacinths, narcissuses, daffodils, and tulips — they reappear and bloom year after year, unharmed by subzero winters and requiring only occasional care.

FEBRUARY

Some perennials, like phlox and iris, grow into large clumps that need to be divided and replanted every three or four years. Others, like peonies and bleeding heart, do not like to be moved, and once established in your border will grow larger and bloom more abundantly each year, sometimes for twenty years or more.

But annuals are a necessary part of the flower border, too. Sometimes gardeners here in the Upper Midwest ask me, "Which are most important for my garden — annuals or perennials?" I answer that question like a true Scotsman, who usually plays safe. My answer is, "Both." Perennials and annuals get along famously together. Perennials and bulbs provide most of the bloom in spring and early summer, while annual plants are still mere seedlings; but from midsummer on we must depend more on annuals to keep a continuous panorama of color in the garden.

The earliest flowers of all in our northern gardens are the perennial wild flowers that start to appear in April, often while snow still lingers in shaded corners. These include the dainty little crocus, pasqueflower, bloodroot, and many others. These are followed by the huskier wild flowers — white and purple violets, trillium, jack-in-the-pulpits, May apples, wild blue woodland phlox, Jacob's ladder, mertensia, and many more. These will all thrive happily in any woodsy corner of your yard, or in a part of the perennial border that is dappled with shade in summer. Many of these are so widely used in cultivated borders that we forget their origin.

Overlapping the wild ones are the so-called "minor" spring-blooming bulbs, like the blue squills, or scilla, and the white snowdrops, followed by the daffodils and spring's most glorious display — the tulips.

From late May to the end of June some of our most beautiful perennials bloom in gorgeous procession. Tulips, bleeding heart, Oriental poppies, iris, peonies, columbine, and many others make this perhaps the most rewarding period of the northern gardener's year. During June and July the roses are at their peak, too.

During the hottest part of the summer, late July and August, there are fewer perennials in bloom — the handsome and reliable summer phlox, varieties of daylilies, lythrum and delphinium, perhaps some veronica and balloon flowers, and a few others. This is the time when most annuals are at the height of their bloom. The brilliant colors of marigolds, zinnias, snapdragons, petunias, cosmos, and many others can keep the flower border colorful until frost.

GRANDMA had in her garden a handsome two-foot perennial that had been growing there for more than a hundred years. It was started by Grandfather's father from a single seed brought from Asia. It was ·called burning bush because on sultry nights a gas from the white blossoms would flash with a bluish light when touched with a match. As I remember, its foliage smelled like lemonade. Rumor was that it would die if moved. It also is called gas plant, dictamnus, and fraxinella, and you can buy it today as seed or as a field-grown perennial. It is a beautiful and fragrant flower for a shady garden spot.

Annuals generally require a more fully sunny location than most perennials need. The sunniest corner in your yard could be rescued for an annual bed, to be spaded up and replanted every year. Showy annuals should be transplanted from this bed into the main flower border wherever their color is needed to fill dull spots during the summer. Annuals also provide a constant source of cut flowers, for the more they are cut the more they will bloom. In this way the longer-lasting perennial flowers can be left uncut to give delight in the garden.

The biennials have a secure place in our northern garden, too, falling somewhere between the perennials and the annuals in their habits of growth and bloom. Such biennials as hollyhocks, Canterbury bells, foxglove, and pansies are beloved favorites in many gardens. Most of them will tolerate more shade than annuals will and their season of bloom, though it starts earlier, usually lasts longer than that of most perennials. They are generally planted from seed or as started seedlings in the place they are to grow.

33

Thereafter they tend to reseed themselves automatically, so that each year there are new year-old plants ready to bloom.

Summer-blooming bulbs, corms, and tubers — dahlias, gladioli, tuberous begonias, canna lilies, and others — are also useful for late summer bloom. These plants are not hardy in our northern climate and their bulbs, corms, or tubers must be planted each spring, dug up before frost each fall, and stored indoors during the winter. This makes a bit more work than most perennials require, but the large, exotic flowers and brilliant colors of most of these bulbs and tubers make the extra trouble seem worthwhile.

By late September and early October, even if no killing frost has arrived, most of our perennials, biennials, and even annuals have bloomed themselves out. This is the time when the late bloomers come into their own — the hardy perennial asters and chrysanthemums, which have been biding their time all summer, and a few tireless zinnias, petunias, annual asters, and salvia, which seldom give up before frost.

Time of bloom is not the only important factor in garden planning. We must try to arrange the garden so that colors harmonize, and so that there is enough contrast of shape and color to avoid monotony. The general effect of your garden is more important than the beauty of individual specimens, and each plant must look well with its neighbors. Part of the fun of gardening is in moving your flowers about to discover where they look and bloom their best. In general the tall and shrubby perennials belong at the back of the garden, the middle-sized ones in front of them, and the smallest plants along the edge of the border.

Try to have clumps of several plants or one variety and color rather than a scattered, one-of-a-kind mixture of plants. Plant in staggered groups, not in rows, for a more natural and lovely effect. If part of the garden is shaded by trees during the summer, choose flowers that will bloom in partial shade. Many perennials will thrive and bloom with only five or six hours of sun a day, but be careful to choose shade-loving varieties. A partially shady spot might be suitable for tulips and daffodils, too, since they will be through blooming about the time the trees are fully leaved.

Choosing Perennials. Perennials can be grown from seed, started from root divisions of growing plants, or bought as dormant or growing plants from a nursery.

For immediate enjoyment in the garden, invest in sturdy, field-grown plants from a good nursery. If planted this spring, they will bloom this year. Buy as many as you can afford the first year, if you are starting a brand-new garden, and a few new specimens each year as you discover from experience where gaps need to be filled. In two or three years many of your first purchases can be divided and replanted, thus increasing your masses of bloom, and neighboring gardeners will also be glad to give you seedlings or plant divisions that are crowding their own gardens.

To my mind, there are four perennials that are almost a must in every garden. They are irises, peonies, phlox, and delphiniums. Also among the favorites, and easy to grow, are bleeding heart, Shasta daisy, sweet william, old-fashioned pinks, columbine, and coreopsis. For backgrounds and in the rear of the border, don't forget the tall double hollyhocks (biennial) and the improved golden glow.

Be sure to save space for some of the newer irises. They now come in glamorous tans and reds, white, and deep purple as well as in delicate shades of mauve and pink and blue.

Peonies are usually planted in August, but by planting them very early in the spring you will gain a whole year's blooming. If you go direct to a peony farm in May, purchase field-size clumps, and plant them as quickly as possible without breaking them up, they may bloom this year. These field clumps will cost more than root divisions, but where quick bloom is important they are worth it.

Golden marguerites, coreopsis, and gaillardia will bloom up to frost if kept well cut after the first blooming in June. In the golden tones helianthus and Riverton Gem helenium are true autumn bloomers, as is also plumbago larpentae (leadwort), with its lovely blue flowers.

Then, of course, there is the silver star Shasta daisy. If kept well watered and fed, and if all old flowers are cut off before they go to seed, it will bloom until frost. The hardy asters or Michaelmas daisy have been greatly improved in recent years and now are dandy flowers. Plants come in many sizes from dwarfs to five-footers. They increase rapidly and should be divided every three years.

The chrysanthemum is perhaps the best of autumn flowers. There are dozens to choose from in almost all colors, forms, and heights. Minnesota is celebrated for its mums, and more hardy varieties are being introduced each year. The new Mesabi and Wanda, as well as Wenonah and Vulcan, which were developed earlier, are Minnesota-grown varieties that will grow well in the North. Chrysanthemums need more winter protection in the northern garden than most other hardy perennials, but with a little extra care they can be kept alive year after year. Here in the North we must be especially careful to choose early-blooming varieties, however, or a hard freeze in late September — not uncommon in the Upper Midwest — may end a chrysanthemum's blooming season before it has barely begun. Study your nursery catalogs for extra-hardy and early-blooming varieties for our northern climate.

For shaded places in your garden, choose plants that are adapted to such spots. In really dense shade, as along the north wall of a house, ferns and other foliage plants are probably your best choice. Plantain lilies and lilies of the valley will also thrive with almost no sun, and in addition to their handsome foliage they have lovely flowers as well.

For parts of the garden that are only partially shaded — from four to six hours of sun a day in summer — there are many handsome flowers to choose from. Daylilies, many kinds of true lilies, some irises, bleeding heart, mertensia, astilbe, columbine, English daisies, Canterbury bells and other campanulas, tall platycodons or balloon flowers, the lovely blue and white veronicas, yellow primroses, pink lythrum and coral bells, scarlet beebalm or monarda — all these and many others will do well in partial shade. Even the stately perennial phlox, the mainstay of the garden during July and August, will stand considerable shadiness.

I have mentioned only a few of the many beautiful perennials suitable for northern gardens. Table 2 at the end of this book lists more.

Choosing Annuals. No matter what your plans are for the perennial border, you will want to plant annual flowers too. If your garden plot is a rented one, or if you are not yet ready to plan a permanent garden, you may want to grow annuals exclusively. The seeds usually are low priced and they are the easiest to grow. Most of them can be planted in the outdoor annual bed, where you want them to blossom, or when small they can be transplanted to other parts of the garden. Many will sow themselves and come up again the following spring without any fussing. Always buy the best seed obtainable and avoid bargain, job-lot seeds.

Among the most popular annuals for northern gardens are the many zinnia varieties. The improved types give a choice ranging from baby zinnias or pompons only 18 inches tall to background plants 4 feet tall with frilled, cushioned, or carnation-like blossoms. They come in all shades and blends in the warm yellow and red color group. Seed may be planted outdoors in May, when the soil is warm, or started indoors for earlier bloom. A recent variety, Blaze, won the only AAS annual award for 1954. Blaze is a free-blooming, bushy plant 2½ to 3 feet tall, with profuse scarlet-orange Fantasy-type blossoms up to 5 inches across. The Fantasy hybrid zinnias have fluffy quilled and curled petals in many brilliant and pastel colors.

Marigolds are another favorite annual, ranging from compact dwarf plants suitable for edging the garden border to tall bushy varieties that bear huge yellow or orange flowers. The early-blooming variety Glitters, an AAS award-winner, is one of the finest.

Petunias are one of the best choices for all-summer bloom provided you can start your seed indoors in March or buy started plants in late May when they can be transplanted directly into the garden. Many of the new varieties are profuse bloomers of the hybrid grandiflora type. These have large ruffled flowers in a wide range of colors — Fire Dance, an AAS selection for 1956, is salmon-scarlet with a yellow throat, Paleface and Popcorn are pure white, Comanche and Fire Chief are bright red, Ballerina is a ruffled salmon, Radiance and Prima Donna are pink. All these varieties were AAS award winners in recent years.

37

FEBRUARY

Two low-growing annuals used for edging garden walks and borders are ageratum and sweet alyssum. These grow only four to eight inches high but spread into low, bushy rows covered with tiny flowers. Most varieties of ageratum are a brilliant blue, while sweet alyssum is white (Little Gem) or deep violet (Royal Carpet, AAS Silver Medal, 1953).

GRANDMA had, in her Ontario garden, a rapid-growing perennial sweet pea plant that covered a rustic summerhouse. She said it was known in Georgia as the Great-flowered Everlasting sweet pea. She had brought the root north with her when she was a bride, about forty years earlier. The blossoms were very large, rose-colored, and three to five on a stem. The roots were long and fleshy with four-foot taproots. The foliage and stems were a light green and beautiful. Grandma often gave roots to neighbors in the spring.

A few more of the most popular annuals should be mentioned. Snapdragons today are magnificent. The huge tetraploid hybrids come in various heights — two to five feet — that will fit into any garden arrangement, with a color range in all shades and blends of red and yellow, also a pure white. Portulaca, commonly called moss rose or sun plant, is excellent for dry, sunny locations and is a good ground cover. In a spot that it likes it will sow itself year after year. Its blossoms, which come both single and double, are like beautiful, short-stemmed roses.

Nicotiana, or tobacco plant, is one of the old-fashioned garden flowers. It grows two to three feet high and has white, tubular, sweet-scented blossoms that open in the evening. The plant itself is rather scraggly in its habit of growth, but its perfume alone would make it worth growing. There is also a pinkish variety and a smaller day bloomer.

Phlox drummondi, commonly called annual phlox, has a much

wider color range than the perennial variety. It is 12 to 18 inches tall and an excellent showy bedding plant that is good for mass display in a garden bed — especially the tall gigantea type.

Pansies, contrary to general belief, don't have to be grown in the shade. Given plenty of moisture and loamy soil, they grow well in a sunny spot and bloom all summer if the spent blossoms are picked off daily.

Pinks also belonged to grandmother's garden, but how they have been improved in recent years! They now bloom on sturdy stems, both single and double strains. Some look like their cousins the carnations, and are just as spicy sweet. Pinks should be started in a greenhouse or hotbed. They are late bloomers. Scabiosa — sometimes called pincushion flower or mourning bride — is easy to grow in different kinds of soil. It blooms all summer, is fine for cut flowers, and comes in white, shades of blue and red, and also a deep purplish black.

Annual salvia, or scarlet sage, comes in several shades of red and is a brilliant bedding plant. The tall, three-foot varieties are excellent for autumn border backgrounds. Seed must be started indoors as it is a late bloomer.

Verbenas are colorful, usually dwarf, plants, and are fine for edging rock gardens, for window boxes, and for cutting. The blooms are white and all colors except true yellow. They grow well in poor soil and stand drought. Giant cleome, or spider plant, is a graceful flower three to four feet high, with huge, airy salmon-pink blossoms. It is excellent for show or cutting, but should stand well back in the flower border.

There are many more annual flowers I could talk about — the lovely big annual asters that now are wilt-resistant, the brilliant celosias or cockscombs, bachelor's buttons, the dainty, lacy cosmos, calendulas, nasturtiums, larkspur, sweet-smelling stock, and gay Shirley poppies — each one sure to be some gardener's special favorite. You cannot plant them all, no matter how much the seed catalogs tempt you. But try each spring to include a few new annual flowers in your garden, just for fun and the pleasure of discovery. Table 1 on page 281 lists annuals that are adapted to the northern garden, with information about their needs and habits of growth.

Most annuals require full sun, but a few will tolerate partial shade. Ageratum, sweet alyssum, foxglove, clarkia, godetia, lobelia, nicotiana, torenia, and feverfew are worth trying. The tender perennial patience plant, often grown as a house plant and available as annual seedlings in May at nurseries and greenhouses, will bloom all summer in quite shaded locations.

GRANDMA saved and kept dry wood ashes from the cookstove and fireplace all through the winter. They were stored in big covered barrels in the yard, but away from buildings, because sometimes the ashes contained live coals. Come spring they were carefully cultivated into the garden soil. Grandma knew wood ashes contained considerable plant food. The plants prospered and had brighter and bigger flowers after application. They were especially good for lilies and they also sweetened moldy, sour soils. Coal ashes from the base burner were used to condition heavy soils and were fine on muddy garden paths. If Grandma were alive today she would no doubt stop the ash men in the street and beg for all their ashes.

Choosing Ornamental Shrubs, Vines, and Trees. In the North, spring is the best time to plant roses, flowering shrubs, evergreens, and trees. The new plants will stand the winter better if they have had all summer to adapt to their new home. Right now is the time to select and order from the catalogs the new shrubs you want to plant this spring. They will be shipped to you in late April or while they are still dormant, and should be planted just as soon as the soil can be worked.

Not many years ago it was considered almost impossible to grow winter-hardy roses in the Upper Midwest. Great progress has been made by growers in hybridizing desirable, hardy varieties. Today there are dozens of roses that can be bought from reliable dealers which, with reasonable protection, will come through our winters alive and smiling.

There are many types of roses, each suited for a particular job in the garden. Probably the most suitable roses for home gardens in the Upper Midwest are hybrid teas, floribundas, and climbers.

Hybrid teas are by far the most important roses. Three quarters of all rose plants sold and 60 per cent of all varieties listed are in this group. When we speak of roses, it is the hybrid tea rose that usually comes to mind. Practically all florists' roses are of this type. Many people know hybrid teas as "monthly roses" because of their habit of producing some flowers more or less continuously all summer and autumn, after starting with a big burst of bloom in June.

Most hybrid tea roses are quite large, fragrant, and fully double, with a high center, at least until full-blown. The tapering buds and high-centered flowers of hybrid teas are the accepted standard of rose flower excellence. The plants are reasonably hardy, although there is much variation among varieties on this point, as well as in other characteristics. Height varies from 2 to 6 feet according to variety, soil, care, and season. The foliage likewise varies in shades of green, texture, and resistance to disease, but is almost universally thin and flexible. The flowers are borne on fairly long stems, singly or sometimes in clusters of three, four, or five flowers, if not disbudded. They are the best of all roses for cutting.

There are hundreds of varieties of hybrid teas, but a few score are the best, and are all the home gardener need consider. These are the ones offered in the average catalog and in local nurseries. Some new introductions (many of them patented varieties) are always featured at advanced prices, but the older, less expensive, "tried and true" sorts are generally best for the beginner.

The floribunda roses were derived by crossing hybrid teas with polyantha roses. They combine many of the desired flower characteristics of the former with the heavy and continuous flower production of the latter. Floribunda bushes generally bear their flowers in clusters. They vary in size and form, but are generally smaller than the hybrid teas, not so suitable for cutting, but even more showy in the garden because of the constant abundance of flowers all through the season. They are among the easiest of all roses to grow.

Climbing roses include several subtypes or classes, such as ramblers, large-flowered climbers, ever-blooming climbers, pillar roses, and climbing hybrid teas. Ramblers are now "old-fashioned" and little planted because the others are more attractive in flower and perhaps more satisfactory in plant growth.

The Brownell roses, a special class of hybrid teas, are known as "subzero" roses. They have been bred back to very vigorous strains suitable for a northern climate.

Another new class or type of rose hybrid is named the "grandiflora." Queen Elizabeth, the first rose to be chosen an AARS winner (1955) in this new group, is a very promising variety.

Still another type of rose is the rugosa, a prickly, small-flowered bush often used for hedges and so hardy that it needs no winter protection at all. For recommended varieties of the main types of roses, study your rose catalogs.

Once you have chosen the roses you would like to try, place your order as soon as possible. You should have them, ready to plant, by the last two weeks in April, or a little later if spring is tardy.

Roses should have at least six hours of sunlight every day and, if at all possible, should be placed where they have some shade from the hot afternoon sun. Roses planted too close to the house may react unfavorably to the intense heat reflected by the wall. A shifting light of shade and sunshine from trees has distinct advantages, provided the trees are far enough away so that there is no danger from their roots.

A prime consideration in planning is to put roses where they will be free from competition with other plants, particularly trees, shrubs, and hedges which have large root systems and tend to monopolize soil, water, and plant food. Roots of elm trees often extend many feet beyond the spread of the branches, forming a close-meshed network a few inches below the surface. These can be stripped out and a protective barrier of galvanized iron dropped three to four feet into the soil between the rose beds and the trees. This will keep out the choking, food-stealing tree roots.

Remember that roses are clannish. They will prosper together, but they resent the proximity of other shrubbery. They may do well in the perennial border, however, provided they are not crowded. It is best to place the rose bed where there is plenty of ventilation and air movement, but where it is not too windy. A close, poorly ventilated spot will encourage fungus troubles.

GRANDMA made Uncle Jerry save the soot when he cleaned the kitchen chimney. This soot, from wood fuel only, was put in a gunny sack and steeped in a barrel of hot water. The liquid when cool and diluted was used to water the roses once a month. The same soot was resteeped many times during the summer. I don't know just what the fertilizing action was, but Grandma's roses were magnificent.

Roses are only one of many flowering shrubs you can choose from to add permanent beauty to your home and garden. Ornamental shrubs require a minimum of care, and with careful selection you can get a succession of bloom from early spring well into summer.

For the earliest bloom among flowering shrubs, forsythia or golden bell is a possibility for a sheltered south corner. This graceful five-foot shrub is covered with glowing yellow blossoms even before the leaves appear, and often when the ground is still covered with snow. It needs extensive winter protection here in the North, however, and in some years its flower buds may be killed by spring frosts. Many northern gardeners are willing to take a chance on it, however, because of its earliness and the beauty of its bloom.

Almost as early but much hardier are the flowering plum and flowering almond, which are very similar. They grow to ten feet, and in late April or early May, before the leaves appear, their branches are covered with dainty pink rose-like blossoms. The plum is the hardier of the two, and the flowering almond is often grafted

43

onto the hardy plum rootstock. The yellow flowering currant is another early-blooming shrub, an old-fashioned favorite with fragrant blossoms that will thrive even in considerable shade.

Usually the lilacs are the next to bloom. Lilacs have been greatly improved in the last two decades. The French hybrids are especially good. They are comparatively low growers, usually five to seven feet. Their enormous trusses of flowers in both single and double florets are much larger than the old-fashioned lilacs. The colors are gorgeous — blue changing to lavender rose, deep pink with a satiny luster, reddish violet, creamy white, dark purple-red, delicate blue, and dark maroon.

For a high hedge or screen, however, plant the old-fashioned purple lilacs *(Syringa vulgaris)*. This is the lilac of Grandma's day, very fragrant and very hardy, but almost too robust for the small city lot. It also comes in a white variety, and these two old favorites are still preferred by many to the newer, low-growing hybrids.

In the same way, the old-fashioned, single-flowered mockorange *(Philadelphus coronarius)* is still the choice of many gardeners in spite of a beautiful new, double-flowered variety, Snowflake, which was developed in Minneapolis. Both bloom profusely in June, with large, fragrant, pure white blossoms, and both are extra hardy for our cold northern winter. Snowflake reaches about six feet in height, while the old-fashioned mockorange may reach eight feet and is more tolerant of partial shade and poor conditions. Two lower-growing mockoranges, Golden and Lemoine, three to five feet high, are particularly desirable for foundation planting, as is the newer dwarf variety, Frosty Morn.

Also excellent for foundation planting are two varieties of hydrangea — *paniculata,* six feet high, with huge conical white flowers that change to pink in the fall; and *arborescens,* four feet high, which has huge snowball-like flowers from July until autumn. The latter will stand a northerly exposure and partial shade.

Among the hardiest of native shrubs are the honeysuckles, which come in several different forms, colors, and times of bloom. You may have a choice of four bush honeysuckles with white, pink, cream-yellow, or red blossoms, all excellent for backgrounds as well as individual plantings. There also is a honeysuckle vine, Goldflame, with fragrant flame-coral blossoms lined with gold. It blooms all summer and is very hardy, fine on a trellis and also as a ground cover. Most bush honeysuckles will bloom in considerable shade. Their flowers are followed by handsome red berries that are a great attraction to birds.

Spirea is another popular shrub for northern gardens. Four that are hardy in the North are the well-known white flowered bridal-wreath, five feet tall, which blooms in late May or June; an earlier variety, Garland; Billiard, a foundation type with long pink spikes; and Anthony Waterer, a low-growing bush with rosy red blossoms that blooms most of the summer and will do well in shady spots. All the spireas are beautiful, but do not plant the bridalwreath variety close to your roses. They do not get along well together. Roses are jealous queens who enjoy each other's company but not that of outsiders.

Several other flowering shrubs are less well-known in most northern areas but are well worth trying for special purposes. The Odessa tamarisk is a six-foot shrub that should be grown more often around the house. Its misty blue-green foliage and deep pink blossoms in long, graceful sprays always attract attention. Euonymus, commonly called the strawberry or burning bush, is a six- to eight-foot shrub. Its leaves are lustrous, turning into a brilliant pink cloud around the shrub in the fall. There is also a dwarf variety that thrives in the shade. Blue spirea — *caryopteris* — is a small, three-foot shrub with true blue blossoms from July to frost. Another small foundation shrub is the coralberry, two to three feet high with red berries so thickly clustered that the branches droop with their weight. Birds enjoy this fruit.

Several kinds of shrubs are grown not for their flowering qualities but because they make good hedges. A thick green hedge along the boundary of your yard can be an attractive aid to privacy as well as a handsome background for a flower border. For low and rather formal hedges that can be trimmed severely you can plant red barberry, variegated dogwood, or Chinese or Siberian hedging elm.

45

FEBRUARY

The Chinese elm, although not desirable as a shade or boulevard tree, makes a beautiful hedge in this area. Plants should be very small and planted about twelve inches apart. Stagger the plants in two rows about two feet apart. If kept well trimmed, the hedge will grow from three to five feet high in a couple of years and will give almost complete privacy — so thick a dog cannot penetrate it.

For autumn color in your hedge, try the purpleosier willow, red-osier dogwood, red-leafed maple, winged euonymus, and Japanese barberry. For a family who are winter bird watchers, plant a hedge that will bear and hold the berries that birds love. Plant red or scarlet elders, high-bush cranberry, snow or wax berry, winter berry, chokecherry, bush honeysuckle, and many others.

For a prickly hedge that blooms intermittently during the summer, investigate rugosa roses — very hardy, fragrant bloomers with red, white, pink, or yellow blossoms and practically pest-proof.

Hardy vines and ground covers should also be considered in planning your spring plantings. Handsome perennial climbers like Virginia creeper, bittersweet, and Boston ivy can add great charm to a brick or stucco wall of your house or can screen an unattractive chimney or fence. Of the flowering perennial vines, the purple clematis is by far the most popular and beautiful choice for growing on a trellis on your house or in your garden.

GRANDMA'S farm faced the old pike road. The front was hedged with hawthorn. It was about ten feet wide, six feet high, and a quarter-mile long. This hedge was so dense and strong that farm animals could not penetrate it. The thick, sharp thorns were more than an inch long. It was a paradise for all kinds of birds. In it they built their nests, absolutely safe from marauders. In the spring the hedge was a mass of rosy, fragrant blossoms followed by small apple-like fruit which fed the birds far into the winter. It had been planted by Greatgrandfather almost a century earlier. Every few years it was carefully fertilized.

Ground covers are densely growing vines that trail along the ground or tufts or rosettes that provide greenery and protection from erosion where grass will not readily grow. If you have a heavily shaded area under some trees or a steep bank where a lawn seems impossible, try combinations of lance-leaved funkia, lily of the valley, woodland phlox, and wild ginger.

Spring is the best time to plant trees of all kinds, so consider now what kinds you may want to order. Great progress has been made in recent years in the development of small ornamental trees that serve a dual purpose. Many of them, like the crabapples, bear fruit in addition to beautiful spring blossoms. The Hopa crab is beautiful, with its profusion of dark pink, rose-like blossoms, and its fruit is excellent for jelly. The Red Silver crab also has handsome foliage and brilliant red blossoms. The Almey crab, a product of Canada, is thoroughly hardy, and its wealth of pink blossoms and red foliage makes it an outstanding lawn and garden ornamental. Its dark red fruit is good for jelly. The Dolgo crab is excellent, also, with rich red fruit for jelly and canning.

For shade trees the graceful American elm is one of the finest for northern homes and gardens. It is very hardy and fast growing for a permanent tree. Along with the black and white oaks it is perhaps our most typical residential tree here in the North. Unfortunately the oaks are not too commonly adaptable to nursery growing, so if your yard is not naturally blessed with them, you must find an alert nurseryman or be content with planting other species. Maples are also a good choice for permanent planting. The hard or sugar maple grows to seventy feet and changes to brilliant colors in the fall. The Schwedler maple is a beautiful tree with crimson leaves turning to bronze green in the summer, while the brilliant Crimson King maple, introduced ten years ago, has crimson foliage all through the summer.

Two strikingly unusual lawn trees with long pendant branches are the cutleaf weeping birch and Niobe weeping willow. For background, accent, or screening, consider the Lombardy poplar, a fast-growing, tall, symmetrical tree, and the Bolleana poplar. The latter resembles the Lombardy, but is smaller and longer lived.

47

FEBRUARY

In planning for trees and shrubbery, do not overlook the ever-greens, both the needle and broad-leafed types. In the summer they give your yard a cool, quiet dignity that can be obtained with no other plantings, and in winter your house and yard form a living Christmas card.

The Colorado spruce — both silver and blue — and the Black Hills spruce usually are used in groups as border plantings. Planted on small premises, they make a beautiful background in a few years. Whether these larger trees are suitable in the front areas of a yard or near the house is a debated question, although a few years ago they were extensively used in these ways. As a result, many houses now are submerged in a sea of evergreen foliage.

Try slow-growing varieties such as arborvitae, junipers, and low-growing Mugho pine for foundation plantings. They will be a trifle more expensive at the start, but they require less maintenance and will not have to be replaced for years.

Overgrown foundation plantings add no beauty to your house or yard. Any plant that keeps out light and air from any room in the house should be replaced. Don't cover up the architectural lines of your house either, but allow them to be revealed and accented and enjoyed by properly designed planting. Careful landscaping will enhance both the beauty and the value of your property. Plan carefully and don't be in a hurry — your trees and shrubs will be with you a long time.

As your plans become more definite, get special information about the problems that particularly concern you. Your library is a good source for special books. You should also write to your state university for its publications list. Many of its bulletins and pamphlets will be of help to you. There are also garden magazines, many of them published by societies interested in growing one kind of flower. Your librarian can help you here too.

REMINDERS

Now is the time to buy tuberous begonias for starting indoors next month. Place your order early while the selection of top quality tubers is good, but be willing to pay a little extra for choice varieties. Don't purchase hard woody tubers; under a little finger pressure they should be slightly resilient.

During February mild spells, tulips sometimes sprout prematurely. This frequently happens along the south side of many houses where the snow has disappeared. This early sprouting means the bulbs were planted too shallowly and probably too close to the warm foundation wall. It also means that if Jack Frost doesn't get them, rabbits probably will. Here's the remedy: get some earth from a greenhouse or from your supply in the basement and cover the sprouting tulips from two to four inches deep. They probably will be all right and will bloom according to schedule in May.

GRANDMA had discovered what to do about the rabbits that ate the little tulips that poked up their noses during warm spells about this time of year. She had found that a pinch of snuff would repel the rabbits — unless they were too hungry. She always had Uncle Jerry buy it and explain to Zeb Klinkhammer, the store-keeper, for what purpose it was to be used. Zeb knew Uncle did not use snuff, and Grandma was always in mortal terror that some-one might think she wanted it for her personal use.

This is the time of year to "slip" geraniums to start new plants for summer bloom outdoors. Cut stems from your old geraniums about three inches long, making clean straight cuts just below a joint. Remove all the lower leaves and loose bark. Dry the slips for two hours and then dip the ends in charcoal or garden lime to prevent decay.

You can start several cuttings in a six- or eight-inch shallow pot, the kind called a bulb pan. Cork up the hole in the bottom and place in the center of this pot a two- or three-inch pot, also corked and filled with water. Now fill the space around the small pot with moist, clean sand or moist vermiculite. Thrust the cuttings one and

49

a half inches into the starting medium. Keep the small pot filled with tepid water and seepage from it will keep the cuttings watered.

If possible, place this rooting pot in a warm spot, but not in direct sunshine. It is especially desirable to keep the bottom of the pot warm — roots will form much more quickly. An inverted glass bowl or plastic hotcap placed over the pan will encourage rooting and growth, but raise it slightly if moisture forms inside.

In three weeks carefully dig up a cutting. If half-inch or longer roots have formed, you can plant each cutting in separate two-and-a-half-inch pots in a soil mixture of two parts sand and one part loam. When you make the second potting into a three- or four-inch pot use a rather heavy, fairly rich garden soil. If the plants are lanky at this stage, pinch out the tops to encourage side growth. By the time warm days arrive in May, the new geraniums will be ready to set out in the garden in full sun and start to bloom.

For a real foretaste of spring, plant morning-glories now to bloom in an indoor window. They are adaptable to pot culture and tend to bloom faster when their roots are restricted. Start several seeds in a 5- or 6-inch pot, planting ½ inch deep. Nick the hard seed coat with a knife and soak twenty-four hours before planting to hasten germination. The soil should not be rich — dilute your regular potting mixture with two extra parts of sand. Keep them in a sunny window and provide vertical strings or wire for the tendrils to climb on. You can pinch out the tips of shoots that seem to be wandering too far. In 8 to 12 weeks the lovely 5-inch flowers should begin to open, and you will have spring in your window no matter what the weather outdoors.

❧ MARCH ❧

MARCH in the North is more winter than spring. There may be mild, sunny days of general thaw, but they are sure to be followed by new snowstorms and cold snaps before the end of the month. Take advantage of these last wintry days and evenings to do some indoor chores in preparation for true spring. There are garden tools to be cleaned and sharpened, flowerpots and seed flats to prepare for indoor planting, perhaps a new window box to build or that cold frame or hotbed you've always wished for. A few March evenings spent in your basement workshop can give your garden a real head start.

MAKING A COLD FRAME OR HOTBED

Either a cold frame or a hotbed will add greatly to the northern gardener's pleasure, since it can extend considerably our rather short growing season and bring earlier bloom to our gardens. Or, if you plan to start annual seedlings in flats of earth in the house, these flats can later be placed in the cold frame to "harden off" — adjust to outdoor conditions — before being placed in the garden.

Before you begin to build the wooden frame, choose the spot where you want it to stand. It should be placed in a sunny spot protected from strong winds and driving rains and the top should slant toward the south. The location should be entirely free from shade, at least in the early spring months, so that the sun will shine directly on the frame. It should be in as inconspicuous a spot as possible also, since a cold frame is more useful than beautiful. A location along the south wall of the house would be ideal, and

51

near a basement window if you want to extend an electrical cable from the house to make a hotbed.

Cold frames and hotbeds are usually built 3 feet wide by 6 feet long, or some multiple of this, to fit the standard glazed storm sash which usually serves as a cover. However, there are so many glass substitutes available now that you can change the size to fit the most convenient location available for the frame in your garden. For a 3-by-6-foot frame, one end of the box should be 15 inches high and the other end 10 inches high, to provide the necessary slope for the glass sash.

GRANDMA knew about soilless horticulture. On moist moss, cotton, or blotting paper in shallow plates placed in the window, she scattered seeds of garden cress, sometimes called peppergrass. In ten days the seedlings, hundreds of them, would be up four inches high and ready to be eaten in her dainty, thin sandwiches. It took four entire plants to make a sandwich, so she raised many crops each winter. For salads she grew a permanent crop in flats of earth. These were more vigorous plants and bore all winter. You can purchase this seed in seed stores.

Ideally the frame should be constructed of one-inch boards of cedar or cypress, woods that are quite rot resistant; or even better, of heavy plywood treated with several coats of shellac. If you use old lumber that is not wind-tight, however, line the inside of the frame above the soil line with heavy paper. Do not use tarpaper because its fumes are harmful to most vegetation. Paint the frame both inside and out with Cuprinol to prevent decay, and hinge the glass sash at the high end of the frame so it can be opened easily for transplanting and airing. If you prefer, the sash cover can be made of transparent plastic material such as is used for windows in poultry houses. Plastic is less fragile than glass, is much lighter, and also permits ultraviolet rays to reach the seedlings.

When your cold frame is built and painted, you may have to wait for warmer weather to install it outdoors. When a mild spell occurs and the ground is thawed, dig a rectangular hole at the spot you have chosen for the cold frame to stand. The hole should be at least one foot deep and slightly larger than the size of the frame. Into this hole put the frame you have built — supported under the corners with stones or bricks — so that six inches of the frame walls are beneath the surface of the ground and the remainder above. Thus the front of the frame is four inches above the surface of the ground and the rear nine inches, with the sash cover slanting toward the south.

After you have placed the frame in the hole, fill in around the outside of it with earth or cinders to keep out drafts. In the bottom of the cold frame itself, place a layer of pebbles, gravel, cinders, or other coarse material to ensure good drainage, then fill to ground level with good, loamy garden soil, or potting mixture from your indoor supply. Seeds can be planted directly in this seedbed, flats of seedlings started indoors can be moved bodily into the cold frame, or young seedlings can be transplanted from flats in the house to the soil in the cold frame. Whichever method you use, read the instructions on the seed packets carefully to determine where and when the seed should be planted.

The temperature and ventilation in the cold frame can be controlled by raising and lowering the glass sash cover. On cold nights cover the frame with a tarpaulin or blanket to keep out frost. To protect the glass from breaking, stretch and nail a strip of small-mesh chicken wire over it. The cold frame can be used not only to start annual seedlings early in spring, but also to start new perennial seedlings or cuttings in the summer months, to shelter semi-hardy plants like chrysanthemums over the winter, or to store tulips and other bulbs, potted in the fall for indoor bloom, until they are brought indoors during the winter to force them into bloom.

If you add a source of heat to your cold frame, it becomes a hot-bed and allows even earlier planting in the spring. If you are able to obtain fresh horse manure, fill the bottom of the cold frame — you should dig the hole three feet instead of one foot deep

— with a deep layer of manure, tramp it down, and cover with several inches of good garden earth. Allow it to heat and then cool to 90 degrees before planting seeds.

An electrical heating cable for the hotbed will be more practical for most gardeners, however. Such cables, with thermostats to regulate temperature, are sold by many garden supply dealers. The current consumed costs little and the even heat gives better results than the old-fashioned manure-heated hotbed. The amount of current needed for heating depends upon the insulation of the frame, and how early in spring heat is turned on, but it seldom adds much to the light bill. The even heat provided by the cable is beneficial to all plants and vital to those that chill easily. It also extends the growing period, since the heat does not become exhausted as does heat from manure.

To make an electrically heated hotbed, the cold frame is sunk into the ground about six inches — a cable doesn't require a deep pit, as manure does. The cable is arranged on the bottom of the frame in loops, so that heat will be evenly distributed. The supply wire and cable both are connected to a thermostat which can be set at the desired minimum temperature.

The cable may be covered with four to six inches of soil in which seeds are sown. It is a good idea to place a sheet of fine-mesh poultry wire an inch above the cable, with soil between. Another method is to grow plants in flats placed above the cable, which may be embedded in the soil on which the flats rest. A special type of cable may also be obtained which can be laid on top of the soil, protected by a grating of wooden slats. To improve insulation and reduce current consumption, the outside walls of the frame should be banked with cinders and covered with soil to within a few inches of the top.

The main things to watch are temperature and drafts. Ventilation is necessary on warm days and for very short periods on cooler days. Sow seeds thinly and water beds moderately when planting. Thin out the seedlings when necessary, and in general follow the same rules for preparing the seedbed and starting the seeds that apply to planting any garden.

STARTING ANNUALS INDOORS

If you do not have the time or space to build and use a cold frame or hotbed, or if you want an even earlier head start on your outdoor garden, you can start annual seeds indoors. Growing healthy seedlings in the average house or apartment is somewhat difficult, but the challenge of the difficult is part of the fun of gardening. The greatest problems are to avoid "damping off" of the seedlings, a fungus disease, and to keep them from becoming spindly for lack of all-around light.

There are two main reasons for starting annuals indoors. First, there are many very desirable ones, like petunias, asters, snapdragons, salvia, tithonia, and verbena, that take a long time to come into bloom, and when they are planted outdoors in the North they do not flower until the end of summer. Second, it's nice to have even the quick-growing annuals, such as sweet alyssum, lobelia, annual phlox, and marigolds, all ready to bloom in June as soon as they can be transplanted outdoors, instead of six weeks later as they would if the seeds were planted outdoors in May.

The trick in starting annuals indoors is to time them so that they are well along but not too large when it is warm enough to transplant them outdoors. Hardy annuals that can withstand some frost should be started six to eight weeks before outdoor planting begins. In most of the North, the average date of the last killing frost is sometime in middle or late May, so that hardy annuals should

GRANDMA had Uncle Jerry get out her canna, dahlia, and elephant ear roots from the potato cellar, where they had been stored all winter, in late March. In the fall they had been placed in a small ventilated box under bushels of potatoes where they had kept beautifully without drying out. Grandma now would divide, pot, and place them in the big sunny kitchen window. Here they would get a good start before planting outside in late spring. They were always the first to bloom in the valley.

be started indoors during the last half of March. Tender annuals like zinnias and marigolds need settled warm weather before being set outdoors and should be started two or three weeks later than the hardy annuals, from early to mid-April in most northern areas.

GRANDMA *was careful about overwatering, but sometimes at this time of year little pests, such as tiny worms and springtails, would appear in the earth of her potted plants. She quickly remedied the trouble. She toasted old bread until it was like charcoal, absolutely black, crushed it into small crumbs and cultivated this carbonized bread into the top earth of the plants. Sometimes she placed some in the bottom of the pots.*

Annuals can be started in the house in any window that receives direct sunshine for most of the day — the more sunlight the better, and you may find that they will appreciate some additional artificial light as well. If your windows are not sunny all day, you may want to try using artificial light exclusively for your seedlings. A fascinating book, *Growing Plants under Artificial Light,* by Peggie Schulz, will tell you how to go about it. Either fluorescent or incandescent lights, or both, can be used, and at very moderate cost controlled greenhouse conditions can be reproduced in a dark basement or garage.

If you are dependent on a sunny window alone, however, some sort of table or bench should be placed at the window to hold the flowerpots or seed flats. Wooden boxes two to three inches deep may be used, but for most home gardeners the shallow flowerpots called bulb pans are large enough and more convenient. The pots or flats should be filled with an inch of broken crocking or other coarse material for drainage, then filled to within half an inch of the top with a light soil mixture. This should consist of one part each, by weight, of light, sifted garden loam, peatmoss, and sharp, gritty builder's sand. The soil must be absorbent yet porous enough to drain quickly, and should be pressed down firmly in the pots or flats.

Sow the seed sparingly over the smoothed surface of the soil. The seedlings should not be crowded, even in infancy. Large seeds like zinnia and calendula should be 1/8 to 1/4 inch apart, medium-sized seeds like aster and marigold somewhat closer, and tiny seeds like portulaca and petunia may be 1/16 to 1/8 inch apart. When the seeds are sown, press them firmly into contact with the soil and with a sink strainer sift more soil, or better still, a layer of rubbed and sifted sphagnum moss over them. Big seeds should be covered to a depth of 1/4 inch, medium seeds 1/8 inch, and fine seeds just barely covered until out of sight. The advantages of sphagnum moss are that it is light, it retains moisture at the surface where the seeds need it, and it is sterile, thus preventing the damping off disease that attacks many homegrown seedlings.

The bulb pans or flats should be watered from beneath. This is done by setting them in two inches or so of water in the kitchen sink until moisture begins to show on the surface of the soil. Then they are removed, allowed to drain thoroughly, and not watered again until the surface starts to look dry. A covering of glass, plastic, or cone-shaped hotcaps over the pots or flats will keep the surface from drying out too quickly. Once the seeds have sprouted, however, these coverings must be removed to allow proper ventilation.

When the first pair of true leaves — not the seed leaves that appear first — have begun to develop, the seedlings are transplanted to roomier quarters in other bulb pans or flats. The same soil mixture may be used, except that the sand may be reduced and abundant plant food added — one cup of bone meal with three of dried cow or sheep manure mixed thoroughly with half a bushel of transplanting soil. The seedlings should be set two inches apart each way, with the soil firmed well around their roots and watering from below continued. They should be turned frequently in their window to maintain even growth. They will remain in these pots or flats until it is warm enough to plant them in the garden. If you have no cold frame to set them out in to harden off, they should spend several days on an open porch or in a protected outdoor spot before being transplanted to the garden in May.

An even simpler way to start annual seeds indoors is to use small, square cardboard pots or plant bands especially designed for the purpose. The small bottomless plant bands are 2 inches square and come twelve to a kit with a waterproof cardboard tray for them to stand on. You partly fill the plant bands with good garden earth, planting three or four seeds in each band. Fine sphagnum moss is used for the top layer of the planting medium, which usually prevents damping off.

When the seeds sprout, cut off — don't pull up — all but the one most vigorous seedling in each band. When the weather is warm enough, you can transplant each plant into the garden — still in the bottomless container — without disturbing it the least bit. In this way one intermediate transplanting process is eliminated. These kits of bands and trays are very reasonable in price. There is also a dandy little illustrated booklet entitled *Sphagnum Moss for Seed Germination,* #243, that you can order for 15 cents from the Superintendent of Documents, Washington, D.C.

TIME TO START TUBEROUS BEGONIAS

The time to start tuberous begonias for northern gardens is the middle of March to the middle of April. If you ordered your begonia tubers in February you should have them now, ready to sprout.

Tuberous begonias should be started in shallow containers such as wooden seed flats, bulb pans, or nonrusting baking pans. The containers should be filled with two or three inches of moist sphagnum moss or vermiculite, obtainable from your garden supply store. Press the tubers about half an inch into the starting medium, placing them three inches apart so that the roots will not tangle. Do not cover them with the moss; instead, leave the upper surface of the tubers exposed. Be sure the indented or hollow side is up and the rounded side, which forms the roots, is down.

The starting medium should be kept constantly moist, but do not overwater. Use tepid water, about 80 to 90 degrees, and be careful not to allow water to get into the indented top. If it should, soak it up with absorbent tissue. If possible, use a long, slender-spouted watering can or a small funnel and apply water between the tubers, in the same places each time. While the tubers are sprouting, the containers should be kept in a warm place but not in sunshine. A warm basement floor near the heating plant is a possibility. One home gardener I know of places the container on top of the radio, which is usually just warm enough to sprout the tubers.

In May, when it is time to pot your begonias, I will discuss the next step in this process.

MARCH CARE FOR YOUR HOUSE PLANTS

Most of your house plants should be flourishing during March, with longer days and brighter sunshine to encourage new buds and leaf production. As long as foliage plants keep putting out new leaves, and your fibrous-rooted begonias, African violets, and other flowering plants keep blooming, be generous with plant food and water. The earth in their pots dries out more quickly on sunny days, so be prepared to water oftener if needed.

GRANDMA cut branches of pussywillows, forsythia, flowering almond, cherry, plum, and sometimes crab-apple to blossom in the house when the buds began to swell in March. She cut the branches at a long slant and placed them in deep pails or washtubs of tepid water in a reasonably bright, warm room — damp if possible — but not in direct sunshine, until the buds commenced to open. Every day the branches were sprayed or dipped in tepid water. If not kept damp, the buds dry out and perish. Grandma changed the water every few days and made a fresh cut on the stems to permit free absorption of water. Why not try Grandma's methods this March and make your living room, like her parlor, a blooming bower of spring?

MARCH

Some of your flowering plants will be through blooming by now. Potted tulips and other bulbs have a fairly short period of bloom. Do not discard them, however, for you may get another blossoming next year, and you have nothing to lose by trying. Keep the potted bulbs watered and fertilized until the foliage turns yellow. Then place them in the darkest, coolest corner of the basement and allow them to rest, without water, until next fall, still in their pots. Then remove them from the pots and plant them outdoors in the garden, five inches apart and about eight inches deep for tulips.

Daffodils and hyacinths grown in soil in pots are also treated in this way, except that they may be planted out in the garden whenever the weather is warm, without waiting for fall. The little bulbs, such as scillas, snowdrops, crocuses, and grape hyacinths, can be removed from their pots when the spring days are warm and planted as a clump, with tops just two inches deep, in the wild flower garden. Usually these bulbs will not bloom the following spring, but the next year, when you have almost forgotten about them, up will come beautiful clusters of these spring beauties. Don't bother to save the golden or Paper White narcissuses that have been forced in water, however, for these bulbs seldom bloom again after forcing.

If you have gloxinias in your indoor garden, you may be having trouble with buds blasting or dropping. The plants may be getting too much or not enough sunshine. In March, two or three hours of the morning sun, or all day in a south window covered with a very thin curtain, should be about right. Keep the plants out of cold drafts and always medium moist, but never dry. One dry spell may ruin all the buds or even the plant itself. A thin layer of charcoal on the soil will keep the soil sweet and repel pests.

Many Christmas poinsettias, if they were kept in sunny windows with cool night temperatures, have only recently stopped blooming. When flowering is over, allow the poinsettia to go almost dry and keep it in a cool, well-ventilated place. When the weather is really warm outdoors, cut off all but five inches of the stems and feed with balanced plant food or repot with your regular potting mixture. Now the poinsettia should be plunged in the garden, pot and all, where it will be protected from wind and midday sun. Keep it well watered and feed twice during the summer. Pinch back the new growth sparingly until about September 1 — this helps to form a bushier plant — but don't pinch off the same shoot more than once or small flowers will result.

In early September the poinsettia should be brought back into the house by easy stages — through the porch or garage, a cool east room, and then into a sunny window. Even after all this care it may shed its leaves and fail to bloom next Christmas, but, if you are successful, the scarlet-bracted flowers are worth the trouble.

BUILD A WINDOW BOX

With seedlings started indoors or in your cold frame, tuberous begonias sprouting on your window sill, and flowering house plants taking a well-earned rest, now is the time to build a window box for this summer's enjoyment.

Window boxes are usually placed on sturdy metal shelf brackets with the top edge of the boxes just below the outside window sill. If placed on the sills, they may obstruct light and ventilation. For an ordinary single window, a box 3½ feet long, 8 inches deep, and 10 inches wide is a good size. If possible, make the box about three inches wider than the window. Where large or multiple windows demand greater length, the other dimensions may be larger in proportion. If made of cypress, your window box should last indefinitely. Have your lumberyard saw the boards to the correct size and you will have no trouble nailing them together.

If you wish a really permanent box, however, use brass or copper screws instead of nails and drill the holes to receive them. Another method is to have a tinsmith make your window boxes of galvanized iron. These will also give good service. In any case, be sure to drill drainage holes and paint with moisture-proof paint.

An inch layer of charcoal in the bottom of the window box will help to keep the soil sweet. Paint the inside with a special chemical paint sold in photo supply stores for waterproofing developing trays and your box will last for years. Rich soil with plenty of humus such as peat or leafmold — the type florists call "potting soil" but with more humus mixed in — should be used. Window boxes need abundant plant food. Add it at the rate of one level tablespoonful for each square foot of soil, and mix in well. More may be added during the growing season.

GRANDMA brought the geranium plants up from the cool cellar in March. She had stored them there the previous autumn, just before freeze-up. Although the big tops looked quite dead, there was a small clump of earth around the roots. This earth had kept the roots from drying out completely. Most of them had sprouted little green buds close to the roots. Grandma explained to me that even in the dark, cold cellar, these almost lifeless roots had felt the call of spring. She would cut off most of last year's growth, remove the dead leaves and pot the roots with the old earth still around them in ordinary garden earth. They were then given a good soaking, placed in a sunny window, and kept rather dry until they were well sprouted. By the middle of May they were flourishing plants, ready to be planted around the veranda and in the window boxes.

Perhaps the finest of all window-box flowers are petunias because they blossom constantly throughout the summer and provide interesting varieties of color. All the AAS prize-winning petunias of recent years — Fire Dance, Paleface, Comanche, Ballerina, Lipstick, and others — are obtainable from your dealer, either as seeds to start indoors, or as growing plants in May. It is of course easier to buy small plants. Nasturtiums, particularly the new double hybrids, are excellent window-box subjects. Fragrant flowers, such as sweet alyssum, mignonette, ten-week stocks, and dwarf snapdragons are doubly attractive. The low-growing Unwin dahlias are also desirable. All these are started from seed now in the house and transplanted outside in May.

Boxes that spend most of the day in shade are a special problem. If the shade is dense, like that of a building, perhaps only foliage plants can be grown, such as ferns, fancy-leaved caladiums, crotons, and other florists' subjects. If there is some sun or considerable blue sky, tuberous begonias probably will do well. *Impatiens sultani*, the Zanzibar balsam, bearing flowers of salmon or rose on bushy plants 18 inches tall, is excellent in semishaded places. Violas also thrive in partial shade, and the list of flowers that will do well increases as the amount of sun increases. Don't plant too many different kinds of flowers in your window box, but try for an overall effect of two or three colors.

GET YOUR GARDEN TOOLS READY

March is a good time to clean, oil, sharpen, and repair your garden tools. In your warm basement now you can do a much better job than when the spring rush is upon you.

Don't forget to call your hardware store — before all your neighbors get the same idea — to pick up your lawnmower for sharpening and adjustment. Do not attempt to do this work yourself as you may ruin your mower. Repairs on a power-driven mower are usually a job for a specialist.

Sharpen all tools that have a cutting edge, such as hoes, spades, shovels, and trowels. For this work get two flat files, one medium and one fine, with handles, and a whetstone for sickles and scythes. However, have your pruning shears sharpened by an expert.

Your tools will last longer and be almost rust-proof if metal surfaces are rubbed bright with steel wool and dressed with an auto body hard-waxing solution. This is also an excellent rust preventive for the cutting edges of your lawnmower if applied after each use.

Some folks get along with broken and misshapen handles on hoes, rakes, and digging tools. Get new handles — they are not expensive and your work will be easier. For some metal broom rakes you can get new tines to replace broken and missing ones.

Mending materials and repair kits are obtainable for plastic garden hoses, also for single- and triple-tube soakers. Small leaks in plastic hoses or sprinklers can be repaired with a tenacious plastic tape, and for pinholes there is a thick gummy material that comes in a collapsible tube. For big cuts use new couplings or slip-in repair links. So don't discard the old plastic hose until you investigate.

MARCH

If you are starting a brand-new lawn this spring, seeding must wait until the ground is dry enough to smooth and rake, probably not until sometime in mid-April. But for rehabilitating a lawn already established, late March is usually a good time to begin. If we should have a fairly warm spell with drying winds, the lawn area may become dry enough for you to prepare it for feeding and seeding. The mat of dead grass and leaves on the lawn should be carefully and lightly raked off, but if the sod is soggy and your raking disturbs the grass roots, wait until the area is drier. However, remember that a mat of dead leaves will smother grass like a heavy plank.

Often in late March and early April we have alternate thawing and freezing that cause a "honeycomb" condition in the ground which is admirable for the retention and absorption of lawn food without a wasteful runoff during spring rains. Every lawn needs an application of fertilizer at least once a year, in early spring, and preferably another in September also. Either an organic fertilizer, like Loma or Milorganite, or a balanced inorganic fertilizer like Vigoro may be used. On an established lawn in good condition you will need about 20 to 30 pounds of balanced inorganic plant food, or 100 pounds of dry animal fertilizer, for each 1,000 square feet of grass.

If applied early, the nutriment is soaked deep into the soil by the spring thaws and rain. Unless the ground has a decided slope and is bare, there will be practically no loss from surface runoff. Where there is a well-established turf, the grass blades act as obstacles to loss from the surface.

Feeding lawns has recently been greatly simplified by slow-dissolving, balanced lawn fertilizers. One application in the spring is usually enough for the entire summer. Another application in August or September may be necessary if the soil is poor, however.

Some people feed their lawns directly on snowfalls in late March or early April. This is a good practice if the turf under the snow is open enough to take the dissolving plant food. Grass seed can also be sown on top of a spring snowfall. This method enables you to see the seed against the white snow and distribute it more evenly. Fertilizer should have been applied to the lawn first, however, and be already well washed into the soil by rain or thaw before new grass is seeded. A couple of days after the snow has melted, a light top dressing of black dirt will help to bury the new seed and also protect it from the birds.

GRANDMA waited until her lawn was dry enough so it wouldn't wet the soles of her shoes. Then she and Uncle Jerry would rake off the accumulation of winter rubbish without disturbing the old mulch of last year's lawn clippings. She knew that this loam-forming mulch protected tender spring grass and kept the lawn green during the hot summer by conserving moisture. When buying grass seed, two of Grandma's old adages always come to my mind: "Don't be penny-wise and pound-foolish," and "No matter how good the earth may be a garden or lawn is no better than the seed you put into it."

Never buy cheap grass seed. It is a waste of time and money. Such seed is almost always low in germination, short-lived, and probably contains much chaff and weed seeds. It will pay you to buy the best, but choosing the best for your particular lawn has not always been easy. Until recently the owner of a lawn that had a combination of full sunshine and deep shade areas had a problem. Today, however, you can buy a mixture of eight or ten different grass seeds that will produce a good lawn in almost any degree of sun or shade. This mixture is also adaptable to many different soils, provided they contain a reasonable amount of plant food and humus. If these are lacking, they can be added to your soil before the grass is seeded. We will talk more about this soil preparation next month when new lawns and gardens can be dug, raked, and planted.

One of the best new developments is Merion bluegrass. Some

nationally-known seed houses are now using it in their standard seed mixtures. Merion bluegrass is slow to germinate, usually taking from fifteen to thirty days. It increases mostly by root extension and takes about a year to become well established. It grows well with ordinary Kentucky bluegrass and looks a good deal like a cross between bluegrass and bentgrass. It resists mold and weeds and stands close mowing. However, it does not hug the ground like bentgrass. The blades are a beautiful dark green and stand nearly upright. It also seems to have a tendency to drive out crabgrass. During hot dry spells in the summer, it remains surprisingly green and fresh with comparatively little watering.

Even an established lawn will usually be improved by a light application of grass seed in early spring, after it has been raked and fertilized. Late March or early April is a good time, and less seed will be required now than later in the spring, when the lawn is drier and seed will not germinate so readily. Later, too, you will have more birds eating your grass seed. Three pounds for each 2,000 square feet should be enough. The seed can be sown by hand or with a spreader. For even hand sowing, divide the seed into two lots. Sow one lot when you are walking in one direction and the other lot when walking at right angles to the first sowing.

Do not walk on the lawn more than necessary at this season. The sod is so soft and spongy that it packs very easily. Erect barriers or rope off areas where people cut across the lawn. If March and April rains prove to be deficient after your grass seed is sown, you will have to get out the hose to keep the lawn moist. Grass seed is rather slow to germinate and needs moisture throughout that crucial period.

Apart from routine fertilizing and reseeding, your lawn may need special attention because of fungus or weed conditions. The melting snow sometimes reveals a condition called snow mold on our northern lawns. This is a cottony fungus growth that becomes apparent some springs soon after the snow has melted. It often appears first as a white or grayish growth on an area about the size of a saucer and spreads quite rapidly into areas of many square feet.

If you had it in your lawn last year, get a snow mold remedy and apply where the mold was last spring. And watch for its appearance elsewhere. Usually it is quickly routed if caught early, but it sometimes will ruin a lawn. Since it is a fungus disease, do not walk on the infected places or rake them into healthy areas, or you may spread the infestation. But there is a bright side to this problem, too. Sometimes after a few dry, sunny days the mold will disappear as suddenly and mysteriously as it arrived. However, to play safe, you had better apply the fungicide as directed and guard against a return of the infection.

In recent years there have been developed several new weed control chemicals for lawns. These, too, are most effective if applied early in the spring before weed seeds get a good start.

Perennial chickweed, often called "mouse-ear," perhaps because of its downy foliage, and the annual variety, "tongue grass," "starwort," and "starweed" ("star" perhaps because of the shape of the small blossoms), are both effectively controlled by a new chemical, disodium monomethyl arsonate. It can be used in a sprayer or a sprinkling can and is harmless to permanent grass when applied as directed. Unless chickweed is killed early, before warm weather comes, reseeding of the bare spots left by dead chickweed will have been delayed too long to establish a good stand of grass on these areas; and unless a good stand of grass can be established, these spots are likely to be taken over by crabgrass or more chickweed later in the season. When applied early, even in temperatures as low as 50 degrees, this new chemical also kills knotweed, a lawn pest for which no other chemical control is available.

Ordinarily, spraying for chickweed and knotweed must be done earlier than for crabgrass.

OUTDOOR GARDEN CHORES

On that first warm day in late March, when the snow has finally melted and the temperature is in the sixties, there is a great temptation to uncover the perennial border and roses from their winter mulch. We northern gardeners should resist this temptation with all our native caution. It's true that spring comes suddenly in the North, but real spring is still several weeks away. There will be more snow and freezing weather before March and April are over, and gardens uncovered now will suffer.

If the March warm spell is prolonged, however, and if the temperature remains above freezing during the night, you can, with reasonable safety, remove about half the winter protection from roses and perennials. Inspect the ground and any new stems and leaves carefully for signs of mildew, and if you see any trace of its powdery, white growth, loosen the leaves or hay thoroughly and allow the warm sunshine and breezes to dry and freshen it. Tulips, plantain lilies, squills, and other shoots may be coming up beneath the mulch, but as long as the winter covering is not matted or causing mildew, it is better to keep it loosened but in place for another two or three weeks. If a real March heat wave should develop, however, remove all the winter covering but keep it handy in case of a sudden cold snap. Don't remove the hilling around the roses until warm weather seems really settled.

A good chore for eager gardeners in March is pruning hedges. A hedge should be trimmed so it is narrower at the top than at the base. Heavy pruning usually results in a thicker, sturdier hedge.

GRANDMA often helped the squirrels. Some years when spring's arrival was delayed and she knew the squirrels had about exhausted their winter stores, she and Uncle Jerry fed them all the corn and culls of winter apples they could eat. This wasn't altogether Grandma's kindness. It was also a bit of common sense. The first year she was on the farm there was a late spring with icy snows and the squirrels became ravenous. High in the branches of the sugar maples they ripped off the bark and ate into the wood for food. Hundreds of gallons of maple sap were wasted. It poured down the trunks, soaked into the ground, and drained the trees. So that was why Grandma always started early feeding the squirrels when there was a late spring. Then she knew the maple syrup harvest was safe.

Late summer and autumn-blooming ornamental shrubs may also be pruned now, but do not trim spring-blooming shrubs such as lilacs, flowering almond, mockorange, forsythia, and ornamental flowering fruit trees until after they have blossomed. Prune grape vines early, before the sap starts to flow. Leave only about forty buds on vigorous branches. Cut out old dead raspberry canes and thin out the new, bearing canes to about four per foot of row. In pruning currants and gooseberries, cut out the old (four years or older) canes clear down to the ground. This will make room for the new productive canes. Now is a good time, too, to give all shrubbery a feeding of well-rotted cow manure or balanced plant food.

Shade trees in the home grounds seldom need to be pruned, but sometimes a damaged branch must be removed. In removing large branches, undercut one foot from the trunk and then cut off, leaving a stub. Next remove this stub by cutting close to the trunk. This prevents tearing of the bark. Remove dead or partially dead branches. Cut out water sprouts and branches that cross and rub one another, and remove unproductive wood. Space branches on young fruit trees so two do not come out at the same place on the trunk. (See pp. 252–54.)

Shade trees should also be protected as soon as possible against the canker or measuring worm that defoliates many northern trees, especially elms, during the summer. The canker worm makes two migrations up the trees each season: one in early spring and one in October. The female climbs the tree to lay thousands of eggs that grow and become the destructive worms.

Probably the best preventive is spraying with a 10 per cent solution of DDT or with lead arsenate. The trunks should be sprayed to a height of ten feet when the leaf buds are beginning to swell, and this spraying should be repeated after ten days. Another spraying program should be done in the fall.

A second method is encircling the tree with a heavy weatherproof paper band, three inches wide, which you can buy in seed stores. The side that presses against the bark is covered with a soft wooly substance. A sticky substance, purchased with the bands, is applied to the outside of the band; this substance stops the migration of the female up the tree. Never apply the "stickum" directly on the bark, as it will always leave an ugly scar and may even kill some trees. Unless the worms are prevented from getting a start, they first defoliate the elm trees and then move to other trees. They can lower themselves by silken threads like spiders and raise havoc in gardens also.

Plant Sweet Peas Early. As soon as the frost is out of the ground, we can prepare to plant sweet peas. Ideally the trench should have been spaded and enriched last fall, for in spring the soil is often too wet for digging till well into April. If the trench is not ready, however, wait till the soil can be worked without sticking to the spade. The earlier the better is the rule for sweet peas. They make their best growth in April and early May when they can send their roots down deep, enabling them to withstand the hot, dry days of summer.

Choose a place where they will get the morning sun, and if possible not more than two or three hours of the hot afternoon sun. Run the rows north and south. When the soil can be worked, dig a trench the width of the spade blade and 12 to 20 inches deep. The deeper the better, provided you have enough compost. Fill the trench with a mixture of old cow manure, compost, rotted leaves, and loamy soil or peatmoss to within three inches of the top after the mixture has settled. The purpose of this mixture is to make a deep, cool, easily penetrated bed for the long, hungry roots of the sweet peas.

Then add one inch of clean garden earth, and on it sow the seeds, after soaking them all night in warm water. Place the seeds in two rows 8 to 10 inches apart with 2 inches between each seed. Cover the seed and add enough loamy soil so the long bed will be mounded above ground level. Water must never stand around sweet pea stems. To ensure steady growth after they have sprouted, dig in one tablespoon of balanced plant food per running yard along each row every two weeks until June.

Pea seeds can be treated with a nitrogen-fixing bacterial inoculant which usually causes the plants to make better and quicker growth. Roll the soaked seeds in the inoculant and plant immediately. Discard the rest of the inoculant because it becomes "dead" soon after the container is opened.

When the seedlings first appear, run supporting cords on each side of each row, about one inch above the soil, to prevent leaf and stem infection from the ground which might occur if the seedlings are blown over. Have a four- or five-foot vine support in place between the rows when plants are three inches high. About every two weeks lightly dust or spray the vines with a mild fungicide to prevent mildew and "yellows."

If plant lice (aphids) appear, spray the vines after sundown with a nicotine sulphate solution mixed with soapsuds, diluted according to directions on the package. Some gardeners have good results with a twice-a-month dusting with an all-purpose garden dust. Keep the soil loose along the rows with shallow but frequent

GRANDMA'S sweet peas of fifty years ago were not the pampered darlings they are today. True, hers were not ruffled and frilled, but how fragrant they were and how they did bloom! During the winter Grandma had Uncle Jerry chop enough brush branches for her sweet pea vines to climb on. Uncle laid the branches on the ground, pressed down with an old barn door. When needed, the flattened branches made a nice support for the sweet pea vines. One winter Uncle cut willows because they were more handy, and they sprouted. Uncle had to keep plucking willow leaves from among the sweet peas all summer. Grandma's growing procedure was not complex. She soaked her sweet pea seeds in water for twelve to thirty-six hours — starting with warm water — until they swelled. She discarded the seeds that did not swell. Uncle Jerry lifted a strip of lawn sod 8 inches wide and 150 feet long, extending from the veranda to the highway, and into it Grandma popped the seeds. She warmed the furrows with hot water just before planting, and the seed sprouted. On wash days she sprinkled the sweet pea hedge with soapsuds to repel insects. Things were simpler in her day.

cultivation. Moderate soil moisture is essential. Water the rows with a gentle stream close to the ground with the nozzle off the hose. Or make a two-inch-deep trench on each side of the row and fill with water whenever the soil is dry. Keep water off the leaves and vines, as it often will cause scalding in hot sunny weather, and the foliage will wither. In May a mulch of peatmoss extending one to two feet on each side of the bed will help to retain moisture and keep the roots cool. These two growing requirements — cool roots and constant moisture — are very important.

A new sweet pea of many colors that has shown much promise in the trial gardens is the floribunda. It is a combination of the multiflora type with the old drought-resistant Cuthbertson strain, resulting in larger, more fragrant blossoms and plants that will withstand heat.

REMINDERS

If you notice scale on your trees and shrubs this month, spray them with a lime-sulphur or an oil spray emulsion for dormant plants. When the young insects appear in late spring, they may be destroyed with a nicotine spray. The lime-sulphur spray is also said to discourage rabbits.

Speaking of rabbits, the rabbit repellent "No-Nibble" is reported excellent for driving the bunnies away from your sprouting tulips and daffodils. And if late March snows linger on the ground, watch your shrubbery and trees for signs of rabbit damage. You can protect the bark from being eaten by encasing it in aluminum foil or wire netting.

When lawns are free of snow and the sod is soft, your grass may be damaged by too much walking over it. Where people have been "short cutting" all winter, you had better put up a temporary barrier across these paths or your grass may be destroyed.

With the arrival of early spring, dog trespassers may become a problem, too. One solution is to keep handy a pail of sand or very small gravel. Throw a handful at the dog and call a loud "Get out!" The sand or gravel will not hurt them but is unpleasant. Dogs are smart and most are very willing to oblige. Usually a few experiences will teach them to pass up your lawn.

Do you know that the seed from an avocado, sometimes called a Calavo or alligator pear, will produce an interesting evergreen plant? Thrust three toothpicks horizontally into the lower part of the seed and lay it on top of a glass of water, pointed end up, with the base just touching the water. Roots and then a stem with glossy tropical leaves will develop. If the first seed fails, try again.

In a month or two, slowly add earth until the water is replaced. Later carefully remove to a large pot filled with garden soil and eventually to a wooden pail or tub. Occasionally seeds will grow when planted directly in a pot of earth. Often the plants last for years and reach a height of five feet. Place them outdoors in the summer in their flowerpots or containers.

✄ APRIL ✄

April brings the northern gardener both the pleasures of spring and the frustrations of late snowfalls and sudden, hard freezes. The winter snow cover has melted, the robins are back, tulips and daffodils are sprouting, and the brown lawn is turning green. But April is treacherous. One day the sun will send the thermometer into the seventies, drying the muddy garden and coaxing new buds from your bushes and new shoots from many perennials. Yet overnight the weather may change, bringing freezing winds and icy snow or drizzle to nip whatever new growth has been uncovered.

Your motto for April should be: Go slow. More harm is likely to be done by removing winter protection from your perennials and shrubs too early than by keeping it on too late. In the same way, spading the ground too early for annual beds or for planting roses, while the soil is still wet and sticky, does far more damage to the texture of your garden soil than a later planting will do to your summer flower display. Most years the soil is not dry enough for digging and planting in northern gardens until the latter part of April or even early May. Don't be impatient; there are plenty of other early spring garden chores to keep you busy.

NEW GARDEN TOOLS

Every gardener needs certain equipment to work with — spade, spading fork, hoes and trowels, a stiff garden rake and a flexible lawn rake, a lawnmower, pruning shears, hoses and sprinklers — all the familiar tools that gradually accumulate after one starts to garden. Part of the fun of gardening lies in adding to this equipment new gadgets and inventions to do each job more easily or with better results. Early April is a good time to inspect and evaluate the new products blossoming out in garden stores.

Perhaps the most intriguing of recent garden developments are the power-driven lawnmowers, priced from $69 up. All you have to do is walk or run behind them — depending on which button you press — and do a little guiding. Some machines, in addition to mowing your grass, will chew up the grass clippings and return them to the lawn as a mulch and future food. There also is power-driven equipment that will plow, furrow, pulverize, and hoe your garden.

Less mechanized gardeners might choose a straight-bladed grass scythe with a long handle and hooked teeth that is operated with one hand, or a lawn sprinkler with a calibrated adjustment that will give a five- to fifty-foot water spread. Another, a ball-bearing sprinkler, has an adjustment that will give a wide spray even when the water pressure is weak. It comes in a low model or on a high adjustable standard. There is also a self-traveling sprinkler that will walk over a lawn, sprinkling at the rate of twenty feet an hour, and shut itself off at a predetermined time. It's the water pressure that makes it work.

For rose growers there is a long-handled rosebush pruner that will clip off blossoms without slippage or dropping the flowers. It has a hardened serrated blade that cuts freely without bruising the stems. For lawn-makers there is a coarse-meshed, rot-resistant netting for spreading over newly-seeded lawn areas. The netting, which is four feet wide, prevents soil erosion and seed loss during heavy rain, especially on terraces and inclines. It is also a deterrent to children, animals, and seed-eating birds. The net can be removed without injury to lawns when the grass is an inch high, and it can be used year after year.

No longer is there any excuse for tools cluttering the basement or tool house. You can buy a wall rack that comes in 18-inch sections and each section will hold eight tools. Indestructible, non-rusting shrub or plant labels are a contribution to the garden's tidiness. The name of the shrub is etched with acid and will last for years. The construction allows for expansion as the shrub grows, and this prevents choking of the branch to which the label is attached. For women gardeners there are lightweight, good-looking hand tools, as well as dainty gardening gloves, waterproof but washable. These gloves are also made in men's sizes, but heavier.

There are many new insect sprayers. A dandy sprayer is a 1½-gallon portable type in which you create pressure with a hand pump. The attached hose and nozzle will deliver five different types of spray, from small drops to a fine mist. There are also substantial, nonrusting stainless steel hand sprayers for fine or coarse delivery.

Another type of sprayer will reach the tops of 20-foot fruit trees, one of the toughest spraying jobs for the home gardener. You slip an insect- or blight-repellent cartridge into it, screw it into your garden hose, and the water does the rest. There also is one that you can operate by finger pressure that gives a fine spray for house plants. It can be used outdoors with a different spray jet, and shoots repellent several feet.

One of the most useful functions of a garden sprayer in our northern gardens is to keep away mosquitoes. One mosquito-killing spray on the market claims excellent results. The concentrated liquid is mixed with water and expelled from a sprayer in fine droplets over the yard. Mosquitoes die in a few seconds. A household

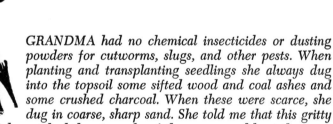

GRANDMA had no chemical insecticides or dusting powders for cutworms, slugs, and other pests. When planting and transplanting seedlings she always dug into the topsoil some sifted wood and coal ashes and some crushed charcoal. When these were scarce, she dug in coarse, sharp sand. She told me that this gritty material scratched the stomachs of the worms and kept them out of the garden. Uncle Jerry claimed that the cinders in the coal ashes gave the cutworms ulcers. I always knew Grandma was right about her garden lore, but I was never quite sure about Uncle Jerry.

sprayer will do the job, but a continuous-pressure sprayer is more effective, much quicker, and will cover a larger area.

There are also many good types of garden dusters. One in particular has a long extension tube leading to the nozzle and will deliver a cloud of dust even to the back of a wide border, either on the top or under side of the leaves.

Other practical garden aids include a lawn conditioning tool which, when pressed with your foot into a compacted lawn, removes two plugs of earth half an inch in diameter and four inches deep. The resulting holes aerate the soil and allow easy entrance of water and fertilizer. An average lawn can be conditioned in this way in a few hours. Another type of spiking tool rides on two wheels for conditioning hard-packed lawns.

You can also buy a liquid film coating for protecting tools from rust. It prevents mud from sticking to them too. The quick-drying liquid is contained, under pressure, in a metal can and is released in a fine spray by pressing a trigger. One coating will last for months.

An electric hedge and shrub trimmer will prevent many a sore back. Just slip the cord through an open window, plug it in an electric outlet, either AC or DC, and the trimmer does the work in jig time. There's another hedge trimmer that you can attach to your quarter-inch electric drill. It will trim the edge of the lawn as well as the hedge.

Then there is a portable trellis made of nondecaying red cedar bars and weather-resisting marine ropes that you can adjust into scores of different designs. It should be fine for clematis and climbing roses, and could be used horizontally for sweet peas. Other intriguing devices include a metal basket hose holder that drains and coils your hose in the basement after it is poked through a hole in the foundation; a seven-bladed, ball-bearing, lightweight lawnmower built especially for bentgrass; a hand-powered grass seed sower; and best of all perhaps, though no longer new, the lightweight plastic garden hose — four pounds for fifty feet — that won't kink, won't burst from freezing, and is rustproof.

The comparatively new triple-tube plastic hose has hundreds of tiny openings and delivers fine sprays of water. It does the job thoroughly and evenly with practically no water wasted. These hoses — and there are several on the market — will deliver as large or small a mist-like rain as you desire. When they are properly used, you can cut your summer water bills in half, and they operate satisfactorily even if the pressure is low.

SPRAYING FRUIT TREES

If you have fruit trees in your yard — apple, crabapple, pear, or plum — a good pressure sprayer is one garden tool you should invest in. The first spring spraying should be done before they blossom. Spraying fruit trees may seem like quite a chore, but it is really worth the effort. But don't spray when they are in bloom lest you injure bees pollinating blossoms.

Spraying should be done under as high pressure as possible. Regulate the disks of the nozzles so that the spray will be in the form of a mist. Cover the tree thoroughly. Spray at the proper time, as a delay of a few days will greatly reduce the effectiveness.

If you do not have a pressure sprayer, an ordinary hand-pump type of flower garden sprayer will do a fair job if used vigorously.

The Minnesota Horticultural Society has a simplified spray program that calls for only a few sprays each year; the society suggests the use of a combination spray or dust for home gardeners. The program, although perhaps not so effective as the complete combination program recommended for commercial growers, will result in cleaner fruit and is better than no program at all.

When buying a spray or dust check the label to be sure it contains ingredients that will be effective. The mixture should contain insecticides, including DDT and lead arsenate, and a fungicide such as Ferbam. The following home-mixed combination spray is suggested where commercial preparations are not available: three parts (by volume) of lead arsenate; two parts (by volume) of Ferbam; two parts (by volume) of 50 per cent wettable DDT. Use 5 level tablespoonsful of this mixture per gallon of aqueous spray solution.

The simplified spray schedule for home gardeners is as follows:

Apples and Pears. First spray: when fruit buds show pink at tips. Second spray: after three fourths of the petals have fallen. Third spray: five to seven days after the second spray. Fourth spray: one week after first maggot flies appear, or about July 15.

Plums. First spray: when three fourths of the petals have fallen. Second spray: when plums are the size of peas.

Fruit trees come into blossom at different times. For trees that are several years old a good feeding of balanced fertilizer will help if applied early in April or as soon thereafter as you can. Apply about ten pounds per tree dug into the soil about three feet away from the trunk and extending to just beyond the tips of the branches. Water this fed surface for several hours. Keep this area well watered during long dry spells. Repeat this spraying and feeding program every spring and you will be surprised at the increase of fruit.

TAKE CARE OF YOUR TREES

Early April is a good time to attend to the needs of all your trees. If you found time to do major pruning jobs during mild weather in March, and if you took precautions then to protect shade trees against canker or measuring worms, water and fertilizer are probably the chief requirements of your trees in April.

Ordinarily spring is the season when the ground has more abundant moisture than at any other time of the year. Sometimes, however, as when a winter of little snow follows an abnormally dry fall, spring rains may not be adequate to supply the large water needs of deep-rooted shade trees and evergreens. Trees and shrubs that have been planted within the past two or three years will need more watering in dry spells than older, longer established ones.

If the ground seems very dry this month or next, get the garden hose and with the nozzle off allow the water to run for hours under your trees. Let the water seep into the ground under the spread of the branches. For quicker and more efficient use of the water and for less runoff loss, you can get a tree-feeding rod from your garden dealer that can be attached to the hose and thrust into the ground. The water is delivered about three feet down into the immediate proximity of the tree roots. You can also feed the trees at the same time with a plant food cartridge obtainable from your dealer to be placed in the feeding tool.

If you do not have a tree-feeding rod, you can achieve much the same results by the following method. Punch holes in the soil about eighteen inches apart in circles under and out to the farthest spread of the branches. If the tree is large, punch the holes about two feet away from the trunk, or about a foot away for a young tree. These holes should be eighteen inches to two feet deep and about an inch and a half in diameter. A crowbar or an iron pipe will do the job. In a pinch, a spading fork can be used.

Water can be allowed to run slowly into these holes for as long as the soil will absorb it, or fertilizer may be added also to do two necessary jobs at once. To determine the amount of balanced plant food required, measure the circumference of the tree four feet above the ground and feed one pound of balanced fertilizer for each inch of circumference.

For large trees over fifteen feet in height, double the amount of plant food. Mix fertilizer with an equal amount of clean fine earth, fill the holes with the mixture, and water well for a couple of hours. If there is some mixture left over, punch more holes. If this program is repeated again in three months, it will save your trees from any possible drought damage, send them into the winter well fed and watered. If balanced plant food is difficult to obtain, four inches of cow manure on the surface of the ground is excellent. Keep it a foot away from the trunk and soak it for at least two hours.

Evergreens are especially susceptible to damage during a dry winter and spring, since the sap in evergreens circulates all winter and the trees continue to transpire moisture even in cold weather. Therefore it is necessary that they have plenty of moisture around the roots to supply this demand. Lack of moisture in the soil during the previous fall, winter, or spring is often the cause of evergreens' drying and dying the following summer. If your evergreens look dry or "winter burned" this April, prompt remedial measures should be taken as soon as frost is out of the ground. Give them water and fertilizer as outlined above and repeat once or twice during the summer and fall to help them through next winter in better shape.

SPRING CLEAN-UP IN THE GARDEN

When all the snow and ice in shady corners has melted, when the ground is thawed and spongy but not too muddy, and when several warm, sunny days have dried the dead leaves or hay mulch on the perennial border and around the shrubs — then the northern gardener can begin the pleasant task of cleaning up the yard for spring. In many parts of the North this welcome moment usually arrives about the second or third week of April. For most of us this is the real beginning of the gardening year.

The spring clean-up should be a gradual operation, for a sudden cold snap can damage even hardy perennials if their winter covering of leaves or hay is removed all at once. Start by loosening the winter covering on your garden and around your roses, but remove only part of it. If you find any trace of mildew, either on the plants or the covering, remove more of the mulch at once and allow warm, dry air and a little sunshine to freshen and sterilize the plants. Be sure to keep the mulch you remove handy for a week or so. We will still have freezing nights. Most hardy perennials can stand temperatures in the high 20s on spring nights, even if they are uncovered, but most roses are not quite that tough. A dip to 10 or 15 degrees can harm even tulips and daffodils if the buds are well developed.

Another reason for not removing all winter protection at once is that tender vegetation can't stand the sudden exposure to strong,

GRANDMA had little trouble in persuading chronically-tired Uncle Jerry to spade the garden in the spring. He was as good as a robin at picking up worms and grubs. He would get enough in a couple of days to give him a summer's supply of fish bait. He stored them in an old horse trough filled with earth mixed with coffee grounds and bread crumbs. One day someone left the cover off the trough, the chickens discovered it, and "bang" went Uncle's supply of fish bait. My, but he was furious. He had to dig bait for the rest of the summer.

direct sunlight. Make the change slowly. Often white or pale green shoots will be discovered under the winter covering, especially on spring bulbs. Shield them for a few days with a light covering of leaves, hay, or straw and they will soon change to a normal green.

A weak spray of Bordeaux mixture on the crowns and new shoots of plants that are showing signs of life will be beneficial. Many summer leaf troubles may be prevented by this treatment. Be sure to make the spray weak, however, about one quarter of the normal strength as given on the Bordeaux powder container (or one level tablespoon of Bordeaux powder mixed in one pint of water). This treatment is a preventive of peony stem rot and various leaf spots and blights of delphiniums, hollyhocks, phlox, irises, and chrysanthemums.

Keep the winter protection on the bulb garden as long as the ground under the covering is frozen. There will be less chance of the bulbs' making premature growth and getting nipped or even killed by a late frost, or eaten by rabbits. By mid-April, however, tulips and daffodils will probably be well sprouted, and their winter covering can gradually be removed. Roses should also have their coverings removed a little at a time. The mounds of earth around the roses should remain a week or two longer still, probably until May, when the weather settles down more dependably.

Toward the end of April, if spring is progressing on its normal northern schedule, the perennial garden may be fully uncovered and exposed to sun and air. Use a light leaf or lawn rake to lift off the old leaves or hay mulch, being as gentle as possible, so as not to injure the young plants coming up underneath. Wear a sturdy pair of garden gloves and use your hands to remove matted leaves and debris from delicate shoots that a rake might injure.

Dead stalks from last year's leaves and flowers will often come loose at a touch, but do not pull or twist if they resist, lest the roots of the plant be damaged. Cut off all remaining dead stalks close to ground level. Use sharp shears on the old peony stalks because their stems are probably damp and tough. Don't twist or yank them loose or you may injure the brittle new spring growth that is just appearing at the surface.

Many plant diseases can be prevented if the perennial border and annual beds are thoroughly cleaned up before new growth or cultivation starts in spring. If you used clean marsh hay for your winter garden covering, you may be able to dry it and save it for next year or add it to your compost heap to decompose into humus. If you depended on autumn leaves for your winter mulch, however, it is probably wiser to burn both the leaves and dead flower stalks after they are raked off the garden. Many of the fungi and bacteria that cause plant diseases nest over winter in last season's plant refuse.

Burn the dry leaves, stalks, and rubbish, placing the damp roots on top. Even though the roots don't burn now, they will get so hot the insect eggs and larvae will be killed. The roots then can be placed on the compost heap with other clean vegetable material to form, ultimately, an excellent mulch.

CARE OF HEDGES AND SHRUBS

If you did not have time or good weather to trim your hedge and shrubs in March, April will do just as well. Bushes that bloom in spring and early summer should not be trimmed until after they have bloomed, or you will lose most of this year's flowers; but most other hedges and shrubs require some pruning every spring, both for general appearance and the welfare of the plants. When trimming and pruning, cut out all dead wood and old bark-bound stalks. Most bushes bloom best on this or last year's wood.

The way to keep the natural look of a shrub is to cut out the old stems right to the ground. Then new shoots will grow in their place. On the other hand, if you want a formal-looking shrub, prune frequently instead of doing occasional drastic cutting.

Hedge trimming should not be a haphazard, hurry-up job. Give the undertaking care and thought. A good-looking hedge should be narrower at the top than at the bottom. If the reverse is true, rain and light are screened from the base, retarding the growth of the bottom twigs and the branches. This results in an unattractive, top-heavy hedge, with a full green top supported on naked stilts.

Sometimes it is best to cut an old hedge, filled with bark-bound old wood, down to half a foot from the ground and allow it to make a complete new growth. If your hedge is somewhat formal and you wish to keep it even, stretch a guide rope or wire close to and parallel to the hedge and at the height you desire the hedge to be. Trim along this guide line. To fill gaps in a hedge, draw branches together with wire before trimming to fill in the empty spaces. To prevent dogs and cats from making runways through the bottom of your hedge, string 12-inch galvanized chicken netting through its entire length, about two inches above the ground. It will be almost invisible, and the netting is rustproof and will last for years.

To do a good job, provide yourself with proper tools. A small hand pruner is necessary for close-in work, and a large scissor type with long handles is best for extensive hedges. An electric hedge-trimmer is a dandy.

Do not trim evergreens such as junipers, arborvitae, yews, and hemlock until their growth begins in May or June. Use a sharp knife, cutting the tips of new growth with an upward movement. Large evergreens (spruce, Douglas fir, fir, and pine) should be grown far enough away from the house so that their growth need not be limited by pruning. Just remove dead branches when necessary, cutting them off close to the trunk.

To keep shrubs and hedges flourishing, they must be fertilized regularly every two months from early spring to August. For most shrubs, one rounded tablespoon of complete plant food should be worked into each square foot of space around each plant. Larger bushes, like lilacs, snowballs, and flowering almonds, should be fed more often until late June. Holes 8 to 10 inches deep and 1½ in diameter, 18 inches apart, should be made around the bush in a zig-zag fashion. Two handfuls of a mixture of half plant food and half soil should be placed in each hole. Fill these holes with soil and water well, allowing the hose to run slowly over the ground beneath the shrub for several hours. This slow, deep watering is especially important if the past fall and winter were dry, or if spring rainfall has been below normal. Shrubs planted in the last year or two will need more watering than older bushes whose roots are deeper.

PLANTING TIME

In the North, early spring is the best time to plant trees, ever-greens, shrubs, roses, and perennial vines. Most of these can also be planted in the fall, but spring planting gives them a better start and time to get established before the rigor of winter. The earlier you can plant the better for most hardy trees and shrubs, so plan to get started whenever the ground is dry enough for digging.

Planting Trees. Dormant shade trees of many varieties, such as elm, ash, catalpa, one or two of the many willows, Bolleana and Lombardy poplars, linden (basswood), a group of birch, and maples with colored foliage, are obtainable in April and early May from your local nursery. These trees have been in winter storage and are ready to take root and leaf out very soon after planting. A good plan is to plant the slower-growing, long-lived trees. Then for quick shade, plant near them trees that grow and mature quickly, such as soft maple and Carolina poplars. These will have passed their prime when the slow-growers are arriving at their best, and the quick-growing trees can then be removed.

When planting a tree, dig a hole large enough for the roots to spread out in without crowding. The hole should have perpendicular sides and should be dug half again as wide and twice as deep as is necessary to accommodate the root ball. Under no circumstances should roots be cramped. Untangle them and cut off with sharp shears any that are bruised or broken.

Set the tree in the hole and spread out the roots. Do not let them cross, wind around, double under, or crowd each other. Keep the subsoil that is removed separate from the topsoil. Mix thoroughly with each bushel of topsoil one-half pint of complete plant food and then fill the hole with enough of this soil so that the tree, when placed upon it, will stand about one inch deeper than it did in the nursery.

After the tree has been set, work more of the enriched topsoil around the roots. When the space is half full, tramp the soil firmly. After tramping, let the rose run into the hole a while to make sure the roots get soaked thoroughly and to remove air pockets from the soil. Now fill the hole to the top, using the subsoil when your supply of topsoil is gone, and then tramp it down again. If you want the tree to live, you will need to water it every week all summer, except for the weeks that have a good natural rainfall.

Since the root system was reduced when the tree was originally dug up from the ground, you should prune off some of the branches to compensate for this loss, sometimes as much as half of each branch. Otherwise the tree will demand more water than the roots are able to take up and it may not survive. A further precaution against excessive evaporation of moisture is to wrap the trunk with burlap from the ground to the first limb. This also protects the bark from sun scald until the leafed-out branches are large enough to shade it.

GRANDMA'S remedy, over fifty years ago, for vagrant rabbits in the garden was blood. When poultry or animals were killed on the farm, Uncle Jerry had a standing order to paint small boards and flat stones with blood and distribute them around the garden — exit rabbits. Don't ask me why. I don't know. Today you can get blood meal in the garden stores. It is a plant fertilizer but is said to be an excellent rabbit repellent too.

All trees should be supported until the roots take hold. Small trees may be staked with one stake, but the stake should be driven 18 inches into the bottom of the hole before planting. For larger trees three guy wires are usually used. Drive three stakes at equidistant points around the tree, keeping them far enough away from the tree roots to avoid damage. Run three strong wires through short pieces of worn-out hose to protect the tree trunk. Stretch each wire to one of the three stakes and fasten securely.

Evergreens are handled in a slightly different manner. They come from the nursery with their roots surrounded by a ball of earth wrapped in burlap. Place the tree in a hole considerably larger than the burlap ball, without removing the burlap. Fill in the rest of the hole with rich topsoil, allowing a gentle stream of water to flow into the hole while filling. In a few hours the soil will settle. Then open the burlap, cutting away as much of the upper part as possible. What remains will rot away. Tramp down the soil to force out air pockets. Then fill in more soil until the tree is surrounded by a shallow saucer-like depression to catch water.

If the weather is warm and dry, sprinkle the entire evergreen tree or shrub frequently to conserve moisture. Drying out of newly planted trees is a frequent cause of loss. An evergreen has an exceedingly large leaf area, which causes the tree to evaporate moisture during all seasons.

Do not try to transplant evergreens from the woods. Such trees seldom survive the trip. They may struggle along for a few years, but the change from the cool woods to an open yard usually is too much for them. Evergreens have extensive root systems and well-developed taproots and they are likely to be damaged badly in transplanting. Death is almost sure if the tiny roots are exposed to the air. Moreover, in most states it is unlawful to transplant trees from the woods, because you might introduce a disease that would infect trees in your neighborhood. Nursery trees are state inspected and certified free from disease.

Planting Shrubs. In planting shrubs, as in planting trees, the most important thing is not to crowd the roots. They should be spread out. To be on the safe side, estimate how large the hole should be and then dig it 50 per cent larger and deeper. Discard all subsoil and in the bottom place several shovelfuls of well-rotted manure or three or four pounds of balanced plant food, mixed thoroughly with good garden earth. Cover this with six inches of unfertilized earth before setting the shrub in the hole. Keep all fertilizer away from the roots. Let the roots seek downward for the plant food as they grow. For small shrubs use proportionately less fertilizer.

All broken roots should be trimmed off. Plant the shrub so it will be an inch deeper than it was previously growing. Cover the roots with good garden loam. As you fill in the earth, allow a gentle stream of water to flow into the hole and pack the earth firmly around the roots to prevent air pockets. At no time allow the sun to shine on exposed roots. Keep them covered with a wet sack until the shrub is in the hole. It is best to plant in the evening or on a cloudy day, if possible, to help conserve the moisture already stored in the roots and branches.

It will be several weeks to an entire growing season before the newly transplanted roots are able to start functioning with their former efficiency, so your new shrubs will need frequent watering during the summer. If a week goes by without rain, be sure to water them thoroughly with the hose.

Planting Roses. Late April is the normal time for planting roses in most of the North. The shrubs are still dormant then and digging is seldom possible much earlier. If a late spring delays your planting until early May, this need not harm the new roses you have received from the nursery provided they are still dormant and kept cool and moist in their plastic wrappers. If they show signs either of mildew or of drying out, however, you should immediately "heel them in."

Choose a relatively cool place in the garden and dig a trench, allowing about 10 inches for each shrub. One side of the trench should be about 10 inches deep straight down, the other side should have a 30-inch slope, extending from the bottom of the 10-inch cut to the garden surface. Unpack your new roses and lay them on the long slope, roots at the bottom, and the tips of the shrubs just above the top of the slope. Now fill the trench with earth to keep the entire plant moist. When the weather is settled and the rose bed is ready, carefully dig them up, one at a time, and plant them. Roses can be kept for a week or more in such a trench. Whether trenching or planting, however, you must not allow the sun to strike the delicate roots of the rosebushes.

Preparing the rose bed should be done just as early as possible. Select a site that receives at least six hours of sunlight each day, is open and airy but protected from wind, and has good drainage. Don't plant roses too close to trees or shrubs whose roots will compete for soil nutrients. If possible, the rose bed should have some

shade when the summer sun is at its hottest. This is usually around
2 P.M. and after during July and August.

Roses can be grown successfully in any good garden soil that is
well drained, moisture-retaining, and rich in plant food. The ideal
mixture for finest bloom and growth is a loamy garden soil plus
15 per cent rotted manure and 25 per cent peatmoss, and a cupful
of special rose food mixed in for each rose planted (Vigoro manu-
factures a special rose food for the purpose).

*GRANDMA had in her garden a musk rose Uncle Jerry
had brought from Italy. Its flowers were white singles,
almost scentless in the daytime, but in the damp evening air their odor was almost overpowering. Grandma
never used the petals in her rose jars. She told me that
roses are probably the oldest known flower and that
Theophrastus, a Greek philosopher and the father of botany, wrote
of them about 250 B.C. Withered rose bouquets were found in
ancient Egyptian tombs.*

The soil should be pulverized to a depth of two feet and enriched
to approximate this ideal mixture as closely as possible. If the
original soil is heavy and drainage is poor, put a four- to six-inch
layer of gravel at the bottom of the bed. Roses are injured by an
excess of standing water in the soil. The layer of gravel will carry
away excess water without interfering with the plants' growth.

When the soil in the rose bed is prepared, you should plant your
roses as soon as possible, preferably in the evening or on a dull or
rainy day. As soon as the plants arrive from the nursery, unpack
them and soak the roots in a bucket of thick, muddy water, about
the consistency of syrup, for six to eight hours before planting.
When ready to plant, take them from the bucket one at a time. Do
not expose the roots to sun or dry wind. Or if your roses arrived
early and you have trenched them, dig them carefully out of the
trench for planting, one at a time.

APRIL

Before planting, all broken, bruised, or decayed roots should be pruned off with a sharp knife. Enlarge a space in the pulverized rose bed or dig an individual hole large enough to accommodate the roots without crowding and deep enough to set the plant at the proper height. In this northern zone, the lower part of the graft bud or crown of the plant should be two inches below the surface of the ground after the soil has settled.

Spread the roots so they point downward and outward. Cover them with loose soil, working it well underneath them so they are in firm position. When the roots are covered, fill the hole three fourths full and tamp the soil down firmly. Pour in a bucket of water and allow it to soak in to eliminate air pockets. Then fill to ground level with soil, using soil mixed with one third peatmoss for the top few inches. Tamp the soil firmly into the hole.

After planting, hill up each bush with soil ten inches high to protect it from drying winds, sun, and cold. As soon as new growth has started well, this hilling of earth should be removed. Immediately after planting, prune each stem of the plant to about six inches in height, making the cuts a quarter inch above a bud that faces outward.

Proper spacing between roses is most important. Hybrid teas should be planted 1½ to 2 feet apart. The floribunda roses have considerable variation in growth habits. Some grow only 18 inches high and may be planted 16 to 18 inches apart. Larger floribundas and rugosa roses will require as much space as a hybrid tea.

After planting, new growth should be apparent in about two weeks. Do not give more plant food to newly planted roses until they are well started and new growth is about four inches long. Then you can work into the soil a heaping tablespoonful of commercial fertilizer in a circle six inches away from the plant.

When new growth is well started, the roses should be sprayed or dusted with a special rose spray or dust. A three-in-one spray such as Triogen will control both insects and diseases. Dusting sulphur containing 10 per cent arsenate of lead also may be used. With dusting sulphur, some pyrethrum, nicotine, sulphate, or rotenone spray must be used in addition to kill sucking insects such as

90

aphids. The dusting treatment is improved by adding 10 per cent Fermate.

The most important thing is to spray often, once a week at least, and after every rain. Avoid spraying or dusting when the temperature is higher than 90 degrees or when the wind is strong. It's best to spray or dust in the morning and when the air is reasonably calm. For your health's sake, wear a filter or a mask when you are dusting. The dusting or spraying program should continue all summer.

Planting Clematis. The Jackman clematis is one of the best ornamental perennial vines for our northern climate. It grows especially well on south or west exposures and fairly well on an east exposure. Do not plant it on a north wall, however, or where the vine will be heavily shaded. Dark purple-blue flowers cover the vine in July and August and make a lovely combination with climbing roses. There are several varieties of clematis that are hardy with some winter protection in exposed locations, but *jackmani* is probably the hardiest and the most vigorous grower and bloomer. When once established it is long-lived and seldom winter-kills. The blossoms, often seven inches across, are a dark purple at first, then change to a lighter shade. On a vigorous plant they almost hide the dark green leaves.

The variety *clematis henryi* is not a free bloomer, but the large, lovely creamy flowers against its dark foliage make up in exquisite beauty what they lack in numbers. There are also Mme. Edward Andre, a velvety red free bloomer; *paniculata,* with a mass of dainty, fragrant white flowers in September; Ramona, with delicate single pale blue blossoms; Texensis, a prolific bloomer with oddly shaped scarlet flowers; and *tangutica,* a golden clematis.

Clematis loves a sunny, well-drained spot, not necessarily against a house. If you do choose to grow it against a house wall, however, plant it at least a foot away from the foundation. It will do well if allowed to climb on a trellis about two inches from the house, or on a low stone wall, a post, or a tree stump.

To plant a dormant clematis root, dig a hole one foot wide and eighteen inches deep. Two thirds fill with rich earth mixed with one cup of vermiculite and half a cup of balanced plant food. A shovelful of well-rotted cow manure mixed with a cup of bone meal should be put in the bottom of the hole, if possible, to feed the plant in years to come. Never allow the roots to come in immediate contact with the plant food or manure, however. Permit the roots, as they grow, to seek and find the food as they need it.

In the middle of the planting hole, pile up a wide, cone-shaped mound of the soil and vermiculite mixture. Carefully spread the roots of the clematis and drape them down the sides of the cone. Slowly fill in the hole with sandy loam, to which has been added 10 per cent air-slaked or hydrated lime, meanwhile gently raising the roots and allowing the loam to sift in between them so that they do not touch each other. This process of filling the hole and arranging the roots should be done very carefully. If it takes you less than half an hour to plant your clematis, you are not being careful enough. Finish with the crown of the plant one inch below the ground level. Tamp the soil firmly and hill up more soil to the level of the woody growth, so that surface water will drain away from the crown. Water thoroughly at planting time and once a week during the summer if rainfall is not ample. Sift a circle of lime around the crown and always keep the growth at the earth line lightly dusted with lime to repel sow bugs.

As soon as the roots reach the fertilizer, the plant will grow rapidly, sometimes climbing two to three inches a day. As the vines become too heavy, tie them to a white trellis with strips of inch-wide cloth of a green or neutral color. Many vines lose a great deal of strength trying to support themselves. This lost strength would otherwise go into blossoms. Spread the branches to give them sunshine and air.

You can also buy clematis vines as growing plants in pots and transplant them into slightly limed soil enriched with plant food as directed for dormant roots. Remove the plants from their pots or containers and plant them without disturbing their roots, which will be surrounded by a ball of earth. Be sure to give them the light lime dusting at the earth line.

Although clematis flourishes in full sunlight, it must have the ground around its roots and stems cooled with a heavy mulch of leaves; or you can plant annual flowers a foot away from the clematis to cast shade over its roots. Keep perennials at least a foot away, however. Their deep roots may crowd the roots of the clematis. Established vines of *jackmani, paniculata,* and Mme. Edward Andre should be trimmed within four feet of the ground in the fall or before leaf budding in the spring. Extra care in planting a clematis pays well. When properly done, the plant lasts a lifetime, increasing yearly in size and loveliness.

HOW TO START A GOOD LAWN

There are several requirements for a good lawn, none of them difficult but all important. You must start with a grass adapted to your circumstances — sun or shade, sloping or level — and to our northern climate. You should buy good seed, tested for purity. Permanent grasses, not annuals, should make up at least 75 per cent of the mixture.

It is also necessary to provide a good soil base, and to feed the lawn at least once a year with a balanced plant food. Early spring (April 15 to May 15) is recommended as the best seeding and fertilizing time, though some gardeners prefer autumn.

If yours is a new house with the yard left in the rough, you probably will find low spots where poor, stony earth can be used for filling. Then, if the contractor has saved the rich black topsoil, spread it evenly over the entire area, the deeper the better. If there is not much topsoil to spread, you will need to buy black dirt to resurface the lawn area to a depth of three or four inches.

A sodded or seeded lawn can adapt itself to quite a range of soil conditions. But where the soil is extremely heavy or light, it is best to improve these conditions. This can be done by adding sandy loam to a heavy soil; by adding clay to a light soil; by resurfacing the area with three to four inches of a desirable loam or sandy soil; or by digging peatmoss into the soil so that you will have a seedbed six to eight inches deep.

Under this improved surface layer of soil, a clay subsoil is very desirable, because it prevents moisture from escaping too rapidly, as is the case when a lawn is made over sand or gravel. When grading for a new lawn, allow the lawn area to drop away from the house, sloping it about one fourth of an inch per foot for a distance of four feet from the house foundation. Allow at least a four-inch total drop to ensure good drainage and a dry basement.

GRANDMA *always scattered three-inch pieces of soft cord around the garden in early spring. These were for the birds to use in tying together the twigs of their nests. She knew that longer pieces were dangerous, however — the birds would get them twisted around their necks and hang themselves. She also had little puddles of mud for them to use in plastering their nests.*

When the lawn area has been plowed or spaded, raked smooth, and graded, an important next step is to eliminate weeds and weed seeds before planting grass or laying sod. Allow the prepared seedbed to lie unseeded for a week or so, and then hoe out the newly sprouted weeds as they appear. A few hours spent in hoeing out the weeds — a scuffle hoe is fine for small ones — or a good weed killer will save days of work in the future. The weeds will never be easier to remove than at this stage. There is little good in just leveling or spading the area, or covering it with a thin layer of good soil. You will just be planting the weed seeds a little deeper and they will come up to pester you for years to come.

Crabgrass and many other weed seeds can remain dormant, buried in the soil for years, waiting for more favorable growing conditions. Covering dormant weed seeds with extra-thick sod is no insurance against the weeds' sprouting up through the sod. Quackgrass especially is bad in this respect.

A quicker method that is growing in favor is treating the cleared and raked area with a solution of Crag, a weed seed killer obtainable in most garden stores. This chemical is dissolved in water and sprinkled on the surface of the lawn seedbed. It kills all germinating seeds. This method, too, involves some delay in seeding your grass, as you must not plant your grass seed until the soil is cleared of the poison, which takes several heavy rains.

When your new lawn area is smoothed, graded, and precautions taken against weeds, the seedbed should be fertilized in preparation for planting. For a good seedbed, work into the top two inches of soil a first-class lawn food. One that contains 10 per cent nitrogen, 6 per cent phosphoric acid, and 4 per cent potash will give quick results; 5-10-5 or 4-12-4 formulas are adequate for ordinary use. Wet it down thoroughly with a fine spray.

Almost all lawn beds will be made more moisture-retentive and more fertile if you work into the soil a pure organic or vegetable humus. This peaty humus is obtained from ancient lake beds, and is ground or dried for easy handling. It is free of weed seeds and is also an excellent soil conditioner for flower and vegetable gardens.

Some gardeners seed their grass when fertilizing, but it is probably better to sow the new seed a few days after feeding the soil, thus allowing the fertilizer to sink into the soil and provide ample moisture and food for the roots.

Seed may be sown by hand or with a spreader. Distribution should be made in two directions, one at right angles to the other. This decreases the possibility of leaving bare spaces. Seed (for a new lawn) at the rate of three pounds per thousand square feet. After the seed is sown, lightly rake it in just enough to cover it, or brush it in by dragging some light, flexible object, such as a sack, over the soil. This aids in spreading the seed and covers it lightly with loose soil. After it is brushed in, roll the seedbed with a light roller or tamp the soil by other means, to bring the soil particles in close contact with the seed. This operation is one of the most important in planting a lawn. Its omission is often responsible for poor germination.

Next, water the lawn bed thoroughly with a gentle spray. To get a good growth from freshly sown lawn seed, it is necessary to keep lawn areas constantly moist until the grass blades are clearly visible. Don't flood new growths with heavy streams of water, however. Usually a thorough wetting in the early morning and again at about 2 P.M. will keep the ground moist during the warmest part of the day. Use as fine a spray as possible to prevent puddling. Do not let the area dry out even once. The soil may harden and form a crust, and the tender grass plants may perish trying to break through.

To protect new lawns and newly-seeded places from soil erosion, you can buy the large-meshed netting mentioned on page 75.

TIME TO SPADE YOUR ANNUAL BED

Most years the soil should be dry enough to spade by the end of April. Never work soil that is wet and sticky, however, for it will tend to dry into hard, rock-like clods. When the earth is moist but crumbly and does not cake or cling to your tools, it is just right for digging.

To prepare your annual bed — and a vegetable garden, too, if you have room for one — use a spading fork instead of a spade. The fork will thrust into the soil much more easily and will also break up clods. Thrust the fork straight down — not slanting — to the full length of the tines. Turn over each forkful, dash it down to shatter it, and strike it a sharp blow for further pulverizing. Don't try to spade your whole plot in one session. If you do, you may stiffen your winter-soft muscles and back for several days. There is still plenty of time, for you will not be planting most of your annual

GRANDMA always gave special care to her weakest and smallest seedlings of ten-week stocks and petunias. She said these weaklings, that most people toss away as too much trouble, often produced rare and unusual plants. The stocks especially were good, double and very fragrant, and the weak petunias often outranked Nature's huskier seedlings. Today her method is a common practice with the world's great seed producers. Grandma was wondrous wise years ahead of her time.

seeds until the soil is warm, probably in May. Spade what you can do easily at one time, then some more the next day. Rest a little at the end of each row. There is something exhilarating in the smell of fresh earth spaded in the warm spring sun. In a week or so you will feel equal to licking a whole army of cutworms.

If possible, let your freshly turned earth stand in the rough a few days before raking, fertilizing, and planting. The sun will sweeten the soil and the birds will eat thousands of weed seeds and grubs. If barnyard manure is available (this should really have been put on the plot last year, but you can use it now if it is well rotted), use at the rate of approximately one pound per square foot. Or you can use commercial balanced plant food with excellent results. Spread it on the garden at the rate of three pounds per hundred square feet before planting, if your plot is good average garden soil, and rake it in well. Break up all clods, large and small, and work the soil into a smooth seedbed to permit easy root penetration.

Most gardeners, especially in the North, feel a strong desire to plant their annuals as early as possible to get a head start on the short summer season. But early planting outdoors is not always a short cut. If cold weather comes and your seedlings stand in cold, wet ground, their growth will be retarded. As a matter of fact, plants from seeds planted late frequently outstrip those planted early. For most annuals it is better to wait until the air and the soil are warmer, in May, or at least until after the average date of the last killing frost of spring. In the Upper Midwest the average last killing frost may occur between May 5 and June 1, and these dates are probably typical for most northern areas.

REMINDERS

If you haven't yet started tender annual seedlings indoors or in your cold frame, there is still time. Zinnias, marigolds, and many other warm weather annuals cannot be planted outdoors until sometime in May, when all danger of frost is over. Start them indoors or in the cold frame now for earlier blossoms this summer.

If you have built a birdhouse or repaired an old one, don't paint it. Birds dislike the smell of fresh paint, varnish, or stain. If it is already painted, dry it thoroughly in the sun and bury it completely — even filling it with damp earth — for at least a week. Then perhaps the birds will accept it this year. Birds are a bit fussy, but they are great companions and helpers in a garden.

Most potted Easter plants will flower longer if there are buds as well as open flowers on the plant at the time of purchase. The one exception to that rule is the hydrangea. Hydrangeas should be purchased in full bloom, since green flowers do not develop normal color unless they are kept in a very bright, sunny location. Keep the plant in bright light, maintain a cool night temperature, and keep the soil moist but not soggy. Fertilize frequently. Hydrangeas can be planted permanently in a sheltered spot in the garden when the weather is warm. So can potted roses, if they are cut back after blooming.

GRANDMA saw to it that Uncle Jerry took down the purple martin house about this time and gave it a thorough housecleaning before the martins returned. The martins arrived from their winter vacation in Brazil almost on the same date every spring. These birds are considered the farmer's friends because they gang up and drive away predatory birds that are hunting a chicken dinner in the poultry yard. Don't paint the martin house if you want them to occupy it this year.

To rid your lawn of night crawlers, earthworms, and grubs that destroy grass at the roots, use the insecticide chlordane. It will also kill ants, chiggers, wireworms, and other grass and garden pests For 1,000 square feet of lawn, get from your dealer a half pound of 40 to 50 per cent chlordane powder and mix it with dry sand or sifted earth — about two pailsful. Strew this mixture evenly over the lawn, then wet the area down with the sprinkler. Make this application now, before young birds are hopping around who might devour dead worms and be poisoned.

A teaspoon of balanced plant food to a running foot of tulip row, dug into the soil three inches away from the sprouting tulips, will add size and color to their blossoms.

Have you ever considered growing grapes? They are just about a perfect fruit for a home garden. In addition to their fruit they are an excellent source of shade when trained on trellises, porches, and summer houses. Grapes grow best in a south or southeast exposure in our part of the country. Avoid low ground because of untimely frost. Grapes produce well in a fairly deep, well-drained, moderately fertile soil. A rich sandy loam is excellent. When purchasing your vines remember that while year-old plants are cheaper, two-year-old plants will bear sooner. There are locally developed varieties that produce large, good quality grapes and are so hardy that they can stand as much as 40 degrees below zero. They should be given some winter protection, however.

Cannas, elephant ears, and Peruvian daffodils should be started now in the house or cold frame to ensure fairly early summer blooming when transplanted into the garden.

In late April and early May, robins and other birds are building their nests. Soft pieces of cloth and cotton to make the nest soft and warm will be appreciated, as will the fluff that comes out of gas or electric clothes driers. Set up a bird bath, too, and keep it filled with fresh water. The birds you attract will consume an unbelievable number of harmful insects and worms.

♒ MAY ♒

MAY is a rewarding month for the northern gardener. The first flowers of the year appear in late April and early May — crocuses, snowdrops, blue squills, bloodroot, pasqueflowers, white and purple violets, yellow and white narcissuses, and many more. They spring up year after year in wild flower gardens or in a shady part of the perennial garden. These dainty early bloomers should be part of every northern garden, for nothing can quite equal the pleasure of their early arrival after our long, cold winters.

A WILD FLOWER GARDEN

If you would like to start a wild flower garden, choose a spot on the north side of the house, or in that shady place where cultivated flowers "just won't grow." You will find it one of the most interesting parts of your garden. Cultivated wild flowers get along so beautifully together, each in perfect harmony with its neighbor. Wild flowers seldom run rampant like cultivated flowers. They require little attention.

The next few weeks is the time to get them from shady ravines and in the woods. Do not dig up individual plants. With your spade, lift a whole section of loamy soil including several plants. A square foot or more is not too much. Place the clumps in shallow fruit crates or flat boxes lined with several wet newspapers. Then sprinkle them and get them home and replanted as quickly as possible. You probably will be surprised by the number of additional wild flowers that will come up later. Sometimes seed will be in the ground for several years before sprouting.

In the woods and glens, you will find snowdrops, ginger root (sometimes called devil's cap), Dutchman's britches, wild phlox, bloodroot, several varieties of violets, columbine, anemone or wind-flower, bluebells, jack-in-the-pulpits, and many others. Later in the summer the Solomon seal, wild lobelia, cardinal flower, and meadow rue will bloom.

Use ferns for a background planting in your wild flower garden. Early in May you will find them pushing through the woodland debris like clusters of folded fingers.

One caution, however — many wild flowers are protected by law. Do not dig, transplant, or molest our Minnesota wild orchid, the lady's-slipper, or any related species of the lady's-slippers, trillium, arbutus, lotus, gentian, or wild lilies of any kind. All these wild flowers are protected by law, and violators are subject to fine or imprisonment of ten to thirty days. However, you can buy at nurseries or greenhouses many wild flower plants grown from seed.

To prepare a wild flower garden, dig out all the ordinary garden soil one foot down, or deeper, and replace it with a loamy mixture of decaying leaves, sand, and moss. Add very little fertilizer. It is best to get this earth mixture from the dell where you get the flowers.

To help you in identifying your collection get *How to Know Wild Flowers*, a dandy pocket-sized book, well illustrated, by Alfred Stefferud. He is a native Minnesotan who certainly knows our northern wild flowers.

GRANDMA used to encircle her trees with old-fashioned tangle-foot fly paper cut in strips to discourage squirrels and cats from robbing the robins' nests. Maybe our modern tree-banding method, using sticky material on heavy paper bands to stop the tree worms, would also serve to discourage marauding cats and squirrels. It might require several bands, four inches apart. The animals wouldn't be injured, but they would be frustrated.

MAY

Other cultivated perennials that will be good neighbors for your wild flowers in a somewhat shady place — as long as considerable blue sky is visible — are Virginia bluebells or mertensia, yellow or orange trollius or globe flower, some varieties of primrose, bleeding heart, lily of the valley, balloon flower, monkshood, moss phlox, lythrum, viola, Sweet William, forget-me-not, pansy, and dog lilies. These will appreciate a richer soil than the native wild flowers, however. The early spring bulbs, like blue squills or scilla and daffodils, will also be at home in a wild flower setting.

MAY CHORES IN THE PERENNIAL BORDER

The reappearance of perennials each spring is like the return of old friends. When the winter mulch of leaves or marsh hay is finally raked away and the new green leaves and stems appear above ground, you can begin to take a careful roll call. If you have planted hardy varieties and kept them well fed and watered last year, there should be few of your plants that have failed to come through the winter all right.

Some perennials start their spring growth earlier than others, however. Tulips, peonies, mertensia, and plantain lilies are among the first to appear. Iris and the spring-blooming blue phlox often keep some of their green leaves all winter. Clumps of summer-blooming phlox may not show signs of life until several weeks later, depending on variety; and physostegia (false dragon head) and platycodon, or balloon flower, often do not come up until well into May, when the anxious gardener may have given them up for lost. For this reason you should be very careful not to dig up prematurely the "bare" spots in the border. It is a good idea to wait until May is well along before concluding that any of your perennials have been winter-killed and must be replaced.

When the perennial border is raked clean and new growth is a few inches high, one or more preventive sprays or dustings of a mild Bordeaux mixture or all-purpose garden dust are desirable. Much summer leaf disease and other trouble can be prevented or greatly reduced by this early spring treatment. Phlox, delphinium, peonies, hollyhocks, and lilies are especially in need of preventive

102

measures. Treatment now will often destroy diseases and molds that are picked up at this time from the soil but do not appear on the plants until later in the season. Dust or spray your peonies with the mild Bordeaux mixture and give the soil of your rose beds a dusting or spraying of insecticide.

When perennials are well started on their new growth, the border should be fertilized. Slow-acting organic fertilizers such as dried sheep or cow manure will help to improve the texture of the soil, and of course nothing is better than the rich, crumbly compost from your compost pile — if you have one. Keep manure away from the irises, however. Bone meal is the best fertilizer for irises, bulbs, and peonies. A little bone meal goes a long way and releases its nutrients very slowly in the soil. Barnyard manure, even if well-rotted, should be applied only in the fall after the season's growth is over, to avoid burning the foliage.

You may also use a balanced inorganic fertilizer in the perennial border, spreading about one third of a cup in a circle around each good-sized perennial plant and digging it shallowly into the soil. This provides the plant with a quick boost but less sustained nourishment than organic materials. If a balanced chemical fertilizer is used, another application should be made later on during the summer. Choose a brand designed for flower gardens, not for lawns, and follow directions on the package.

If the spring season has been advanced this year, new growth and early flower buds may be well along in early May. This is a dangerous situation for our northern gardens, since May can be unpredictable. A sudden change in the weather, bringing frost or even snow, can do much more damage to flowers and foliage that are well advanced than to perennials just sprouting. Even two or three degrees of frost could kill flower buds that have appeared prematurely in an early spring.

To minimize this danger, be ready to protect your garden as much as possible with covers of sheets, canvas, gunnysacks, heavy paper, and what-have-you. If the day has been cold and the evening becomes calm, or the thermometer is rapidly falling, be prepared to cover as much of the garden as possible. Often on the morning after a freezing temperature, a fine spray from the hose over the garden seems to hold damage to a minimum.

Roses. In a normal spring in our northern climate, it is safe to remove the hills of earth around your roses by early May. When new leaves start to appear, the plants should be given a preventive spray or dusting with an all-purpose rose spray or dust. When new growth is four or five inches long, fertilize with one of the special rose foods you can buy in your garden store, or with a balanced fertilizer.

GRANDMA was ruthless when frost threatened. Everything in the house that could be used for cover went into the garden, even her prized Irish table linen that was used only on holidays and when the minister stayed for supper. Poor Grandpa grumbled bitterly when he had to sleep between scratchy blankets. Grandma had borrowed the sheets from his bed to protect the plants. Or, if frost threatened on an almost windless night, she would have several smudges of hay or straw covered with partly dried grass. The smudges were put in old metal washtubs covered with coarse wire netting to prevent sparks from flying. They often smoked all night, forming a protective canopy over the garden.

If cold weather caught you unaware last fall and you did not have time to hill up and mulch your roses, they may show no apparent signs of life this spring. Don't be in a hurry to dig them up and discard them, however, even if they appear to be dead. They may be alive and vigorous just below the dead top growth. Before tearing up a frosted rose, carefully pull away some earth around the stock and just above the bulge of the root graft, which should be two inches below ground level if the rose was planted correctly. Should the soil be sticky, wash it off the stock with a small, gentle stream of water.

If you see new buds above the graft, replace the earth and trim off the dead top growth. The chances are you will have a blooming rose plant in less than sixty days. However, watch out for new growth below the graft. If allowed to grow, it will produce only small, wild roses which are far less attractive than the original hybrid. Always remove such growth or eventually it will kill the desirable rose.

In May you can still purchase dormant roses to plant in your rose beds, or, if you prefer, potted rose plants already started. Sometimes these potted roses even have flower buds almost ready to open. They usually come in heavy composition containers with a good clump of earth around the roots. They can be transplanted into your garden as long as obtainable.

For this type of started rose plant, prepare the hole in the garden in advance, a few inches wider and deeper than the container and with fertilizer mixed with the soil in the bottom. The rose plant still in its composition pot is placed in the hole, and the pot is cut loose and carefully peeled off. The extra space is then filled up with good garden earth. It is possible that this way of planting may cramp the roots, however, and they will not be so widely spread as they should be to develop into a sturdy, winter-hardy bush. But there is no question but what they do produce a quicker bloom. Also they are very handy when you wish to fill in a gap quickly where one of your regular roses has died. It is exciting to have a rose blooming in your garden in a week or two or sometimes even just a few days after planting.

In planting roses or any other growing plant, never place fertilizer or manure in contact with or very close to the roots. Mix it with the soil a little distance below or away from the roots, and let them seek and find the nourishment as they grow. Many plants are burned and killed by plant food coming into direct contact with their roots.

If you wish to feed dormant stock planted late but not in a fertilized hole, wait until the new shoots are four inches long. Don't give them more than a heaping tablespoon of balanced plant or rose food. Work it into the soil in a circle six inches away from the plant.

105

MAY

Dividing and Planting Perennials. As May progresses, the border that looked so bare when the winter mulch was first raked off seems pretty well populated. Most gardeners tend to forget, in the spring, how full or even crowded the border looked last August when each plant was in full foliage. If you are just starting a perennial border this year or if your border is only a few years old, crowding is probably no problem for you. Just remember to give new plants plenty of room to grow in when you set them out, and you needn't worry about dividing perennials for a year or two.

But the average garden more than two or three years old is likely to become a jungle. Perennials when bought are small, and most gardeners plant them too close together, unable to believe that in a few years they may grow to clumps two or more feet across. Perennials need enough space between them so that they have plenty of air and the sun can shine in around them down to ground level. Otherwise the earth tends to become dank and moldy and disease flourishes. There should be room enough to cultivate the soil around each plant to keep it aerated and weed-free.

Most perennial clumps should be divided every three to five years, some even oftener. Some, however, continue for many years to enlarge and thrive without division — peonies, bleeding heart, and Oriental poppies, for example. These three perennials are usually planted in August, after their blooming period is over, and they should be divided or transplanted then, too, if it is necessary. Most other perennials should be planted, transplanted, or divided in the spring, generally in May here in the North, before the new growth of leaves has progressed too far.

If new perennial plants are ordered by mail from a nursery, they should be planted just as soon as they arrive in late April or May, while still dormant. If new perennials are bought at a local or nearby nursery, they are dug up with earth around their roots and replanted within a few hours, so that most of them can be bought and planted in your garden any time from May through July or even August.

How can you tell if a perennial plant needs dividing? It isn't always easy, but here are a few symptoms: (1) Stalks at the center

106

of the clump have died out, leaving a ring of growth about a sparse center. (2) The plant does not bloom as heavily as in the past and has small or malformed flowers. (3) A great many of the lower leaves wither away, and the foliage that remains wilts easily and seems in poor health.

To divide a perennial plant, dig around the clump with a spading fork and lift gently. Try to dig up as large a ball of roots and soil as possible. When the ball of roots is loose, lift it out of the ground and with your hands or a trowel carefully separate the clump into several divisions, the number depending on the size of the original clump. In general each division should make a good handful of roots and earth and have several stalks growing from it.

When replanting the divisions, follow the same rules that apply for planting or transplanting any growing plant — perennial, annual, rosebush, or small shrub. Dig a hole wider and deeper than the mass of roots and soil, so that the roots will not be crowded. Dig in compost, bone meal, rotted manure, or other fertilizer at the bottom of the hole, cover it with plain garden earth, water the hole if dry, and set the plant in with its neck at ground level, unless otherwise specified. Work good soil down around the roots to fill the hole, tamp it in firmly, and step carefully around the plant when finished to compact the soil. Water well to remove air pockets and protect from strong sun and wind for a week or so until it is well established. Planting and transplanting are best done on cloudy or rainy days or in the evening. Continue to water thoroughly whenever the plant appears dry during the next few weeks.

The question of which perennials to plant in a new border, or what variety will best fill a bare spot in the garden, has so many different answers that your own personal preferences must determine your choices. Personally, if I could have only four perennials in my garden, I would choose irises, phlox, delphiniums, and peonies.

Phlox. Perennial phlox is the queen of the late summer garden. No other flower gives so much pleasure with so little care. The color range is from glistening white to deep, dark red and all shades of pink and salmon. The plants range in height from eighteen inches to about three feet, with tall stalks bearing large, long-lasting flower heads usually of intense fragrance. Different varieties provide constant bloom from late June until frost. There is also a separate species, *Phlox divaricata* or wild blue woodland phlox, a low-growing, spring-blooming cousin with fragrant blue flowers that make a lovely color pattern with pink or yellow tulips.

The tall, summer-blooming phlox will grow in almost any soil and location, but will do best in a rich soil and a sunny place. Never allow it to drop its seed, because the seed seldom runs true to the parent plant and eventually will revert to an undesirable magenta-colored strain. Remove weak-colored poor clumps and replace them with good ones.

There are many outstanding varieties of phlox. Among them are Miss Lingard, white and the earliest to bloom; Mary Louise, a pure white with florets of silver-dollar size; and Daily Sketch, an English novelty which has enormous heads with large flowers of bright salmon pink and crimson eyes. The brilliant reds include Fireglow, Struthers B. Comte, and Beacon. Lillian is a soft pink. Plant them in a sunny spot where they will have ample air circulation and do not crowd them. A properly placed perennial phlox is almost never winter-killed. They are among the hardiest of all perennial flowers for northern gardens.

Most varieties of phlox will also tolerate some shade. Give them plenty of humus and fertilizer each spring and during summer to ensure maximum bloom. The tall varieties are among the best of all flowers for background planting in the border. They make excellent cut flowers as well, and if the dead flowers are cut off promptly, your phlox will continue to bloom for six to eight weeks or longer.

Peonies. These large and handsome plants with their dark green leaves and huge, fragrant flowers in late June make perfect accent points in the background of the perennial border. They like full sun and a rich, well-drained soil, but otherwise are one of the easiest flowers to grow. Peony blossoms are large and showy but never coarse. Some are single, but most of them are double, resembling magnificent roses. There are many beautiful varieties in white, all shades of pink and rose, and deep crimsons and wine reds.

One of the oldest but still one of the best is Festiva Maxima, with deeply double white blooms tinged in the center with streaks of crimson and very fragrant. See the list of recommended varieties at the end of the book for more suggestions.

Peony plants should be staked or fenced with specially made low wire peony supports to keep the luxuriant foliage and heavy-headed flowers from being beaten down by summer rainstorms. Three stakes for a large clump should be enough, with soft twine or torn strips of cloth to circle the plant and tie it to the stakes. The stakes should be put in early in May, before the new growth is more than a foot or so high, but the foliage and flower buds need not be tied up until they reach their full growth at blooming time in June. Place the stakes several inches away from the peony stalks so they will not damage the roots.

Peonies are usually planted in August, when large clumps may be divided, but it is possible to plant them in May and gain a whole year's blooming. If you go directly to a peony farm or nursery and purchase five-year-old field-grown clumps, and plant them as quickly as possible without breaking them up, they may bloom this year. These field clumps will cost more than divisions bought and

GRANDMA always had a large sunny corner in her garden where the soil was rich and plants grew extra well. It was known as the "give-away garden," and into it went surplus plants, divisions from clumps, and husky seedlings. Only thoroughly healthy stock was planted here. This plot was weeded, watered, and tended by Grandma as carefully as the rest of her garden. Anyone was welcome to these plants, especially old timers, mostly farm folk who were taking it easier in the twilight of life and now had time to have a flower garden. Also most welcome to these flowers were newcomers to the valley and young couples who were just starting homes; Grandma always lived her belief that it was more blessed to give than to receive.

planted in August, but where quick bloom is important, they are worth it.

Dig a hole as large as a bushel basket and two to two and a half feet deep. Use plenty of well-decomposed cow manure, bone meal, or commercial plant food mixed with the earth in the bottom. Do not set the plant too deeply in the hole, however, as the buds or eyes on the rootstock must not be more than two inches below the surface. Otherwise the plant will flower sparsely or not at all. Space peony plants at least three feet apart.

If you planted small peony divisions last August or two years ago, don't expect prolific bloom for another year or two. Peonies grow slowly, increasing in size each year, but do not reach their maximum bloom until they are at least five years old. There may be only a few blossoms this year, a few more the next, but ultimately your patience will be rewarded with a gorgeous display of ten to twenty blooms per plant, continuing for twenty years or even longer. For best results, pick off all but one flower bud on each stalk as they develop in May, leaving only one terminal bud per stalk. If ants crawl over the flower buds, ignore them; they do no harm.

Peonies are "hardy as an oak" and love our cold northern winters. All they ask is plenty of bone meal or well-rotted manure dug in around the clumps once or twice a year, and they will be a permanent joy in your garden.

Iris. Great progress has been made in the breeding of iris in the last few years. Some of the new ones are almost breathtaking in form and size. They come in glamorous shades and blendings of blues, tans, reds, pinks, mauves, purples, and also in true blue. (See recommended varieties at the end of the book.)

By carefully choosing the proper varieties, you can have irises in bloom next year from early May into late June. The bearded — sometimes called German — iris is the most popular. In this group there are more than two hundred listed varieties, from six inches to more than four feet high.

In late May and next month when they are in bloom, you can make your choices from among the many different irises by sight.

There are many good nurseries and some public iris gardens in the Upper Midwest and most northern regions where you can view irises in June and buy them later, at planting time in July and August. Your new plants will be well settled by winter and be ready to bloom next summer. Although new iris can be planted now, don't expect much in flowers this year.

When planted in a well-drained spot with plenty of sunshine, good soil, and not too much watering, irises grow so lustily they usually have to be divided every three or four years. They appreciate bone meal and gypsum worked into the soil around the clumps. Plant with the rhizomes just below the surface of the soil. Keep manure away from irises, as it tends to cause rot in the rhizomes, and don't mulch them heavily in the winter. With very little attention your irises will bloom and flourish for many years.

Delphinium. Delphinium, a flower of our grandmothers' gardens, is increasing in beauty and popularity every year. Dark blue was its characteristic color, but with the new hybrids we can also get delicate shades of light blue, mauves, and magnificent whites.

The present most popular types are the tall elatum or garden hybrids, with dense spikes of light blue or white flowers; the bellamosum, similar to the belladonna but with dark blue flowers; and the Chinese, a three-footer with loosely arranged blue or white flowers. The Chinese strain is an easy grower and free bloomer. Unlike the other delphiniums, it will bloom the first year from seed sown early.

Delphiniums should be planted in rich, well-drained soil. Completely decayed cow manure should be mixed into the bed before planting. Plant in a partially sunny spot but avoid all-day sunshine. Plants should be at least two feet apart and far enough from other vegetation so that the sun can shine part of the day on the crowns. Place three or more supporting stakes around each clump when planting. When growth reaches two feet, circle the stalk with soft twine or cord and tie to the stake. Do not permit more than four or five stalks to grow from each plant. A small handful of fine tobacco dust sifted over each clump will repel most insects.

Chrysanthemums. "Plant your chrysanthemums when the tulips are in bloom," according to a garden adage I've heard. Here in the North most tulips are in full bloom during the latter part of May, so that timetable seems just about right. Chrysanthemum plants can be set out in the perennial border or in their own special beds any time after the weather is settled and danger of killing frosts is past — from late April to about June 15.

Until a few years ago, the only chrysanthemums the average northern gardener was acquainted with were a few very late, rather unexciting varieties that bloomed, if at all, just before winter cut them down. Now, however, new developments in Minnesota nurseries and in other northern states have resulted in new varieties that make the chrysanthemum the most important of our autumn flowers. The early chrysanthemums break into blossom in late August and from then on there is a continuous procession of ever-changing color to late October and often into early November.

By carefully choosing your plants, you can have almost every color and blend — except blue — in blossoms from little buttons to large pompons and in singles, doubles, and semi-doubles of yellow, gold, bronze with red predominating, and, of course, white. There is also the cushion chrysanthemum, a long bloomer that is a low, rounded mass of blossoms from the soil to the top of the dome.

The blossoms can stand several degrees of repeated frost, and often will be riding high above November snows in the garden and in window boxes.

For better blooms, divide old plants every two years. Chrysanthemums should be planted in an open, sunny location where they will not be shaded by buildings or trees, except during late afternoons. Soil that will grow good flowers or vegetables will grow mums. However, compost, leafmold, or well-rotted cow manure worked into the garden earth will grow better ones.

It is a mistake to plant too many varieties. Best effects can be obtained by planting three of the same variety together but about twenty inches apart. Arrange them in your border according to height and your choice of color harmony. Use clumps of white mums for highlight spots and as buffer zones between two strong colors. There are many fine varieties to choose from. See the table of recommended varieties at the end of the book for some suggestions.

When chrysanthemum plants are eight inches high, pinch off with your fingernails one-half inch of the terminal end of each branch to encourage stocky growth. Continue to pinch them back in this way every two weeks until late July. Do not pinch the early-blooming varieties after early July, however. Water from underneath by allowing the hose to run along the ground. Water every week during hot weather. Avoid sprinkling on foliage and blossoms. Loosen the earth around the plants by frequent light cultivation — but not too deep because of their shallow root system.

Several sprayings of Black-Leaf 40 (nicotine sulphate) during July and August should keep the plants clean. Two light dustings of 5 per cent DDT during the bud-forming stage will eliminate the tarnish bug.

Always remove all faded blooms and buds. Mums can prolong the beauty of your perennial border by being transplanted into just the spots where they are needed, even when in full bloom. In this way they can grow all summer in an inconspicuous bed of their own until they are ready for public view at blooming time. They are amazingly beautiful as a second planting for your window box early in the autumn. If very cold weather or early winter should threaten some of the late bloomers, just dig them up, pop them into a large pot, bring them into the house, and they will burst into bloom in your living room just as beautifully as outdoors.

Tulips and Others. Toward the end of May the tulips in most northern gardens are in full bloom. Their drifts of bright color in the perennial border are a lovely sight, especially when blended with the graceful pink sprays of bleeding heart, the clear lavender-blue of *Phlox divaricata* and Jacob's ladder, and the pinky-blue of the dainty mertensia or Virginia bluebells, which bloom at about the same time.

Tulips often last well into June, but all too soon their flowers will be gone for this year. Then their old flower stalks and rather floppy leaves present something of a problem in the border. When the blossoms fade, immediately remove the heads to prevent seed pods

113

from forming. This will permit the tulips to use all their strength to store up food for next year's blooms. Do not remove the leaves or stems until they are faded and withered and their juices have returned to the bulbs. If you cut tulips when they are in bloom, take only one leaf with the flower stalk.

GRANDMA followed the lovely old custom of planting flowers on graves. In May she always replaced plants that had not wintered. When she saw cemetery plots owned by families who were unable to attend to them, she would plant something there. On shady graves she planted ferns, forget-me-nots, bleeding hearts, lilies of the valley, moss phlox, and fall-blooming asters. She reseeded sunny plots or tucked in transplants from her own garden that did not require much shade. On the grave of a little girl who had loved wild flowers Grandma planted wild violets, ginger root, jack-in-the-pulpit, and snowdrops. They came up every spring.

Keep the earth in which tulips are planted cool all summer with a mulch, or plant shallow-rooted annuals over them. Tulip bulbs may bake and perish if not protected. Pansies, sweet alyssum, or any small annuals can be used to shield the tulip bulbs and hide the unattractive foliage until it is dried — usually sometime in July — and can be removed. These small annuals will provide color in that part of the border for the rest of the summer.

May is the time to plant other perennials and plants of all kinds. If you made a garden plan and chose the flowers you wanted back in February, now is the time to put your plan into practice. Day-lilies — which are not really lilies at all but hemerocallis, with tuberous roots — may be planted now and are a hardy and easy-to-grow choice for your border.

True lilies that grow from deep-planted bulbs may also be planted now, just as soon as the soil is warm and all danger of frost is past. Among the finest lilies are the golden-throat regals, the beautiful but fickle gold-banded auratums, and the rubrum, white shaded with rose and black. All are sweet scented. Then there are the beautiful but more common candlestick lilies (orange-red), Golden Fleece (yellow), Vermilion (crimson), *elegans* (royal red), and tiger lilies (red, both single and double). Most lilies prefer full sun and a deep rich soil. They will bloom and multiply year after year if given the conditions that suit them.

Planting Gladioli. Toward the end of May, when the soil is dependably warm, the northern gardener can begin to plant gladiolus corms. These corms — or bulbs, as most people call them, though the name is not strictly accurate — will grow and bloom for several years like perennials; but since they are not winter-hardy, they must be dug up each fall and stored indoors. When May and warm weather arrive, the corms can be planted outdoors again in much the same way that annual seeds are planted. For this reason they are usually planted in beds of their own or in the annual bed, rather than in the perennial border which cannot be dug up each fall.

Even though May is well along, don't hurry your gladiolus planting. They can be planted as late as July and still bloom before frost, but too-early planting can do real damage. Even a few days in cold soil will often cause corms to rot.

In most northern areas cautious gardeners do not plant their glads until after May 15 or 20. They lose only a week or two of growing time and this is soon made up in continuous warm growing weather. Gladioli can be planted in light, sandy soil in a warm exposure much earlier than in a heavier black loam. Do not plant all your corms at one time. Plant a few every week or ten days into mid-July and you will have constant bloom from July well into late autumn, instead of a flood of blossoms for only a couple of weeks.

Gladioli grow well in full sun and in soil that will grow good annual flowers or vegetables — but they require lots of sunshine and must be away from shrubs and trees. Plant the corms about four inches apart, staggered in flat-bottomed trenches. The trenches should be eighteen inches apart. Balanced commercial plant food,

115

worked into the soil before planting at the rate of five pounds per hundred feet of row, will make for better blossoms, or two to three pounds may be worked into the soil on each side of the rows after planting. Plant standard-size corms four inches deep in heavy soil or up to six inches deep in sandy soil and about six inches apart.

After the glads are about a foot high, drive several stakes along the row and intertwine a double cord through the rows of growing plants to protect them in strong winds. Do not plant them in the same soil where you had them last year lest they pick up some disease from the soil. In dry weather water once a week in the morning or evening.

If you are planting last year's corms, give them a treatment for thrips. Thrips are insects that live in the corms all winter and play havoc with blossoms the following summer. Even though you treated the corms last fall, some insects may have survived. To be on the safe side, soak all your corms for three hours in a solution of four tablespoons of Lysol in three gallons of water. Drain them and plant while moist.

New corms purchased from reliable dealers should be practically free from insects, so you should not have to treat them. But many gardeners, to be on the safe side, give all their corms a dusting of 5 per cent DDT or chlordane a few hours before planting.

Mulch the rows during the hot months with compost, vermiculite, lawn clippings, or moss. A diluted DDT spray or dust is reported to be excellent if, in spite of precautions, thrips do appear on stalks, leaves, and buds. When the plants are about to bloom, an application of liquid manure will increase the size and color of the blossoms. If you are growing glads for cutting, plant in rows, but to lend color in a border, plant the corms in groups of three or more.

ANNUALS IN MAY

When the soil is warm, start planting annual seeds in the beds that you prepared in April. Rows or masses of annuals make an attractive garden by themselves, and individual plants will fill in beautifully in the perennial border during the "between" periods when there is a lapse in the continuity of perennial flowering. Annuals, a constant source of cut flowers, allow the slower-growing perennials to remain a delight in the garden.

For earlier blooming (and to sidestep considerable trouble) the amateur gardener can purchase most of the desirable annual flowers as seedlings of transplanting size from greenhouses or nurseries at reasonable cost. There are, however, many desirable annuals that do not stand transplanting well and should be seeded directly in the garden, preferably in the annual bed, but also in small bare spots in the perennial border. Among these are blue lace flower, balsam, nasturtium, cleome, clarkia, kochia, moonflower, anchusa, morning-glory, zinnia, tithonia, four o'clock, and cynoglossum.

The following annuals can be directly seeded, then thinned and the seedlings transplanted with care: nicotiana, calliopsis, ageratum, marigold, scabiosa, alyssum, annual dahlias, gaillardia, linum, celosia, verbena, stocks, salpiglosis, and lobelia. A special outdoor seedbed can be used to start these in a made-to-order, light, humus-filled soil. Transplant on a cloudy day or in the evening. Water plants an hour before moving and also water the soil where they are going. Protect from sun and wind for several days after transplanting.

Much the same technique should be used in planting seeds as in sowing in a seed box indoors or in the cold frame, particularly as to shallow planting and covering the seeds with porous soil. Identification of the seeds, and of their location, is important, since some are slow to germinate and it is easy to forget exactly where they were sown.

GRANDMA used the grayish-green warp or cord that she wove into her beautiful hand-loomed rugs for her annual vines to climb on and for tying plants to stakes. This warp was strong enough to last all summer and was not conspicuous. I have used it for years. It still is obtainable in the stores and is surprisingly low priced — fifty cents for half a mile.

MAY

Practically all seed companies put up their products with full directions printed on the seed envelopes. Always buy the best seed obtainable — fresh seed put up and sold by reliable established firms. Sow your annuals in beds where they will get sun at least half the day, preferably more. The beds must be well drained and the soil must contain enough loam or humus so it does not pack readily, but will retain moisture. The surface soil should be raked and smoothed to a fine texture so the roots of the tender seedlings may penetrate easily. The soil should be enriched with well-rotted manure or balanced plant food several days or a week in advance of planting. Very fine seed, such as petunia and portulaca, should not be buried. Just scatter it on the surface and press into the soil, or cover it lightly with powdered charcoal.

Sometimes a cold spell will delay proper germination, however, and fungi may attack and kill the seedlings. Some of this trouble can be prevented by using a disinfectant such as Spergon or Arasan. Take as much of either as you can lift on the broad end of a toothpick, drop it into the seed packet, and shake it well to coat the seed. As a further precaution against fungi many gardeners spread a layer of fine sphagnum moss over the seed surface and sow the seed on it. They then sift over the seed an even finer texture of the moss. This method prevents damping off. You can learn more details from the U.S. Department of Agriculture pamphlet, *Sphagnum Moss for Seed Germination,* mentioned in the March chapter.

If sphagnum moss is not available and if you have a compost pile, there is no better way that you can use the humus from it than in preparing a special soil with which to cover seed. This should be mixed with sand, half and half. In addition to making it certain that the seed sprouts will be able to emerge, this loose soil will hold moisture and keep the soil beneath it from drying out. This is especially desirable when you are planting in hot weather.

Until the seeds sprout, the soil must be kept moist. This requires frequent sprinkling with a fine spray, taking care not to wash the seeds out of the soil. You should know when to expect the seeds to sprout. For this information, look on the seed packet.

When tiny seedlings appear in the annual bed, thin them when

118

they are an inch or two high to stand the distance apart recommended on the seed package. Thinned seedlings can be replanted in another part of the bed. Be careful to disturb the roots as little as possible, and water and protect from sun after moving them as in all transplanting operations. Keep the annual beds free of weeds by hoeing frequently, and water if necessary.

If you started annual seedlings in indoor seed flats or in a cold frame, they should be good-sized young plants by May and ready to set out in the annual beds or perennial border whenever the weather is warm. If you are buying annual seedlings instead of raising your own, middle to late May is usually the time when nurseries have their widest assortment to choose from.

Follow the rules already outlined for planting and transplanting and you will have blooming annuals in your garden in a very few weeks, long before the other annuals sown outdoors in May begin to bloom. If there is a brief return of freezing temperatures, it is not difficult to protect your seedlings with hotcaps, inverted flowerpots, sheets, or newspapers arched over them and anchored with stones or handfuls of earth on the corners.

Another use for annuals is to soften the bare lines of a new house or a fence, to give quick shade over an arbor or porch, or to hide an unsightly spot on your property. For this purpose nothing can equal the quick-growing annual vines. They will take care of the interval until you can landscape with permanent vines and shrubs. For quick results, plant seeds of the four good morning-glories — Heavenly Blue, Blue Star, Scarlett O'Hara, and Pearly Gates. Nick the seed coat and soak the seed overnight in warm water before planting. Or plant moonflower, a night-blooming climber that has enormous white blossoms. There is a pink variety, too. The moonflower often stays open until the following noon. These moonflowers, once out of the ground, quickly will climb cords fifteen feet high, and they have luxuriant foliage. There are also the quick-growing hyacinth bean, scarlet runner, and heart and honey vine.

The perennial kudzu vine with large, tropical-looking green leaves is useful for shade and covering fences and unsightly places. It can be planted from seed, and although it takes from thirty to fifty days to germinate, when once established, it will grow fifty feet in one season.

POTTING YOUR TUBEROUS BEGONIAS

When the sprouts on your tuberous begonias are two to three inches long, they are ready to be potted. This will usually be sometime in early May. Some gardeners whose indoor space is limited first pot them in two- or three-inch pots, setting the tuber half an inch below the surface. Then after four to six weeks they are carefully transferred to the large seven- to eight-inch pots where they will spend the summer or stay until transplanted to the garden. Wide pots are better than deep ones, as the roots tend to spread horizontally. One way to save space on your window sill is to use milk cartons cut down to four inches in place of the small pots. Later the plants can be removed easily by tearing away the cartons.

The potting mixture for tuberous begonias should be rich in humus and organic plant food. A good mixture is one third each good garden soil, somewhat sandy, peat, and well-rotted cow manure. For each eight-inch pot you can add a coffee-measuring scoop of fish meal, cottonseed meal, or soybean meal, or a combination of all three. Some gardeners place the sprouted tubers in sphagnum moss in the upper third of the pot and use the enriched potting

GRANDMA waged a never-ending war against ants in the house—and how those ants did love maple syrup and maple sugar! Grandfather had a big sugar bush on his farm—though why it was called a bush, I don't know. Most of the maple trees were more than fifty feet high. Every spring he harvested large quantities of syrup and sugar. No matter where Grandma put the syrup and sugar, the ants would find them. She used bottles, jugs, and metal boxes, but still the ants always would be around trying to find an opening. After much experimenting she found that a mixture of borax and saleratus usually would drive them away.

mixture only in the lower two thirds of the pot. Fill the pot to within one inch of the rim and cover the top of the tuber one-half inch. Use a curved piece of broken pot over the drain hole, and then in the bottom of the pots put about an inch of coarse gravel and charcoal mixed.

When the tubers have been potted, set the pots in a cool place in the house in full light but not in direct sunshine. Do not allow the pots to become dry, but do not overwater. Before the begonia stalks grow too high, thrust into the pots small stakes to hold the plants upright if they become top-heavy. Allowing only one stalk to grow from each tuber will produce larger but fewer blooms. Turn the pots often so that the plants develop as evenly as possible all around.

In late May or early in June, whenever the weather is dependably warm, the begonias may be taken from their pots and set out in the garden, or the potted plants may be plunged in the earth up to their rims. With either method, be sure to choose a location that is semishady, protected from strong winds, and that does not become too warm. If you plunge the pots in the garden, place them on a layer of ashes to keep out worms and insects. If you plant the tuberous begonias directly in garden earth, the soil must be well drained and, if possible, have a gravel or sandy subsoil. A cool, loamy soil mixed with compost and well-rotted cow manure is best. The addition of peat will also be beneficial in maintaining the loose, friable soil texture that begonias like. Never allow the soil to become either dry or soggy. Begonias will lose their buds and leaves from too much or too little watering. In hot weather, spray the plants at least once a day.

Tuberous begonia plants have a front side which must face the source of greatest light. Watch for this when placing your potted begonias on shelves or planting them in the garden. Three blossoms are usually produced from each stem. To obtain large blossoms, pinch off the side buds when they are small. Feed your begonias with a liquid fertilizer every two or three weeks during the summer and you will have an abundance of gorgeous flowers from June until frost.

MAY

During May your early spring lawn work begins to pay dividends. Fertilizer, reseeding, spring rains or faithful watering, and warm weather all make the grass grow luxuriantly. All too soon it begins to need weekly mowing, and all too soon the summer crop of lawn weeds must also be coped with. The best way to fight weeds in your lawn is to maintain healthy grass by the routine care I have already outlined, and by mowing not shorter than two inches, especially during hot weather. But even good care cannot always keep weeds from appearing, so specific remedies must be used as well.

Crabgrass is one of the northern lawn's worst enemies. It is an annual grass that sprouts in late May, flourishes in the hot, dry weeks of July, crowding out desirable perennial grasses if given a chance, then dies out in August leaving ugly dead patches in your lawn and thousands of weed seeds to sprout again next May. Crabgrass is easily recognized. Even in the early two-leaf stage it is different from other grasses. It has rather heavy leaves, yellow-green in color, about a quarter of an inch wide. These first two blades are opposite and as they grow, they curve outward and down.

There are several ways to fight crabgrass, chiefly hand weeding when the plants are still small or spraying with special chemical weed killers before the plants are fully mature. The most promising method of all, however, is a recent development that uses a chemical spray in late spring to kill the crabgrass seeds before they have sprouted. This chemical, sodium 2, 4-dichloro phenoxyethyl sulphate, is sold under the trade name Crag, and will kill crabgrass seeds before they sprout.

The spray must be applied in late May, before the crabgrass seeds have germinated. A solution of three tablespoons of the chemical to three gallons of water is needed. It can be sprinkled on with a watering can, but a much more effective job will be done with a garden hose siphon sprayer used in accordance with directions on the herbicide can. The application should be repeated two or three times at three-week intervals, into June and July, to catch any crabgrass seeds that might sprout later. The application will also have to be repeated next May and possibly for a year or two more to catch buried crabgrass seed that may work up and be within sprouting depth in the next few years. Crabgrass can remain alive for several years when buried in the soil.

The herbicide does not injure seriously, if at all, lawn grass that is already growing. It should not be used on bentgrass or new lawns, however. Do not sow seed on the treated area for at least a month after application.

GRANDMA showed great bravery by eating tomatoes in an age when many people considered them deadly poisonous. Some people still called them "love apples." They were smaller than ours today and usually grown only for ornament. But Grandma knew they were not poisonous, and she would eat them calmly while her neighbor children stood around watching in horror.

The few crabgrass plants that do sprout and grow this summer after the preventive treatment can be removed by hand weeding or a narrow, pointed hoe, or if necessary by a thorough spraying with good crabgrass killer. We will discuss these methods in more detail next month, but with good luck, they should not be needed.

Another nuisance that appears in our lawns in May is the dandelion. If you have a good thick stand of grass, there is not much chance that the wind-blown dandelion seeds will reach the ground in your lawn, and if they do they will not create much trouble provided you mow your grass two or three inches high. Dandelions have to have sun and a chance to flatten out when growing.

One-inch-mesh chicken netting dragged over the lawn will pull off the dandelion blossoms, but you must pick or rake up the heads, because they will ripen even after they are cut off. Do this for a few years, and dandelions will disappear. However, if they already have a start, the ever-ready pocket or putty knife plus some elbow grease is the next best answer. Stab well below the crown to make sure you remove the entire root system. Or you can stab them with a "killer" stick containing 2, 4-D solution. For a mass infestation of dandelions, spraying with any of the weed killers containing 2, 4-D is best. However, weed killer is hard on clover and bentgrass. Don't allow the spray to reach any of your flowers or shrubs. Apply on a windless day and take great care not to allow contact with any broad-leaved plants except the dandelions you are trying to kill.

PLANNING A BRAND-NEW HOUSE AND LAWN

If a new house is among your plans for "someday," or if your plans are about to become reality, you should remember that you will not only be laying the foundation of a new house, but of the lawn and garden as well. Care and foresight now can save you hours of work later.

First of all, have a clear understanding — or better yet a written agreement — with your builder or contractor that all existing trees on the property will be protected during excavating. Too many new residential developments show the obvious symptoms of "bulldozeritis." Even trees not dug up are severely and often irreparably damaged by having the earth close to their roots disturbed. Worse still, careless bulldozer operators often bump into and gouge the trees.

If a tree you want to save is very close to the site of your new house, and it is possible that some of its roots will have to be sacrificed, call in a tree surgeon. Follow his advice to the letter. He will probably advise removing some of the branches to compensate for the root loss.

Often you hear, "Don't bother to save oak and elm trees. They soon die anyway when they are near a house or from people walking over their roots." This is utter nonsense. Many of our finest park trees are oaks — and hundreds of children play around them.

Have the trees protected before bulldozing and excavating begin. Tie or wire to the trunks wide boards or large sheets of heavy galvanized iron. Do not permit the workmen to drive spikes or even nails into your trees to support scaffoldings.

124

When actual excavating starts, see that the black topsoil is carefully saved — not mixed with clay or gravel subsoils or buried. Then you can use the topsoil to form a good foundation for lawn and garden, instead of buying loads of black dirt as many new home-owners are forced to do in order to build a lawn.

If the grade or level of your lawn is raised more than two or three inches around the tree trunks, place a circle of rocks a couple of inches from the trunks to prevent the earth's rotting the bark. In a few years, with the drifting in of leaves and dust, the tree will gradually become accustomed to the change.

The amount of fill that can be safely added is six inches for young trees, seven inches for medium-aged trees, and eight inches for old trees. For a tree twelve inches in diameter, sixteen inches of gravel, ten inches of sand, or six inches of soil can be added. Use gravel or coarse sand if possible to allow drainage and aeration.

If, on the other hand, the grade is lowered, you will need to take precautions against root damage. The amount of topsoil that can be removed without injury is approximately four inches for young trees, six inches for medium-aged trees, and eight inches for old trees. But try to maintain the original level at least under the spread of the branches.

Oaks, sugar maples, beeches, birches, hickories, and hemlocks are most susceptible to grade injury. Elms, poplars, willows, planes, locusts, and boxelders are least susceptible.

GRANDMA expected Uncle Jerry to keep the front lawn clear of dandelions, Jerry said they were "a pain in the neck" to him and also a pain in the back, from bending over to knife them out. One spring when Grandma went visiting he got a brilliant idea. He turned a herd of twenty sheep on the lawn for two days. Results: no dandelions for several years, also no lawn to speak of for most of the summer.

MAY

If your new house is being built on really wild land, you will need to take special precautions to make a gradual change from forest conditions, where a deep humus provides ideal moisture retention around the roots, to lawn conditions. Supply a great deal of water and food to the trees during the first seasons, and the trees may survive the change without serious damage.

As your house nears completion, you must not relax your vigilance. Be sure to prevent the builders from dumping the accumulated rubbish or short boards, shingles, and bricks into the working space around the foundation, covering the rubbish, and then leveling off the ground. This buried rubbish can form pockets where water will settle and slowly seep into your basement.

GRANDMA always encircled her little vegetable garden with bright-colored annual flowers. She explained that she and the birds enjoyed the colors and, incidentally, the birds enjoyed the cutworms and other grubs. She never forgot to keep her birdbath filled. She knew that parent birds have not only their own thirst to satisfy, but also many little babies that are crying for water. The birds were so numerous that often the bath had to be refilled several times each day. Perhaps that was the secret of Grandma's pest-free garden.

REMINDERS

Watch the seedlings in your cold frame carefully, making sure they are not getting too warm. The glass sash should be opened during the sunny hours for ventilation. By the end of May or early June, all the annual seedlings in the cold frame should have been transplanted into their permanent places in the garden.

Lilacs, flowering almond and currant, and pink honeysuckle bloom in late May in most northern regions. Like all spring-blooming shrubs, they should not be pruned before blooming. But cut as many blooms for the house as you care to, for this is a pleasant and effective way to prune. With lilacs especially, cutting flowers from the top of the bush will encourage a new lateral growth. Lilac branches that produce blooms this year are not likely to bloom again next spring in any case, though some varieties do. Most shrubs bloom best on branches that are only one year old. When blooming is over, complete your pruning of these shrubs and fertilize again for summer growth.

For taste appeal all summer long, reserve a tiny patch near the kitchen door for parsley, chives, and mint. A little will go a long way. The chives and mint will come up year after year, but the parsley should be reseeded early each spring.

Don't forget to stake your peonies before they grow too tall. Remove all the tiny, subsidiary buds around the main flower bud on each stem. Most peonies set more buds than will ever bloom, so nip off the extra ones early to make one large flower per stem.

Set out pansy plants in partly shady spots. Keep them blooming all summer by removing faded blossoms every day.

Remove the lower leaves of delphiniums that touch the ground. Dust stems and soil with an all-purpose garden dust.

Mow your lawn two inches high and often. If clippings are short, don't rake them. They form a mulch on the turf which discourages crabgrass and conserves water. Don't use weed killer spray on windy days. It could drift and kill your flowers.

Take only one leaf when cutting tulip blossoms. If a seed pod forms, remove it. Don't cut tulip leaves and stems after blooming. Let them dry up naturally.

Put up a bird bath. An inverted garbage can cover will do. Robins have finished the framework of their new homes, but they must be plastered. Provide puddles of plastering mud somewhere near the garden and soft yarn cord and fluff from the laundry drier for baby bird beds.

Fertilize the earth in old window boxes or replace it with a rich, loamy, water-retaining mixture.

Protect the trunks of newly set out, thin-barked trees from sunburn during their first summer. Heavy paper wrapped loosely about the trunks will do the trick.

✖ JUNE ✖

June in the North is an exciting month, bringing roses and peonies, picnics and thunderstorms, the first summer heat wave or a chilly wet spell. Each year the timetable for June bloom is a little different, varying as much as two or three weeks. Sometimes tulips and even lilacs last well into June; and sometimes peonies, which in other parts of the country bloom around Memorial Day, may not reach their peak here in the North before the Fourth of July.

In spite of June's vagaries, the northern gardener can expect a steady procession of color and fragrance throughout the month. As the tulips begin to fade, the first of the irises burst into bloom, followed by roses and later the massive peonies. The low-growing blue and pink phlox, Jacob's ladder, and mertensia continue to add color among the taller specimens, with yellow trollius and primroses for contrast and masses of lilies of the valley in shady corners. The arching branches of bridalwreath are covered with white blossoms in June, and the handsome mockoranges, both single and double, fill the air with sweetness.

EARLY JUNE IN THE GARDEN

This is a month of pleasure and reward for the gardener, but there are chores to attend to also. It is still not too late to plant roses and even shrubs, provided they are growing in pots or can be dug at a nursery and replanted at once. Many annual and perennial plants can be planted or transplanted all through June and July, even when they are in bloom.

Bare spots in the perennial border will be apparent now, and can be filled either temporarily with annuals for this year's bloom, or permanently with new perennial plants.

When your tulips are through blooming, cut off only the old blossom heads, not the stems or the leaves. The annuals you plant among them will help to disguise the dying tulip foliage. Most gardeners do not disturb their tulips from year to year until the blossoms deteriorate in quality and the old bulbs need to be replaced. Usually tulip bulbs blossom well for three to five years.

If for some reason it is necessary to use the tulip bed for other purposes, however, tulip bulbs can be dug up after the foliage is completely dry, dried in an airy place but not in the sun, stored during the summer, and replanted in October or November for next spring's blooms. The bulbs should be dusted with sulphur after they are dug up and placed in onion sacks or old nylon stockings. Hang them in a dark, cool basement. Any bulbs that are soft or diseased should be destroyed at once.

When bulblets are found growing from the side of the mother tulip bulbs, they may be replanted at once in a bed of rather fine soil. In the fall replant them four inches deep. If in a year or two they have small buds that show color, clip and discard them. The next year the bulbs may develop fair-sized blossoms, and they will be the same form and color as the parent bulb.

As tiny weeds sprout among the flowers in the perennial border — chickweed is one of the commonest intruders — cultivate with a delicate hand, just enough to get the weeds out and to keep the surface loose and porous. Every day or two cut off all dead or faded flowers to prevent your perennials from going to seed.

If you have not already fertilized the perennial border this spring, do so in early June. A circle of balanced plant food or bone meal dug in around each plant will be of great benefit. Do not allow the fertilizer to touch the roots or stems of the plants. Well-rotted or dried animal fertilizer is better applied either in early spring or in the fall after frost to avoid the possibility of damage to sensitive foliage. Feed your roses with special rose food to encourage many big blossoms.

June often brings a spell of hot, damp weather, which unfortunately is ideal for the growth of molds and mildew in the garden, especially on roses and phlox. Continue to give your entire garden a thorough dusting every week with an all-purpose dust that contains Fermate and sulphur. For thrips on gladioli, dust or spray with DDT or chlordane.

Green, red, or black aphids, or plant lice may also appear in the garden during June. They cling to the under side of leaves or on the growing ends of many flower stems, multiplying with amazing rapidity.

They pierce the leaves and stems and suck the sap of tender perennials and shrubs, reducing the vitality of the plant so that it produces poor flowers or may even be winter-killed the following season.

Aphids are particularly troublesome on the new shoots and buds of roses, and on the tender new branches of bridalwreath that appear after the bridalwreath has bloomed. DDT has no effect on aphids, but a contact poison like nicotine sulphate will control them. Black Leaf 40 is a good nicotine sulphate spray. Mix it with soapsuds according to the directions on the package and spray as soon as you notice the aphids and two sprays each week thereafter until they are gone. Rotenone, pyrethrum, and various all-purpose garden dusts also contain ingredients toxic to aphids.

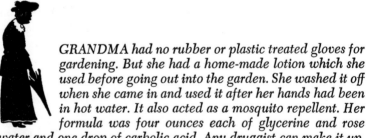

GRANDMA had no rubber or plastic treated gloves for gardening. But she had a home-made lotion which she used before going out into the garden. She washed it off when she came in and used it after her hands had been in hot water. It also acted as a mosquito repellent. Her formula was four ounces each of glycerine and rose water and one drop of carbolic acid. Any druggist can make it up. Grandma also rubbed a thick lather of soap around and under her fingernails before working in the earth. This kept her nails free from stain. In spite of hard work she had beautiful hands, and she was proud of them.

Another early summer insect pest that may appear in your garden is the cutworm. Cutworms are caterpillars of various moths that hide by day and at night cut off young plants at the surface. Cutworms usually can be controlled by dusting plants and the ground around them with 10 per cent DDT powder.

During June you can finish pruning spring-blooming shrubs which are past their blossoming season. Cut out all dead wood and old, thick-barked branches. Prune old lilacs from the top of the bush as well as at the base, but with most other flowering shrubs, such as flowering almond, flowering currant, or honeysuckle, cut out old or weak stems from the base when the bushes become crowded. Never chop off branches in an unnatural pattern, but try to maintain the natural balance and form of the shrub. Shrubs that flower in June or later, such as mockorange and bridalwreath, should not be pruned until September.

Early this month, if not before, the weather should be warm enough to set out your tuberous begonias and house plants for their summer out-of-doors. Both should have a protected, airy summer location with a good deal of shade, especially at noon. Tuberous begonias may be planted directly in the garden, but they will be more adaptable if left in their pots and buried to their rims. In this way you can move them about during the summer to provide color in various places where it is temporarily needed. For a few days or weeks you can keep them in a shady part of the perennial border, then move them to your porch or patio, or to a window box with a northern exposure.

Most of your indoor house plants, both foliage and flowering, will appreciate the same kind of summer treatment as tuberous begonias. The north side of the house or a shady window box, provided it is protected from strong winds, should suit them well. Leave them in their pots but plunge them up to their rims in earth, with a layer of cinders or gravel underneath to keep out earthworms. Keep them well watered and out of strong sun and they will thrive.

Fibrous-rooted begonias and patience plant will often bloom prolifically all summer. Geraniums will also, if they have not been

131

blooming all winter, but unlike the other house plants they prefer full sun outdoors and freedom from their pots. In the fall you can start new slips for indoor bloom over the winter, and lift the large old geranium roots and store them in the basement for outdoor bloom next summer.

There are a few house plants that do better if kept indoors. African violets and gloxinias, for example, are better off indoors, because summer rainstorms damage their brittle foliage. Large-leaved philodendrons and similar large foliage plants may also be damaged by winds and heavy rains outdoors. A sheltered porch or an airy window sill indoors will do just as well for house plants like these.

If your window box is in sun rather than shade, fill it with young annual plants all ready to bloom. You can buy these at a local greenhouse or nursery, or use the early annual seedlings you started indoors or in your cold frame.

Most of the low-growing annuals are suitable for window-box culture. Try velvety, deep-toned trailing petunias, with perhaps a few gay geraniums and an edging of bright blue lobelia and white alyssum. Fragrant flowers, such as ten-week stock and mignonette, will perfume the house, both inside and out, in the cool of the evening. The best window-box flowers are those that bear flowers freely and continuously. In these respects the petunia has no superior. Fragrant double nasturtiums are also fine window-box material, as are lovely Heavenly Blue morning-glories.

PLANTING DAHLIAS

Dahlias are late summer flowers that grow from fleshy tuberous roots and come in many colors, sizes, and flower forms. The time to plant them in the North is late May to mid-June — when all danger of frost is past and warm weather can be counted on. Dahlias need reasonably good soil and sunshine, but are not at all difficult to grow. As background flowers for September bloom in the border, the tall dahlia varieties have no equal. They grow from three to six feet high with mammoth blossoms as much as twelve inches across. The smaller, low-growing varieties are equally desirable for late color in the foreground of the border or in small beds by themselves.

Dahlia enthusiasts are very common among northern gardeners, and dahlia clubs and fall dahlia shows are well-established in most northern cities. Luckily the Upper Midwest and most other northern areas are ideal for dahlias. Any gardener can become a successful dahlia grower and even an exhibitor, if he observes the requisites of good gardening. Attention to seemingly little details wins the blue ribbons.

Dahlias should be planted in well-drained, loamy soil in which humus, such as compost or well-decayed leaves, has been thoroughly mixed. Slight acidity of the soil is desirable but not a necessity. Plant the roots in six-inch-deep holes, one to a hole. Be sure that the root has at least one eye or developing sprout. For tall-growing dahlias, drive a six-foot stake in the bottom of the planting hole beside the root before covering it with soil. The root should lie on its side with the sprouting end close to the stake. Plant the tubers two to three feet apart, depending on the variety.

As the dahlia grows, its stem should be fastened securely to the stake with one-inch or wider strips of cloth. Do not bind the stem tightly to the stake. Allow enough slack for growth. To get tall plants and large blossoms, allow only one stalk to grow from each tuber. Pinch off subsidiary stems when they appear. After the stalk has developed three pairs of leaves, pinch off the top or growing tip of the stalk to make a strong bushy plant with six lateral canes. If you wish, you can let all six grow for several weeks, then remove the two weakest ones.

Dahlias should be kept in continuous, active growth once they have sprouted. This means that you should feed them frequently during the growing season and water generously. Never allow them to go without water in dry spells. Feed one tablespoon of complete plant food per square foot once a month during the growing season. Work the plant food into the soil around the plant. Be careful it does not touch the dahlia stem.

Cultivation is essential. Stir the soil freely to eliminate weeds and prevent a hard crust from forming, once a week up until the first of September, when all cultivation should stop. By then the feeding roots are close to the surface, and hoeing will do more harm than good. A mulch may be used to hold moisture and keep weeds down during this late-summer period.

Insects and other troubles can be controlled with a weekly application of an all-purpose garden dust. Dust thoroughly, but if the dust is visible on the leaves you are applying it too heavily. Stand away from the plant and dust so a very light cloud surrounds it. Dust in early morning or evening when there is practically no wind. This dusting procedure is a good one to apply to all garden plants.

Sometime in July buds will begin to appear usually in groups of three on all varieties of dahlias. If you want large blossoms, break off the two side buds in each cluster of three, leaving only the center bud to bloom. Only one terminal bud should be left on each branch if you want large, perfect flowers and long stems. Go over the plants about once a week during the growing season to remove these excess buds. If you start with good-quality roots and follow these directions, you may well have prize-winning dahlia blooms to exhibit in September.

An interesting and quite comprehensive book on dahlias for the beginner is *Dahlias,* by Marian C. Walker (M. Barrows and Co., New York, $2.95). It covers the growing of dahlias from roots, green plants, and seeds. There is a very good chapter on how to put on a dahlia show. The book contains 128 pages of text and also numerous illustrations in black and white and in color.

SUMMER CARE OF ROSES

June is considered the month of roses in most of the country, but in the Upper Midwest and most other northern areas our rose season lasts from late June through September. This good fortune results from our comparatively cool summers, and especially the cool nights, which roses like. The first peak of bloom usually comes in late June in northern rose gardens, with the sturdy rugosa roses showing a mass of blossoms a week or two earlier. Different varieties will reach their peaks at different times during early summer, but types like hybrid teas and floribundas can be counted on for at least some recurrent bloom until frost.

Roses are not hard to grow, but they must have a fair amount of cultivation and protection from pests and foliage troubles. Cultivation is important for roses, but it can be overdone. Roses have many fine, almost hair-like roots, often close to the surface, and these are likely to be damaged. Light cultivation is excellent, however, to kill weeds and to loosen the soil surface close to the plants, so that water can be absorbed readily and will never stand on the surface.

GRANDMA'S dahlias sometime were bothered with stalk or stem borers, a destructive grub that would drill a dahlia stem near the ground and devour the soft pulp all the way up the stem. Then Grandma would have Uncle Jerry, after dark, raise and lower a lighted candle behind the translucent stem. When a dark spot showed up it was a borer. Uncle would carefully slit the stem a little and remove the pest, or sometimes just a jab with a darning needle was effective.

If your roses are far enough apart so that you can do some rather deep, narrow-blade spading between them without disturbing the roots, fine and dandy. But remember that you may do more harm than good if you cut the lateral roots, so go slowly.

After cultivation many rosarians favor mulching the rose bed, using organic material such as peatmoss, ground corncobs, or loose material from the compost heap consisting of almost completely decayed or shredded leaves and other coarse vegetable matter. Well-decayed cow manure is excellent as a mulch because the roses get a gentle feeding with every rain. All these mulches are most suitable for keeping down weed growth and keeping the beds moist and cool. They slowly return essential elements to the soil and ultimately they can be mixed into the garden soil.

135

Another mulch that can be used on rose beds is a two-inch layer of Canadian moss. When spread over the rose bed, this material reduces the need for watering by almost 75 per cent and retards weed growth. Before applying this moss mulch, some gardeners lightly cultivate a dressing of well-rotted cow manure into the soil. The moss is reported to inhibit black spot, a fungus disease of roses, by preventing the splashing of water drops from infected leaves. Another good practice is to dust the moss surface with an all-purpose garden dust that is both an insecticide and fungicide.

Black spot is probably the most troublesome of rose diseases. It is caused by a fungus and appears as black, irregular spots on the foliage, which eventually turns yellow and drops off. All leaves with black spot should be removed quickly from the rosebushes, and also picked up from the ground, and destroyed. Don't put them on the compost heap; burn them or wrap them and put them in the garbage can. Wash your hands thoroughly before touching the rose plants again.

Fortunately black spot, mildew, and most insect attacks on your roses can be prevented before they get a start by regular dusting or spraying. If you began this preventive program early in May, as soon as your roses put out leaves, you will have healthy foliage and flowers all summer. Regularity is the most important requirement. Dust or spray once a week and after every rain heavy enough to wash off previous applications with an all-purpose mixture containing DDT, Fermate, and other insecticides and fungicides.

Pay special attention to covering thoroughly both the upper and lower surfaces of the leaves. Less dust is lost if it is applied when the plants are slightly moist and there is little or no wind. These powders or sprays are also excellent for preventing leaf troubles of phlox and other garden perennials. If plant lice or aphids become very troublesome, a good spraying of Black Leaf 40 (nicotine sulphate) mixed with strong soapsuds or a liquid wetting agent will soon do away with them. An application of arsenate of lead to the soil, followed by a light cultivation once in June, is advocated by some growers to destroy rose bugs and chafers.

Along with regular spraying or dusting, your roses will need

136

periodic feeding and watering when dry. Dry weather with hot sunshine is hard on roses, but sprinkling them in such weather is also bad. The hot sun shining on the drops of water will frequently scald the leaves and often is disastrous to the opening buds. Use a modified irrigation system instead of sprinkling from above; allow the hose to trickle on the ground into furrows around the rose plants. The water will soak down to the roots where it is really needed. Be sure to saturate the ground to a depth of at least ten inches each time you water. This watering should be done during the day if possible. Avoid watering in the evening because it is likely to cause mildew.

A root feeder, a garden tool that attaches to the hose and carries dissolving fertilizer cartridges or plain water directly to the plant roots, is fine for feeding or watering roses. A moderate stream from the hose with the root-feeder nozzle thrust into the soil for about a minute, will irrigate each rose thoroughly enough to last for days. If more conventional methods of fertilizing are used, a tablespoon of commercial fertilizer or special rose food should be dug in around each plant when new growth is three to four inches long, then again after the first blooming period, and once a month thereafter.

Up until the latter part of June it may still be possible for you to buy and plant new roses, if they are already started in temporary pots. If you intend to plant this month, or if you are visiting rose gardens to make new choices for next year, consider the varieties that rose experts and the All America Rose Selection committee regard most highly.

Among the hybrid tea roses, many consider the variety Peace to be the finest rose ever developed. It has been described as "sunset caught in a rose." The buds are golden with a flash of pink along the petal edges. They open slowly, showing delicate tints of yellow, cream, and ivory with a varying flush of pink. The long-lasting blooms are often four inches wide. The Peace rose has proved so worthy and has improved so much since it was first introduced that the AARS committee recently raised its rating. It is now the highest rated rose in the world.

Among other roses, so many varieties are outstanding for color, form, and perfume that it would be impossible to name them all. See the list of recommended varieties at the end of the book for some of the preferred ones.

You can also write to the American Rose Society, 4048 Roselea Place, Columbus, Ohio, and ask for their free *Guide for Buying Roses,* which contains a list of over four hundred of the best roses with their national ratings and descriptions. Included are the forty-seven roses that have been chosen for the All America Rose Selections award over the last sixteen years.

Anyone Can Grow Roses, by Dr. Cynthia Wescott (D. Van Nostrand Company, New York, $2), is one of the best books on roses that has appeared in years. The author thoroughly knows roses, their troubles, and most of the remedies. Her book is an excellent treatise both for the amateur and for the more advanced rosarian. *Climbing Roses,* by Helen Van Pelt Wilson (M. Barrows & Co., New York, $3.95), is another good book for rose lovers, the first book in many years devoted entirely to climbing roses.

Grandma's Rose Jars. Grandma's custom of making little rose jars each summer is almost a lost art today, but one that is worth reviving. Rose jars recreate the fleeting beauty of summer during our long northern winters and make delightful gifts. I have one of Grandma's rose jars that is at least one hundred years old, and when the cover is lifted for a short time, rose fragrance perfumes the entire room.

Grandma collected rose petals from roses that were not completely open, early in the morning before the sun had shone on them. She explained that the sun's heat quickly evaporated from an open rose the oil or essence that contains the perfume. She preferred petals from old-fashioned damask and province roses because they were highly perfumed, perhaps more so than any other roses growing in her day; but I think we now have hybrid tea roses that are as fragrant as the old-fashioned ones.

Grandma gathered petals from all sweet-smelling roses and also the green leaves from the sweetbriers. She pulled the petals from healthy roses only, discarding marred or diseased blooms. The petals were then spread on clean white paper to dry in the open air, but never in the sun. When well dried, the petals were salted.

In a crock — a quart fruit jar would do — she placed a layer of dried petals. These she sprinkled with table salt — pure, not iodized — that had been dried on the stove and crushed with the rolling pin to remove lumps. Then she added more petals and more salt in layers until the crock was full. The salt absorbed the last vestige of moisture in the petals without absorbing the rose oil.

GRANDMA was so fond of her roses I guess she felt no one was too young to develop that same fondness. So, whenever a new baby arrived in her neighborhood, Grandma would send the new arrival — and the mother — a bouquet of "baby roses" — moss roses, sweetbriers, and dainty double pink miniatures.

In twelve days the contents were removed from the crock and thoroughly sifted to remove the salt. The petals were then slightly crushed and, with a crumbled, dried leaf of rose geranium, put in little ornamental vases or jars with covers. Grandma rubbed the inside of the vases and jars with a half-and-half mixture of glycerine and good rose perfume to seal the containers and remove any foreign odors.

Making a rose jar was something like making cake. You were not always sure how it would turn out. This was especially true in a hot summer when the roses retained or produced less of their perfume essence. When this occurred, Grandma was greatly disappointed, but being of Scotch descent she would transform the rose jars into potpourri jars by mixing with the dried rose petals a mixture of allspice, cinnamon, orris root, myrrh, sage, mint, and verbena powder or leaves — just a pinch of each. You can find these spices in your own cupboard, grocery, or drug store, and if you live near a public rose garden, the caretakers will probably be glad to let you have discarded blossoms or dropped petals. Why not try making a potpourri of your own?

SUMMER LAWN CARE

If you started preventive war on crabgrass in the latter part of May, you should be reaping benefit already. Use of the new chemicals to inhibit crabgrass seed from sprouting is one of the best ways to fight the enemy of healthy lawns. One or two more applications of this "before-sprouting" crabgrass killer should be made during June as well, to catch any late-sprouting seed that may have escaped.

Suppose you were not able to apply this preventive method — what then? How will you recognize crabgrass when it sprouts in your lawn and how can you stop it once it's started? Crabgrass is not difficult to recognize. It usually becomes apparent in June — although in far northern regions it may not appear until July. First it is a light green, two-bladed plant. The first leaves are somewhat hairy, pointed, about a quarter inch wide, and curved downward. Ordinary Kentucky bluegrasses are a much darker green and have decidedly narrower blades than crabgrass.

The two-leaved plant soon becomes a many-leaved cluster with jointed tentacles or runners spreading in all directions. Each joint drops roots and forms another complete plant. They grow rapidly and send up many seed stalks which terminate in multiple fingers, each finger producing scores of seeds. If crabgrass is allowed to spread, it will cause bare areas in the spring and brown areas in the fall after it has gone to seed. It will smother good grasses and it is green only a couple of months, usually in July and August.

Even after crabgrass is well started, there is time to reduce the growing crop with one of the many "after-sprouting" crabgrass killers. There are many different herbicides for killing or at least controlling this weed at different stages of growth in early, middle, and late summer. This is most easily done when the plants are small and tender, of course. But there also are killers that are applied every two or three weeks, if the crabgrass is not caught in its early stages.

Besides herbicides and chemical weed-killers, there are other ways to discourage recurrence of this weed. If your lawn is only lightly infested, you can pull crabgrass with forefinger and thumb while the plants are quite small. Keeping at the job every few days will go a long way toward cleaning it out. Wetting the turf the day before pulling will make the chore much easier.

Crabgrass will not grow well unless it gets strong sunlight. It will not grow well in shade, and its development is discouraged greatly by a thick, long growth of grass, even on a lawn that gets the sun all day. To keep a lawn free of crabgrass, you must have a heavy stand of grass with cool, damp roots. Feed your lawn two or three times a season, preferably in early spring, midsummer, and autumn.

In dry weather, water your lawn *well*, not this everlasting skimpy evening sprinkling. Use a whirling or stationary sprinkler that you place on the lawn, and let the water run until the sod is wet at least four inches down. Then move the sprinkler to another section of the lawn. It may take several evenings to soak your lawn properly, but this method will result in deep grass roots that will not burn or scorch as shallow roots do. Shallow roots are a result of short shower baths from the hand sprinkler. A lawn that is well soaked should not require another watering for perhaps a week, unless the weather should get very hot with strong, drying winds.

In May and June, when moisture is usually abundant and grass is growing fast, your lawn can be mowed fairly close, about an inch and a half high. During the hot summer weeks, however, mow your lawn high, at least two or two and a half inches, and mow often. Allow clippings to fall into the turf, where they will form a mulch and help keep the grass roots cool and moist. Of course, if your mowing has been delayed and the grass clippings are too long to fall between the growing grass blades, then you must rake them up to keep them from smothering the grass. Save them for your compost pile or for mulching in the garden.

To be sure your lawnmower is not cutting too close, set the stationary blade of the mower as high as possible by lowering the roller. If your roller brackets will not give enough elevation, you can gain more by winding a large rope tightly around your present roller, or purchasing a larger one. Another method is to have a pair of longer brackets made.

This rule for high mowing applies to all lawns except those consisting of bentgrass. This grass makes a close, low growth and requires frequent close mowing. During May and June, when ordinary lawn grass grows very rapidly, half an inch usually is high enough for bentgrass. Bentgrass makes a handsome, thick, short turf but requires too much care to make it practical for the average homeowner. A combination bentgrass and bluegrass lawn may be quite satisfactory, however. If you want to experiment with bentgrass, you can buy plugs of it and plant them every few feet in your bluegrass-mixture lawn. Or if you have a neighbor who has a creeping bent lawn, ask him for some of his grass clippings and scatter them over your own newly mowed lawn. Then throw on a little top dressing and many of these clippings will take root, eventually producing a mixed bluegrass and bentgrass lawn.

One other exception to the high mowing rule applies if crabgrass gets far ahead of you during hot weather in late June, July, or August. As crabgrass matures, the plants will sprout several five- to nine-fingered stalks, each finger producing hundreds of seeds in late summer. In addition to using a chemical crabgrass killer, your second line of defense should be to prevent these stalks from ripening and dropping their seeds.

Some of these crabgrass stalks stand upright, but others lie prostrate, hidden by desirable grasses. The low-lying stalks must be

GRANDMA said every bird had its useful purpose in the world. If she were here today, she would be holding the torch for the English sparrow. This maligned little fellow has done much to prevent the spread of crabgrass. Have you ever noticed in the fall the huge sparrow flocks on ripened crabgrass areas, consuming millions of seeds?

raked into an upright position and then cut off short, with the other, upright stalks, to prevent reseeding of the weed. Adjust the stationary blade on your mower so it will cut the grass very short — about one inch. Before mowing, rake the lawn with a stiff iron rake to loosen the jointed roots of the crabgrass and cause the seed fingers to stand upright. Then mow from the opposite direction. Do this four times, raking after each mowing, and mow in four different directions. If possible catch all clippings in a basket attached to the mower or rake them up at once and remove them. When they are dry enough, burn them. Wash the mower thoroughly before using it on uncontaminated grass and clean the grass catcher well. Repeat this close mowing in a couple of weeks in case you missed some of the crab. This method is not a cure for this year's crabgrass infestation, but since crabgrass is an annual that dies off every September, it should help greatly in decreasing crabgrass trouble next year.

Crabgrass is not the only weed that invades northern lawns, though it is probably the worst. Chickweed (mouse-ear), a tiny low-growing annual, is another frequent intruder. Fortunately, one of the herbicides that controls crabgrass (Weedone Crabgrass Killer), will also eliminate chickweed from lawns without killing clover, bluegrass, fescue, or other deep-rooted perennial grasses. It contains potassium cyanate — which is relatively nonpoisonous and not to be confused with potassium cyanide, which is poisonous — plus a wetting agent and a special activator to increase its effectiveness. It can be applied with a regular garden sprayer or sprinkling can, is very soluble in water, and easily washed from the sprayer. It has no toxic effect on the soil and may even act as a fertilizer for perennial grasses.

Other lawn weeds include the broad-leaved perennials — dandelions, plantains, buckhorn, thistles, and others — which tend to reappear year after year. Hand weeding or spot treatment with a 2, 4-D stick applicator will usually be adequate if the weeds are not too numerous. If there is a heavy infestation, a spraying of a selective weed killer containing 2, 4-D will be necessary. Consult

143

your garden dealer on the type best suited to your conditions and follow directions on the container.

Spraying with 2, 4-D should be done at a time when weeds are growing rapidly. This means early summer, with its warm temperatures and adequate moisture. Hot, dry weather and cool, wet weather are not good times for selective weed control applications. The disappointing results some gardeners have experienced with 2, 4-D probably came from spraying at the wrong time.

Tough old dandelions sometimes require two treatments with 2, 4-D. They are perennials and after several years develop long, thick taproots which give them a lot of vigor. This taproot seems to keep nourishing the plant even though 2, 4-D interferes with the growth process. Usually a second treatment a week or so after the first will complete the job. Weed killers are most effective when applied during the heat of the day.

Though 2, 4-D is termed a "selective" weed killer because its action is confined largely to broad-leaved plants, it may also harm closely cut bentgrass. Homeowners having bentgrass lawns should not use 2, 4-D at all on closely clipped grass, and should use a very fine spray only if the grass is allowed to grow long. White Dutch clover, which is almost always present in bluegrass and other mixed grass lawns, receives only a temporary setback from 2, 4-D. Unfortunately 2, 4-D does little harm to crabgrass.

You can apply selective weed controls with a regular 3½-gallon pressure sprayer or through a gravity spray attachment which may be fastened to a gallon jug. If you use your garden sprayer for this purpose, be sure to rinse it thoroughly with a strong solution of household ammonia when you have finished. Otherwise the small 2, 4-D residue remaining may damage your garden flowers or vegetables later when you spray with insecticides and fungicides.

Be extremely careful when you use weed killers as a spray. They are a great aid to gardeners and farmers, but careless handling can ruin thousands of plants and devastate whole gardens. Hold the spray gun close to the ground and make application only when there is no wind. Otherwise the spray may drift into your garden, or what is worse, into a neighbor's garden, and ruin it. If that happens it is your duty to replace and replant the loss, but you can never replace the months or years of devoted gardening that have been destroyed.

If you know or even suspect that your garden has been exposed to weed-killing spray, sprinkle your flowers and shrubs well with the garden hose as quickly as possible and you may be able to prevent or reduce the damage. If you remember the rule never to apply weed-killer spray when it is windy, and if you use caution and good sense, you should have no trouble.

GRANDMA had always had Uncle Jerry cut the grass with a hand sickle and shears. Then he heard of a mechanical contrivance with whirling blades that would bite off the grass. He sent for one. It weighed more than a hundred pounds and cost what was a mighty sum. It took two men to shove it even slowly and it made a tremendous racket. Uncle had a brilliant idea. He harnessed old Hazel, the family horse, to the front of the mower. Then they started, Hazel pulling, Uncle guiding. The noise frightened Hazel and she bolted over a little bridge where the mower and Uncle Jerry fell in the creek. Nothing was injured but Uncle's feelings, but he could never get Hazel near the mower again.

Mushrooms are a minor nuisance in some northern lawns. They usually can be routed with a strong solution of any of the mercuric remedies used for spring snow mold in lawns. If an old stump under the sod is causing the trouble, expose it and its attached roots, and drench them with a strong drain-cleaning compound.

PUBLIC GARDENS AND FLOWER SHOWS

One of the best ways for gardeners to learn more about flower growing is to visit flower shows and public gardens, both at commercial nurseries and in public parks. Private gardens belonging to neighbors or friends, or even to accommodating strangers, are

145

also of great interest to other gardeners for looking, learning, and comparing, especially if the gardener-owner is willing to lead a guided tour and talk about his gardening methods.

Most amateur gardeners have little opportunity to talk personally with garden experts, but anyone who lives near a large city is pretty sure to have expertly tended public gardens available for visiting. In the Twin Cities of Minneapolis and St. Paul, for example, there is a woodsy wild flower garden of several acres in Theodore Wirth Park, where nearly every native northern wild flower grows and blooms, all in their natural state except for unobtrusive markers to identify the plants. And the Lehman Chrysanthemum Gardens at Faribault, Minnesota, with acres of glorious color, provide a view of one of the largest mum farms in the world.

All summer long but especially in June, the Lyndale Rose Garden in Minneapolis contains examples of every class of rose and hundreds and hundreds of different named varieties. Here the home gardener can see and compare, choose the varieties he would like to plant in his own garden, and learn what a healthy, free-blooming rosebush should look like. Here there are test rose gardens, too, where new varieties as yet unnamed are being grown on

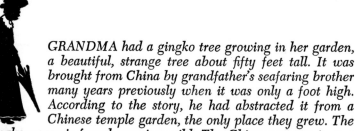

GRANDMA had a gingko tree growing in her garden, a beautiful, strange tree about fifty feet tall. It was brought from China by grandfather's seafaring brother many years previously when it was only a foot high. According to the story, he had abstracted it from a Chinese temple garden, the only place they grew. The gingko never is found growing wild. The Chinese revere it as a symbol of longevity. The gingko also is called the maidenhair tree, since its leaves resemble our garden fern. It belongs to a primitive group of plants that grew in many parts of the earth long ago, following the carboniferous period. This is the only known variety that has survived. It seems to be immune to insects and fungus troubles. In Minneapolis there is a gingko tree growing in Lyndale Park, south of the rose gardens near Lake Harriet.

north

trial for the National Rose Society and the Minnesota Rose Society, and may later emerge as All America rose award-winners.

St. Paul has beautiful public gardens in Como Park, where there is also a huge glassed-in conservatory with exotic plants and trees of all kinds on display both winter and summer. In St. Paul, too, is the Horticultural Building on the State Fair grounds, where late every summer at State Fair time exhibits of prize flowers are held. Other northern cities have other types of special gardens — tulips or peonies, perhaps, or iris gardens, or maybe chrysanthemum displays in September and October, which is another Minneapolis specialty. Whatever city you live in or visit, be sure to visit its public gardens. A real gardener is always eager to look and learn.

June is especially the month to visit rose, peony, and iris gardens. Today there are nearly as many new iris varieties as there are of roses, and by far the best way to choose among them is to see them in bloom. If there are no iris gardens in your local parks, visit a large nursery to see the many new iris varieties in all their glory. The best planting time for iris is July and August, but right now is the time to choose the varieties you want. Peonies also are planted in August as a rule, but June is the month to go to see them.

Another way to learn to know new varieties of flowers and what fine specimens should look like is to attend your local flower shows. Nearly every city has garden clubs, African violet clubs, rose, peony, or iris societies, or groups of dahlia or chrysanthemum or delphinium enthusiasts. These clubs usually hold annual shows where the choicest blooms are displayed, and here too the garden amateur can learn a great deal about choosing and growing flowers. Better still, you can join one or more of these clubs yourself. Soon you can be one of the "experts" and exhibitors, with a lovelier garden and more perfect flowers, but best of all, still learning new gardening pleasures.

Preparing Entries for a Flower Show. You need not be an expert to enter flowers in most local flower shows. Any amateur gardener may enter exhibits at his state fair and at most garden club shows. If you have grown some handsome flowers that you are proud of, by all means consider entering them in a show. You will find it an exciting and instructive way to learn things from other gardeners about better flower growing.

In preparing your entries, there are many things to consider in order to have your flowers as nearly perfect as possible. Flowers that are beautiful in your garden may lose many good points before they reach the exhibition hall, unless given correct treatment. Flower buds should be cut in the early morning or late in the day, twelve to twenty-four hours before the show. Immediately immerse the entire stem but not the blooms in a deep pail of cold water that has been taken into the garden.

Cut long stems with a sharp knife — never use scissors — and at a long slant to allow ample absorption surface. Remove excess foliage so that the absorbed water will benefit the flower primarily and whatever foliage is left on to complement it. Don't crowd too many flowers into the pail, and keep them in the shade and out of the wind. When all are cut, remove the pail of flowers to a cool basement or garage.

Hollow-stemmed flowers and flowers with milky and sticky sap that readily gums when exposed to the air should either have the ends of the stems singed, or should be held in boiling water three or four minutes. Then put the treated flowers in cold water again.

To speed the opening of a bud, place it for several hours in warm sunshine, or immerse the stem in deep, hot water with the bloom directly over the water so that the rising vapor will act upon it. To prevent a bud from opening, place the flower stalk in cold water in a moist refrigerator temperature, 45 to 50 degrees if possible.

Frequently much damage is caused in transportation. Each exhibit should be brought to the show ready for immediate entry. Exhibits of one flower specimen only should be set up in separate bottles and these bottles secured tightly in a carton. In transporting your exhibits, keep the windows of your car in a position where there will be no wind on the flowers.

Most flower arrangements for exhibit have too many flowers rather than too few. Use no more than necessary for the desired effect. Each flower should stand out by itself in full view. A focus of interest toward the bottom or center of the arrangement frequently is helpful. Flowers of any one kind or color should be grouped together rather than "polka-dotted" through the arrangement.

An exhibitor at a flower show should know something of the judging points that will determine which entries are prizewinners. Judges will give points for color, form, size, condition, stem, and foliage. Color is given full value provided it is typical of the flower, unfaded, and clear. The form of the bloom should be typical of the variety. Blooms should be well centered on the stem and terminal blooms should look to the sky. Petals should be of uniform size and well spaced.

GRANDMA always gathered — she said "culled" — her roses and peonies and most other flowers in the cool of the morning or late in the evening if the temperature then was cool. She explained that at these periods the flowers were full of sap. She never culled them when the sun was high. Grandma laid the flowers on the kitchen table and with a thin paring knife cut off the bottoms of the stems with long, slanting strokes. She then placed them in tall pitchers with water up to the blossoms and buds until the cuttings became fully charged with water. Then most of the water was poured off and the pitchers were placed in the spring of almost ice-cold water that ran through the old stone milk house. The flowers would stay wonderfully fresh for at least a week. Several years ago when I roamed over the old deserted farm the milk house was in ruins, but the stream still was running and just as cold as ever.

If the entry requirements call for a specific number of blooms, all should be of uniform size. Three medium-sized blooms are better than one large and two small. The condition of both blooms and foliage is important. Flowers should be mature and fully developed, but not past their prime. Minimum recommended lengths in inches for stems are: roses, 12; peonies, 18; delphinium, 36;

149

dahlias, 12 to 24; asters, 12; large zinnias, 18; small zinnias, 10; gladioli, 24 to 30. All foliage below the water line — except for gladioli, which should have one leaf attached — should be removed. For peonies, remove all except the top brace of leaves.

The exhibitor must follow as closely as possible what the schedule of entry requirements calls for. If the schedule calls for three blooms, do not exhibit four. The exhibitor is supposed to be able to select his best three. For the same reason, exhibit three stems or stalks — no more, no less — when the schedule calls for three. Unless you remove side buds where the schedule calls for three blooms, you take a gamble that a bud will open and disqualify you before the show. A bud becomes a bloom at the moment it shows color. Remember that your exhibit wins or loses its prize at the moment the judge sees it, not the day before in the garden or two hours after he has gone home. The object is to get perfection at the judging hour.

GRANDMA would explain to her grandchildren every summer that when we saw a young robin or other young bird on the ground, or barely able to fly, we should leave it alone. Almost always, the parents were nearby and were giving it flying lessons. If, after half an hour, we were certain it was alone, we could feed it earthworms and berries and give it shelter for the night. But we would return it the next day to where we found it, for likely the parents would be looking for it.

For more information about flower shows and preparing your entries, try *The Flower Show Guide,* by Anne Westner Wood (M. Barrows and Co., New York, $3). This is a well-written book by a capable writer and nationally known flower show organizer and judge. Whatever you want to know about staging, exhibiting, and judging a flower show can be found in this 200-page volume.

REMINDERS

Keep planting more gladioli every ten days until mid-July for a continuous procession of bloom in late summer.

Continue to spray or dust perennials, especially phlox and roses, with an all-purpose garden dust every ten days and after heavy rains. Pay special attention to covering the under sides of leaves.

Do your transplanting on a cloudy day or in the evening, if possible. Keep the hot sun off transplants for a day or two with newspapers, boards, or shingles, until the plants no longer droop and wilt.

Remember to keep the bird bath filled with cool, fresh water. If you own cats, feed them well and keep them indoors for a couple of weeks to give baby robins a chance to grow up. The little fellows are getting their flying lessons now from their parents.

☙ JULY ☙

July is the month for vacations, and for outdoor pleasures of every kind. Our northern summers are too short to waste many moments indoors, so get out your lawn chairs and your charcoal grill and really enjoy the lawn and garden you have tended so faithfully. On warm July nights the fragrance of sweet peas, stock, and nicotiana will drift from the annual beds, and white phlox in the border will gleam in the darkness. Even mosquitoes can't spoil your pleasure if you spray your shrubs and gardens with the efficient new anti-mosquito sprays.

The first of the phlox and daylilies should be coming into bloom in early July, and the blue spires of delphinium, pink hollyhocks, and white dictamnus or gas plant make a lovely background. Yellow-eyed daisies, pink coral-bells, blue veronica and campanula, and deep rose spikes of lythrum will bloom this month and on through the summer if faded flowers are cut off. The annuals you started indoors or in your cold frame are already blooming or about to bloom, and even the poppies, portulaca, annual phlox, and bachelor's buttons that you sowed directly in the annual bed should soon be flowering. No more planting, for the moment, and the flowers are well ahead of the weeds by now, so our motto for July is — take it easy.

TOO DRY OR TOO WET

Take it easy — but of course a true gardener can always think of a dozen chores undone. July in the North may be cool or hot, wet or dry; but whichever it is, it is sure to mean garden problems of some sort. Lots of rain means the grass must be cut more often — and watch out for slugs on the perennials. Dry weather means frequent watering. Hot damp weather brings danger of molds and mildews, and cool damp weather in July makes everyone cross.

Watering and Mulching. If July this year is hot and dry, be sure to water thoroughly and regularly. Don't tease your lawn or garden with hand sprinkling. For the lawn, use a good sprinkler and let it stay in one place until the area is soaked several inches down. For the flower border and the rose bed, take off the nozzle or sprinkler. Lay the end of the hose on a sheet of metal, a shingle, or a flat stone to prevent gouging the soil and practice a modified form of irrigation. Allow a trickle of water to surround the plants and rose shrubs, slowly soaking in. Leave the hose in one place until the ground is deeply soaked, then move hose and shingle to a new spot, until all the garden has been covered. A canvas or plastic soil soaker attachment for the hose may also be used to soak the perennial or annual beds. Water flowers during the day rather than at night to reduce the danger of mildew.

Keep the water off the foliage and blossoms. In hot dry weather water is too precious to lose in quick evaporation, and the foliage does not take kindly to cold harsh city and well water, even though the roots accept it thankfully. Rainwater is soft and seldom cold, and does not injure foliage under normal conditions. The only exception to the no-sprinkling rule for flowers applies to tuberous begonias. They like a moist and humid atmosphere, and a very fine spray over their leaves in hot, dry weather is helpful.

For trees and shrubs use a stationary lawn sprinkler or soaker inside the spread of the branches, and allow the water to run and soak into the ground all night. A root feeder is even better for getting the water down to tree roots without runoff or waste.

If water is not available, "dust farming" will help. Cultivate the soil surface to form a dust mulch which will help to conserve what moisture is yet in the soil. This loose topsoil will also absorb dew and light rains more readily than hard, sun-baked soil.

When your rose beds, annuals, and perennial border have been thoroughly watered, the use of a mulch one or two inches deep

153

around the plants will prevent quick evaporation and retain moisture in the soil much longer. There are several materials that make good mulches. Well-rotted animal manure is good, but don't allow it to touch the plant stems or leaves. Soft, loose, year-old material from the compost heap is excellent for this purpose. So are well-rotted leaves.

GRANDMA loved to share her flowers. Just as day was breaking, she would cut the choicest flowers and put them in a tall pitcher of cold water — to which a teaspoon of sugar had been added — right up to the blossoms and buds. The pitcher was placed in the ice-cold spring in the old stone dairy house. Late in the day Grandma would wrap bouquets in damp cloths with ice against the stems. When the bouquet reached an invalid or a new mother, the flowers were beautifully fresh and would last for days.

In some localities, ground corncobs and hulls from grain and other crops, such as soybeans and buckwheat, can be purchased very reasonably and make a satisfactory organic covering. Sometimes canning factories also have vegetable refuse available that makes good mulch and fertilizer.

One of the best mulches is dry Canadian peatmoss, thousands of years old. It comes closely packed in 10- to 12-bushel bales and is a little less expensive than sphagnum moss. When loosened and dampened it increases in bulk approximately three and a half times. Sphagnum moss can also be used. It is mostly a bog moss and your dealer has it for about a dollar and a half a bushel. There is also an excellent imported German peat that can be used as a mulch.

Mosses are very moisture-retentive and should be well loosened and moistened before they are spread in the garden. Cultivate the soil lightly and water thoroughly before spreading the moss. Some gardeners dust the soil surface well with an all-purpose garden dust that is both a fungicide and insecticide before applying the moss layer. Sometimes the moss layer can be scraped up in the fall and used again next spring. Where the garden soil is hard and compact, however, the moss should be hoed into the soil in the fall to loosen it. New mulch should then be added the following summer.

A mulch on the garden is useful even when July rains are plentiful. Heavy rains pack down the garden soil and then the hot sun bakes it. This condition calls for cultivation just as soon as the garden is dry enough to hoe. Unless the soil is broken your plants will suffer from lack of air. In a sense, the garden earth must breathe, so that air can penetrate to the plant roots. But cultivation can be greatly reduced if a mulch of light material is spread over the garden. A mulch prevents the soil from becoming packed, keeps the entire area cooler, retains moisture, reduces weeds, and protects plant roots from the drying effects of sun and wind.

Molds and Mildew. Hot, damp weather is also a breeder of mildew, and molds, and various insect pests — including mosquitoes which attack not plants but people. Mildew appears as a powdery white growth on the lower leaves of phlox, roses, zinnias, and many other plants. It gradually spreads to higher leaves as well, and although it seldom causes permanent damage to a perennial, it greatly reduces the vigor and attractiveness of the plant and may inhibit blossoming.

Prevention of mildew and other molds is far more effective than attempts at cure. Spraying with a mild Bordeaux mixture early in spring and regular dusting or spraying with an all-purpose mixture every week or ten days thereafter will greatly reduce the chances of mildew's appearing, even in hot, damp weather. Proper watering is important in preventing mildew, too.

If mildew appears, dust all foliage with dusting sulphur or with an all-purpose dust that contains both sulphur and Fermate. Very badly damaged leaves should be removed and burned. Dust once a week and within twelve hours after each heavy rainfall. If wet weather brings out insects as well, use a DDT spray or dust for thrips on gladioli, and Black Leaf 40 for aphids wherever there is a heavy infestation. Apply "612" or a similar repellent to the gardener suffering from mosquitoes.

Slugs. Wet weather often brings slugs to the northern garden, probably the most destructive and repulsive pests the gardener must deal with. Slugs are not insects but molluscs, and are essentially snails without shells. They somewhat resemble very short, fat, pale earthworms, but compared to the slug the earthworm or night crawler is a gentleman. Earthworms do little harm in the garden and help to aerate the soil, but slugs are real villains.

Slugs hide during the day in shady places in or near the garden, usually under leaves, boards, or stones on the ground. When night comes they crawl out to feed on soft or new leaves and flowers. They can be very destructive, especially to such soft-leaved plants as petunias, hollyhocks, almost all lilies, violets, pansies, and delphiniums. In the vegetable garden they cause havoc with rhubarb, melons, lettuce, and other large-leaved plants, eating large, irregular holes in the leaves. One slug can seriously damage a large petunia plant in one night. In addition to eating foliage and blossoms close to the ground, they will climb three-foot dahlia stalks and rosebushes.

Slugs are a brown or grayish tint, sometimes almost pink. When at rest they look like short, fat worms, about a quarter inch to one inch long, but when traveling they can stretch into three or four inches of animated, repulsive slime. Wherever slugs crawl they leave a track of silvery slime. Their eyes are on one pair of antennae, and they have another pair used for feeling. They are hermaphroditic, with both male and female reproductive organs present in each, so unless you manage to annihilate them all, some offspring will remain to plague your garden.

The first step in controlling slugs is to clean up your garden. Leave no rubbish or loose boards and stones around where slugs can hide during the daytime. There are several slug baits on the market that will attract and poison slugs if scattered under plant leaves on the damp earth about your garden in the evening. Repeat as often as necessary, and follow directions on the container. This bait is poisonous to pets, so use with caution.

Slugs can also be discouraged by scattering garden lime, wood ashes, or soot around the garden. Five per cent DDT powder or 40 per cent chlordane dusted on the soil around plants twice a week will also be very helpful. Some gardeners report success against slugs after spraying a solution of one part sulphate of copper to four parts of garden lime dissolved in water. This solution is sprayed on the edges of lawns around gardens just as it is getting dark and the slugs are moving from the lawn into the gardens. Slugs often hide in adjacent lawns after being disturbed in gardens. They are also more troublesome in rich, heavy soil than in sandy loams. If all else fails, an after-dark hunting expedition with a flashlight will enable you to catch many of the sluggish villains at work. Scoop them up with spoon or tweezers and drown them in a can of water mixed with a teaspoon of kerosene.

BEFORE YOU GO ON YOUR VACATION

If you are going to be away from your garden for a two- or three-weeks' vacation, make sure that everything is in the best possible condition before you leave. Give the perennial border a light midsummer feeding to encourage continued bloom and sturdy growth after blooming is over. A thin circle of balanced plant food or well-rotted animal fertilizer dug in around each plant will be of great benefit. Do not allow this to touch the roots or stems, however.

GRANDMA had no prepared peats and mosses for garden purposes, but she fully realized that a good mulch kept the soil cool and lessened the need for watering. So in the cool days of early summer she had Uncle Jerry bring in wheelbarrow loads of loose-textured, dark brown mulch from under the big trees in the maple grove and the nearby forest. Here it had been forming from fallen leaves for hundreds of years. This leaf mulch was spread one to two inches deep on the garden. Uncle was delighted to do this chore because the mulch reduced his weeding to almost nothing.

JULY

The annual beds should also be fertilized again, using the same method as for the perennials unless the annuals are growing in rows. For rows of sweet peas and other annuals dig or hoe in a balanced fertilizer along the row at a rate of one quart per hundred feet.

Your shrubbery and roses, too, should be given a feeding of balanced fertilizer or cow manure. Cultivate it into the soil around each plant, but don't disturb the roots near the surface. Some gardeners spread a layer of earth or compost over the fertilizer. This is an excellent procedure because much of the food in fertilizers escapes in gases unless dug into the soil or covered.

GRANDMA and I were both horrified when Uncle Jerry got to a certain place in reading aloud from Reliable and Complete Compendium of Flora Culture for Ladies and Gentlemen, *a book more than a hundred years old. At the end of the chapter on the historic tulip craze in Holland he would read with a voice of doom,* "During the craze, a hungry sailor in a dealer's garden mistook seven tulip bulbs for onions and ate them for breakfast. The loss to the dealer for this meal was over $3,500. The poor sailor was hanged." *Uncle gloried in horrors.*

Any tall plants in the garden that have not already been staked should be tied up now to protect them from storms during your absence. Slender metal stakes or green wooden wands can be bought very inexpensively at your garden dealer's. For tying the plants you can buy a spool of warp, a sort of cord used in repairing carpets and rugs, that contains almost half a mile of cord. It comes in a pleasant, inconspicuous green and is strong enough to last all summer. It is fine for tying up vines and plants and should provide enough cord for several years' supply.

Don't tie the stems too tightly to the stakes or they will be injured when they grow larger. It is much better to make the initial tie around the stake and then tie the plant to it. This prevents the plant from slipping and also allows one to arrange the shoot more gracefully.

House plants are always a problem when vacation time comes. Those that are being kept indoors this summer can be watered in advance by placing the clay pot in which the plant is growing in a large vessel or jardiniere. Pack an inch or more of sphagnum moss or Canadian peatmoss completely around the flowerpot. Then soak the moss with water. This treatment will usually give the plant enough moisture for several weeks if it is placed in a sunless window. Outdoors, house plants in pots can be left in their buried summer locations in the shade, or they can be placed in bottomless fruit crates with four-inch side walls and packed about with damp moss like the indoor plants. If the pots are well packed in the moss and the plants and moss are thoroughly watered before you leave, your plants should stay moist for about two weeks in a shady, protected spot. Don't forget to place garden lime or ashes under the pots to prevent the entry of worms.

If you will not be gone for longer than a week or two, you can mow the lawn, water the plants, and give the garden a final dusting or spraying with all-purpose dust just before you leave, and be fairly sure that no damage will be done before your return. For a vacation of more than two weeks, however, you should make arrangements for someone to tend your garden and lawn in your absence. A lawn left unmowed for three weeks in July, or a garden unwatered during a long dry spell, can suffer considerable damage.

My own prescription for vacation garden help is to hire a neighborhood Boy Scout — preferably one whose father is also a gardener. I have always found my Boy Scout helpers thoroughly trustworthy and reliable, and usually their dads can give them advice if an urgent garden problem should arise.

Before you leave, instruct your new hired hand in his weekly duties. Show him how to water the perennials and annuals with the nozzle off, allowing a gentle stream to flow on a square of tin or shingle. This irrigation project can be going on while he is mowing the lawn or doing other chores. Give him a lesson in dusting the garden with an all-purpose dust, and show him how you always dust (I hope) with the breeze at your back. If the dust should irritate his throat — or yours — the remedy is to tie a thin cloth over the nose and mouth. Instruct him to dust the garden once a week and after each heavy rain.

Give your hired helper full charge of the garden and show him that you trust him. Explain to him that flowers should not be allowed to go to seed, and give him a pair of clippers or stout scissors to clip off all faded and dead flowers. Encourage him to cut flowers to take home — even the roses — and show him how to cut them just above a leaf joint. This small bonus of flowers in addition to his regular pay will help him to take pride in his responsibilities.

One other major chore should be taken care of before you leave on your vacation. This is another feeding and deep watering for your shade trees and evergreens. Few of our shade trees die of old age here in the North, but many are weakened by lack of food and water and fall victim to disease and insects. In cities especially, the roots of trees growing where the ground is mostly covered with hot pavements and sidewalks cannot spread out naturally to get food and water. Fertilizer spread on the ground and in gardens helps a little, but much is absorbed by other plants or washed away before it has a chance to reach the tree's roots.

For all these reasons, it is important to repeat in July your early spring fertilizing of your shade trees and evergreens. Feeding at root level, either with a root-feeder attachment on your hose or through holes dug around the tree, is the best way for both fertilization and thorough watering. Follow the instructions given in April, and try to make your holes at least eighteen inches to two feet deep.

The amount of plant food a tree requires can be determined by measuring the circumference of the tree four feet above the ground. Apply one pound (about a pint) of bone meal or balanced commercial plant food for each inch of circumference. Thoroughly mix the fertilizer with soil and fill the holes to the top. Water well and sow a little grass seed on top to cover the scars in the lawn. If you cannot feed your trees this month, don't put it off later than September 1. New growth stimulated too late in the year will not have time to harden properly before cold weather comes.

Inspect Your Evergreens. A tiny insect commonly called the red spider mite often attacks evergreen trees, especially spruces. The tree takes on a gray or brown appearance when attacked by these pests — very different from its natural deep green or silvery blue. If you examine it closely, you will find the needles may be discolored, gray or red, and interlaced with fine webs. With a magnifying glass you probably can find tiny red eggs and small spider-like insects. If the tree is neglected during this attack, the needles will dry and fall, and in a year or two the tree may die.

GRANDMA could not rely on Uncle Jerry to water her house plants when she had to leave the farm for a few days. So she would place a large pitcher of water on a shelf high above the flowerpots. In the pitcher she dropped lengths of woolen yarn tied to a stone in the water. The other ends of the yarn she thrust into the pots. The yarn acted as wicks and kept the earth moist.

A heavy wind-driven rain often helps to dislodge the pests. A cold, strong stream from the garden hose directed at the underside of the branches is even better, if done thoroughly and repeatedly for several weeks. Very fine sulphur — obtainable at your garden dealer's but not the kind sold in drug stores — may be helpful. It should be dusted into the branches on a quiet, warm day when the temperature is not over 80. When done thoroughly, this dusting creates a mild sulphuric gas that is deadly to the red mite.

Don't confuse the red-mite discoloration and death of the needles with winter drying, which is somewhat similar in appearance. The latter trouble results from lack of water and is more easily prevented.

If the strong winds of a July thunderstorm have broken off the

161

leader or spire branch on the top of an evergreen, you can start a new one. Choose a healthy, growing top branch of the tree and strap it to a narrow flat board. Then strap the board upright to the top of the tree, forcing the growing branch into a vertical position like that of the former spire.

The board should probably remain in place for a couple of years. Use soft ropes or folded cloth bands for the strapping, but don't strap or bind continuously along the entire length of the branch. Make several bindings three inches apart the entire length of the branch. Better examine it occasionally during this summer and next, for insects might nest under the bands.

POISON IVY

When at last you are off for your vacation, or even if you should stay at home, a noxious weed — poison ivy — may spoil your pleasure. Poison ivy is more likely to be a problem at summer cottages or on the farm, but even in city gardens it is a fairly common intruder.

Poison ivy can be easily identified by its three glossy leaflets, usually somewhat drooping on an upright stalk. The seeds are contained in greenish berries. All parts of the plant are poisonous. When several plants are growing together, they look like a shrub. Poison ivy grows in the open along dry paths, roads, vacant lots, and shores of lakes. In woods where the ground is rich and moist, it grows both as a shrub and as a vine, and even climbs trees. It is often confused with woodbine or Virginia creeper, which is quite harmless, and has five leaflets to a stalk while poison ivy has three.

Ivy poisoning results when the skin comes in direct contact with the milky sap or juice of the plant. The skin itches terribly, blisters often form and break, and the inflammation spreads. Usually there is a fever, but fatalities are few. Anyone who handles clothing or anything that has ivy sap on it is taking a chance, even though the sap is a year or more old and dry. All such articles should be washed with a strong soap. Animals seem to be immune to poison ivy, but your dog or cat can bring the sap home on its fur and pass it on to you. A person can also be poisoned badly about the face and sometimes in the eyes by getting in the smoke of a bonfire of poison ivy.

If you find even a few seedlings of poison ivy growing on or near your property, an ounce of prevention right now will be worth many pounds of cure later. It is difficult to eradicate a large stand of poison ivy in one summer. If a few plants live and drop seed, your troubles will continue next summer. However, two years of vigorous work by a neighborhood group should clean up every back yard and vacant lot for several blocks, or even the entire area around a summer cottage colony.

The U.S. Department of Agriculture recommends ammonium sulfamate to eradicate poison ivy. This compound is not inflammable and is easily mixed for spraying. When used according to directions, it is not hazardous to animals. A pound of these crystals to a gallon of water is suggested for hand spraying. Leaves of the ivy plants should be soaked, but not so much that they drip. Do not use this solution on the skin. Ammonium sulfamate is also destructive to ragweed, plantain, dandelions, and many other weeds. It is an effective herbicide and does not leave a spray residue hazardous to livestock.

Boraxo, a trade name for commercial borax, will also destroy poison ivy when applied at the rate of ten pounds to one square rod. Many eradicators that contain 2, 4-D are effective against poison ivy too, if they are used in extra-strong solutions. Salt, strong salt water (three pounds to a gallon of water), or old crankcase oil poured on poison ivy will usually kill the plant, but the soil will be sterile for years. For quick-killing action on large vines, cut them off at or below the soil level and then soak the roots with brine.

After the plants are dead, they should be raked up and buried. Do not handle them with bare hands because the dry, dead ivy is almost as poisonous as the green. Use a pitchfork or rake and then wash the tools thoroughly with gasoline or cleaning powder to remove the ivy sap.

If in spite of all precautions you do contract a case of poison ivy, Minnesota's Hennepin County Medical Society gives the following information and advice:

JULY

About 50 percent of the people are allergic to poison ivy. The eruption appears from several hours to several days after exposure. It begins with an itching, burning redness on some localized area of the skin. Crops of blisters may develop later. Smearing of the noxious agent to various parts of the body occurs. Scientific studies show the watery contents of the blisters are not communicable, however.

It has been a common practice of prevention to scrub exposed areas of the skin with soap and water. There is a question as to whether this is of much value if 15 minutes or more have elapsed after exposure. The poison is impregnated well by this time. The use of a harsh brush in scrubbing irritates the skin and any prevention remedy used should be mild so as not to irritate.

The treatment of the damaged skin depends on the severity of the eruption. In a mild case, the application of a drying lotion such as calamine lotion is adequate for comfort and control. The United States Public Health Service recommends the application of a 10 percent solution of tannic acid in alcohol several times a day to the involved areas. This astringent will tend to dry the blisters.

In severe cases, a physician should be consulted. In general, oils and salves increase the itching and aggravate the condition by serving to spread the irritating substance over a greater surface. It requires from 7 to 28 days to recover from an attack.

A poison ivy ointment that contains zirconium and an antihistamine drug has recently been reported to be effective.

TIME TO DIVIDE AND PLANT IRIS

The month of July and on into August is a good time to divide and replant your iris, and to buy and plant new varieties. Iris can

GRANDMA made us memorize: "Leaflets three, let it be." When any of us contacted poison ivy, Uncle Jerry would get from swampy places handfuls of jewel weed, sometimes called snapweed and spotted touch-me-not, with which we would rub our skins vigorously. It is an old Indian remedy, but I think that perhaps today the doctor's advice and drug store remedies are better.

be planted any time from June to early September, but the last half of July is probably best. The irises then are well rested after their heavy blooming in June. Divided and replanted rhizomes will make a good growth, dropping their stringy roots and getting well settled before cold weather arrives.

Most varieties of bearded iris form large clumps which should be dug up — a spading fork is best — and gently pulled apart with both hands. They should be separated and replanted about every three or four years. Plants growing in sandy soil will require dividing more often than those in heavier soils.

Do not make your divisions too small. Be sure there are several sprouts on each hand-size piece of rhizome. Although a single-sprouted rhizome will make a good plant, it will not bloom as soon as a larger one, probably not for a year or two. When you dig up all or part of a clump, pull it gently apart with both hands. It will separate at the weakest necks of the rhizomes. Plant only clean, healthy rhizomes and burn all diseased stock. Several small divisions of the same variety may be planted four inches apart in a group, but larger divisions or new clumps of iris should be spaced at least three feet apart. Low-growing annuals may then be planted between the clumps until they spread.

Prepare the iris bed at least ten inches deep, with plant food mixed in the bottom. Bone meal is the best fertilizer for iris. Then partly fill in with good soil and plant the iris very shallowly, so that when the ground settles the rhizomes will be just barely covered with earth. The rhizome should ride the soil as a duck rides the water. Each rhizome can be planted on a mound of soil like a potato hill. This mound will settle, and eventually the surface of the ground should be level with the top of rhizome. When the iris divisions are replanted, cut back the leaves in a fan shape six inches high to prevent too much evaporation until the plant roots are well started. Do not trim leaves until autumn on irises that are not transplanted, however. If the soil is of good fertility, eliminate the fertilizer. Too much food, although it will produce fine blooms, may cause a soft growth that is more susceptible to root rot.

JULY

Plant your irises in a sunny spot in well-drained soil where they will not be crowded by other plants. Untidy housekeeping in the garden is the usual cause of trouble with iris. Keep weeds and rubbish away from the clumps. If you have a slight slope in your garden, use it for iris and avoid the rot sometimes caused by poor surface drainage. The character of the soil should be such as to provide good subsurface drainage, too. If the soil is heavy and clayey, mix in plenty of sand and peat for better drainage. If your iris bed is not on a slope, it is desirable to have each clump a little higher than the surrounding soil so water or ice will not remain on it. Iris thrive best in a garden on the dry side, and should have at least half a day's sunlight, preferably more.

When you are dividing and replanting iris, don't neglect to get at least a few new and better varieties, too. The cost is so little now, and in a few years these new ones will improve the appearance of your whole garden. Root out the old, common, yellowish-whites and the small, space-stealing yellow-and-browns and replace them with some of the fine, tall, colorful, big-blossomed varieties. And don't wish off on your friends and neighbors your old, discarded iris plants. Do your part to encourage better iris gardens here in the North.

The following are all fairly recent irises, fine in color and form, very different from the old types: Gudrun, white; Sable, black; Floriole, light blue; Sierra Blue, medium blue; Ola Kala, dark yellow; Elsa Sass, light yellow; Golden Treasure, yellow and white; Red Douglas, red; Wabash, bicolor; and Amigo, two-toned blue. These have all proved hardy in the North, and one plant each of the entire list should not cost more than $6 to $10, depending on the size of the rhizomes.

This list gives you an idea of the colors obtainable, but there are hundreds more varieties to choose from. A good way to learn more about them, and about iris culture in general, is to write to the American Iris Society, Washington, D.C., and get particulars on joining the society. This will cost you about $3 a year and will bring you a wealth of seasonable and reliable information about iris.

It is exciting to buy one or two really choice varieties, for per-

166

haps a dollar or two each, and enjoy them for years. Each year you can add just a few new specimens, and in a short time you will have a collection your neighbors will come blocks to see.

Irises are not hard to grow, but there are two chief troubles to guard against — the iris borer and rhizome rot. The latter is a bad-smelling, soft, cream-colored rot, which usually starts in a wound in the rhizome made by the iris borer, a larval pest that eats its way down the inside the leaves to the rhizomes. The wound or cavity allows the entry of rot fungi and possibly other diseases.

GRANDMA'S irises were a novelty in her day. She had three kinds — a pale yellowish-white, a short, sturdy yellow and brown, and a tall, dusky one with turban-like standards and dark purple falls, which Uncle Jerry had brought from abroad. He called it the "Hindoo." They were the only irises for miles around and folks came long distances to see them. The minister was quite sure they were orchids. He preached a sermon about them and called them "lilies of the field." After that folks when looking at them spoke in whispers, like they did at a funeral.

Iris rot, if not taken care of, usually will kill the entire plant and may even spread and destroy an entire iris bed. The signs of rot are the withering and browning of leaf tips, with a sodden, water-soaked appearance near the base, eventually followed by a flopping over of leaves and stems. If you notice these symptoms, remove at once all imperfect or diseased rhizomes and burn them. However, if a plant is valuable you might save some of it by cutting off all infected parts, then washing the healthy pieces in the gutter with a garden hose. Place the salvaged sections in sunshine to sterilize them for a couple of days. For additional protection, roll the rhizomes in dry sulphur or gypsum.

Iris growers with very choice varieties remove all soil where diseased irises have been growing and replace with fresh soil. Some growers have saved their plants after discovering rot by sterilizing the garden soil and killing the rot with a much-diluted solution of the disinfectant mentioned above. At the end of each day's work clearing out diseased plants, wash and sterilize all tools used. Do not handle other iris without thoroughly washing your hands with hot water and soap.

The borer enters the leaf when very small, usually near the top, boring a small hole on the leaf edge. This gives the leaf a wet, stained appearance. The borer then eats a passage down the interior of a leaf, rapidly increasing in size until it reaches the rhizome. It then is a fat, pink creature, often 1½ inches long. The quickest way to destroy borers while they are in transit down the stem and before they have reached the rhizome is to slip the suspected leaf firmly between two fingers and draw upwards. This pressure will crush the borer.

The presence of borers is usually indicated by ragged edges on the upper part of the leaves, followed by a watery appearance extending downward. If the borer is discovered and killed while it is still in the leaf and before it has reached the rhizome, no great harm is done. If it has reached the rhizome, dig up the section and wash with a much-diluted solution that contains coal tar and other fungicides. This disinfectant for irises is obtainable at garden

GRANDMA had a method all her own for slugs. She placed a saucer half filled with stale beer in the garden with the saucer edge almost level with the soil. The following morning the saucer would be almost full of dead slugs. We never knew whether they drowned or died of acute alcoholism. Grandma, an ardent prohibitionist, bought only a pint bottle of beer at a time and was careful to explain to the grocer how she was going to use it. She always showed the dead slugs to Uncle Jerry as a horrible example. He would sadly remark that the horrible part was such waste of a good beverage.

stores. Then dry the rhizome in the open air and replant in a new spot. If borers are in evidence, it may help to dust every ten days with DDT or an all-purpose garden dust. Chlordane dust may also deter iris borers.

Leaf spot, a less common disease of iris, is indicated by oval, reddish-bordered spots with gray centers which appear on the iris leaves. This fungus disease may become very destructive if ignored. Remove all affected leaves and dust or spray with a mixture containing Fermate, sulphur, and DDT. This same mixture will also help to repel iris borers if used once a week until buds are about to open.

Chances are that your irises will remain healthy, however, and will need little care after blooming. Do not cut off the leaves. Allow them — unless they are crushed or diseased — to remain until late in the fall. This foliage is necessary to create and build up material for next spring's growth and bloom. After frost you can cut the leaves off to six inches, using sharp shears, and remove the severed leaves and rubbish from around the clump. Protect newly planted iris stock with clean, dry straw or marsh hay during the first winter, but thereafter the hardy varieties will do better if left unmulched during the winter.

OTHER GARDEN PERENNIALS

July is a month of prolific bloom for many less well-known perennials, as well as the favorite roses, delphiniums, and many varieties of daylilies. If you are starting a new perennial border this year, or if there are empty places in your garden that you would like to fill permanently, get to know some of the lovely but less familiar hardy perennials. July is a good time to visit your friends' and neighbors' gardens and commercial nurseries to see many of these in bloom. Most of these perennial plants can be moved into your garden this month if dug up and handled with a minimum of disturbance to the roots.

Astilbe, for example, has attractive pink, red, or white feathery, plume-like blossoms during late June and July. It grows as high as three feet, with delicate cut-leaf foliage, and will bloom in either

169

sun or partial shade. Columbines in many shades of pink, red, blue, yellow, white, and lavender are another graceful flower that add a delicate note of contrast to the heavier clumps of peonies, phlox, and daylilies in the border. Forget-me-nots make a permanent, low-growing edging for the border and are covered with tiny brilliant blue flowers most of the summer. They do very well in shady places, too, unlike most of the low-growing annuals that are often used for edging.

GRANDMA always applied a generous quantity of damp baking soda — she called it saleratus — when we youngsters were stung by a bee or hornet. The soda, being an alkali, quickly neutralized the strong acid in the "sting-venom" of the insect. Then she made the whole operation very interesting by extracting the "stinger" with the help of tweezers and a reading glass.

Gaillardia, with its red and yellow daisy-like flowers, is a good perennial for cutting and blooms all summer. Coral bells, or heuchera, is a smaller plant with slender stalks of tiny flowers rising above a flat, low rosette of leaves. Coral bells also bloom all summer and are fine for cutting, and unlike gaillardia will do well in partial shade as well as sun. Red or pink monarda, also called beebalm or bergamot, and scarlet cardinal flowers are two tall, semi-wild perennials that bloom profusely in the border from July on, bringing color to either a sunny or shady spot.

Two of the loveliest white flowers blooming in the July border are physostegia, or false dragonhead, with its tall spire of bloom, and dictamnus, or gas plant, which sends up large, loose trusses of white flowers from a handsome, bushy plant with aromatic leaves. Both of these perennials are very hardy, blooming for years in sun or part shade without needing division; and both come in rosy-pink varieties as well as white.

Shasta daisies follow the June-blooming painted daisies or

pyrethrum, blooming from early July until frost. They come in assorted colors and with large flowers which make them suitable both for background clumps in the border and for cut flowers. Most daisies require full sun, except for the common yellow-eyed white daisy, which will bloom happily in almost any spot in your garden through late June, July, and most of August if the flowers are kept cut. Both Shasta daisies and the common field or garden daisy are members of the chrysanthemum family but are hardier than most fall-blooming chrysanthemums.

Among the campanulas, I recommend *persicifolia,* a three-footer that has both white and blue bells, and *glomerata,* another three-footer (sometimes a little less) with blue, white, and violet bells.

Two nice border bluebells are *carpatica* and *garganica* which grow about eight to ten inches high, with starry blue and white flowers. These two plants are excellent for rock gardens and walls, used frequently for border edgings.

For a background in your border or to fill in an area where most perennials grow reluctantly, try the new Morden pink lythrum. It is hardy, and comes to us from Canada. The Minneapolis Park Board reports it quite satisfactory.

CODDLE YOUR CHRYSANTHEMUMS

Chrysanthemums require special care now to produce the best blossoms in late summer and autumn. During the hot months, shallow cultivation around the plants must be maintained at regular intervals and also after heavy, beating rains just as soon as the ground is dry enough. This is necessary to keep the soil aerated, moisture-receptive, and weedless. It is almost impossible to keep a garden free of insect plagues if weeds are numerous.

Chrysanthemums should be fed with a balanced commercial plant food this month and in early August. A small handful cultivated into the soil around each plant and soaked in will assure better blossoms. Never wet the foliage of mums by sprinkling from above. Wet foliage frequently causes disease. Water them about every ten days in hot weather, using shallow ditches between the rows through which the water can run.

Chrysanthemums are singularly free of insect troubles when good housekeeping in the garden is practiced. However, if aphids or plant lice should appear they can be controlled with a nicotine sulphate spray. For other insects, such as leaf rollers, leaf hoppers, tarnish bugs, and stalk borers, dust or spray with 10 per cent DDT, and with Fermate for foliage trouble.

In order to have sturdy, well-branched mum clusters, it is necessary to pinch back terminal shoots a couple of times in the first half of the growing season. This simply means removing about half an inch of the soft growing tips of the main shoots, when they are about six inches high, to encourage lateral branches. When the laterals are ten inches long, give them the same pinching treatment. Do no more pinching after August 10, however, because by that time flower buds are forming. A properly pinched-back plant usually will not require staking. But without pinching the blossoms are few and often formed on long weak stems.

DO'S AND DON'TS FOR YOUR GARDEN HOSE

DO remember that the life span of a garden hose is cut at least 50 per cent by careless handling.

DO repair a leak at either end of the hose by checking first to see whether a new washer is needed and then, if necessary, buying and attaching a new fitting.

DO repair a pinhole leak along the hose by applying liquid rubber, rubber cement, or tightly-wound plastic tape.

DO repair a larger leak by cutting out the damaged section and using a metal coupler to rejoin the two parts.

DO buy a swivel device to use where the hose is connected to the faucet. It allows the hose to be moved freely without wear and tear at that point.

DON'T leave the hose lying on the grass when it is not being used. Drain it and coil it on a reel or hanger so it has no abrupt bends in it.

DON'T pull the hose around the corner of the house without checking to see that it is not scraping against the foundation.

DON'T smother the flow of water by kinking the hose.

172

DON'T forget that when the outside cords of a rubber hose are damaged — but there is no leak — further trouble can be prevented by wrapping the area with plastic or friction tape.

DON'T neglect to change the position of the hose on your lawn occasionally while it is in use. When left too long in one position, the grass underneath it will suffer.

GRANDMA'S mosquito repellents — sixty years ago — were extracts of wintergreen and citronella. She smelled like a drug store — only nicer. Uncle Jerry's mosquito repellent was a powerful dark oily linament that was marked "good for man or beast." He smelled like a race horse with a strained tendon. No self-respecting mosquito would go near him, but neither would we.

REMINDERS

Give your annual beds a midsummer feeding with a balanced commercial fertilizer for continued heavy bloom.

Cut zinnias, cosmos, marigolds, bachelor's buttons, and annual phlox for bouquets in the house, and remove faded or dead blossoms from all others before they go to seed. Dust zinnias and sweet peas with sulphur or all-purpose garden dust to prevent mildew. Cultivate after rain as soon as the soil is dry enough. Transplant blooming annuals, three or more of one kind, into flowerless spots in the perennial border.

Delphinium and coral-bells will usually give a second blooming if old stalks are cut back, but retain some foliage. Cut off the entire top flower cluster on perennial phlox when petals begin to fade, and the plant will bloom again. Gladioli will not bloom again this year after the flower spike is cut, but successive plantings during June and early July should keep more blossoms coming. Leave most of the foliage when cutting gladioli blooms or the corms will be underdeveloped.

173

JULY

To rout night crawlers (huge earthworms), ordinary angle-worms, ants, and other insects in your lawn, apply half a pound of 40 to 50 per cent chlordane powder per 1,000 square feet of lawn area. Mix the powder with dry earth or sand and distribute it over the lawn, using gloves or a small fertilizer spreader. Wet down the lawn well after distribution. Areas so treated may not be troubled again for as long as three years. Moles will also cease to be a problem in lawns where their food supply of insects and worms is eliminated.

There is also a 45 per cent liquid chlordane that will do the same job the dust does. Eight ounces dissolved in eight gallons of water — applied with a sprinkling can — will cover 1,000 square feet of lawn.

Crabgrass is still young and tender in most northern areas during July and in prime condition to be sprayed with a crabgrass killer. Keep fighting this pest as long as its seeds keep sprouting in your lawn. If crabgrass plants are already mature, use the raking and close mowing technique to cut off all seed stalks before seed has ripened.

Permit grape hyacinth and other minor spring-blooming bulbs to ripen and scatter their seed. Cover lightly with compost. For late autumn flowers, you can still sow seed of some annuals — baby's breath, mignonette, Shirley poppies, cosmos, godetias, and annual phlox. If you have a hot sandy spot where nothing seems to prosper, try little plants of multicolored portulaca, or moss rose.

Water regularly when rain is scanty. Never allow phlox to become dry, because then they are most susceptible to leaf blight. Water window boxes regularly, but don't flood, and fertilize lightly. Give the flowers a haircut when window boxes get a shaggy look. Mow lawns high during hot weather and allow the clippings to fall back into grass.

To kill weeds in a gravel or crushed-rock driveway, apply any weed killer that contains 2,4-D. Apply double the strength recommended for weeds in the lawn. Several applications of coarse salt will also do the trick — but keep it off the lawn!

During hot, humid weather, dust the garden frequently. This is the time when most leaf fungus trouble develops. Use a dust that contains Fermate and sulphur. Dust your glads and the soil around them with chlordane.

After a climbing rose has bloomed and is sending up new canes, the oldest of the past year's canes can be removed. Cut off, also, all quick-growing sucker branches or shoots that start below the graft union of roses and flowering almonds. Continue to give your roses plenty of water and feed them periodically up to the middle of August.

Make cuttings now for next winter's indoor garden from geraniums, fibrous-rooted begonias, ivies, and coleus.

❧ AUGUST ❧

Aᴜɢᴜꜱᴛ is a month of hot weather and lush foliage in the northern garden, but with a strong hint of the end of summer. Cicadas begin to sing in the treetops, perennial phlox and the annual beds are in their glory, but most of the border is already past its peak of color. Now the dense shade of oaks and elms, and the cool green of the peony and iris foliage, the lilac hedge, and the well-watered lawn seem just as appealing as the brighter colors of flowers still in bloom. This is the time for gardeners to rest a little, enjoy the fruits of their labors, and take stock and make plans for changes and improvements.

PHLOX IS QUEEN OF THE GARDEN

If there is a queen of flowers in midsummer gardens it is *Phlox paniculata* — the tall perennial phlox. By growing early, medium, and late varieties, you can have continuous bloom from late June into October, but it is at its peak of perfection in late July and August.

There is no other flower so beautiful and easy to grow as the phlox and few that equal its long blooming season. It seems to enjoy itself thoroughly in almost any garden and requires little attention. Phlox are thoroughly hardy in the North and require little if any winter covering after their first winter.

The perfume of perennial phlox is cool and sweet but never overpowering. Its range of color is very wide, from pure waxy white through all the reds and carmines, salmon pink, an almost-blue violet, dozens of two-tones, such as deep carmine with a darker

176

eye, salmon with a carmine eye, white with a pink edging, and many other lovely combinations. Often the individual florets that compose the large cone-shaped, spherical, or flat flower clusters are as large as silver dollars.

Different varieties of phlox grow to different heights, from about eighteen inches up to stately four-foot plants, and can be placed accordingly in different parts of the border. The low-growing spring-blooming varieties of phlox — *Phlox subulata* (pink, lavender, red-purple, rose, and white) and *Phlox divaricata* (the wild blue woodland phlox) — are lovely in the perennial border, but they cannot match the summer-long, spectacular display provided by their taller cousins.

August is the time to see the new varieties of phlox in all their glory — and to plan to add them to your garden. There are dozens of outstanding phlox in bloom this month in public gardens and in every commercial nursery. Some of the handsomest are Sir John Falstaff, largest of all phlox, an English import twenty-four to thirty inches tall with huge clusters of two-inch, luminous salmon-pink florets; Blanchette, similar to Falstaff but perhaps a shade darker; Pink Charm, a dainty, luminous pink; and It's Magic, a magnificent white with large pink eyes.

Other fine varieties include Sun-ray, a large, starred pink; Prunella, a deep, pure magenta; Bright Eyes, strikingly pink with rayed petals and a dark eye; Harriet, a fascinating magenta with a white splash in the center; Mary Louise and World Peace, both mammoth and pure white; Daily Sketch, salmon pink with a crimson eye; Leo Schlageter, brilliant scarlet; Harvest Fire, bright crimson with dark red eyes; and Rokoko, a huge delicate lavender-pink variety that grows somewhat lower than most.

Violet Beauty is a striking new variety. It has an almost blue eye, and its white petals are tinged with violet blue.

Today's magnificent, large-blossomed phlox are the result of years of careful breeding and selection. Plants that were considered good just a few years ago do not rate very high by today's standards of what makes good phlox. If your phlox are all older varieties, why not consider making some additions or substitutions?

177

AUGUST

Measure the size of the flower heads and individual florets on your phlox and compare with those growing at your nursery. Consider, too, that the newer varieties of phlox have much less foliage trouble than the older, more common types.

You will probably want to buy a few of the new phlox plants on the spot, or at least place your order for next spring. If the day is cool and cloudy and the nurseryman digs up the plant with plenty of earth around it, you may be able to transfer it quickly to your garden, and it will keep right on blossoming. Plants will cost about thirty-five to seventy-five cents each, but this is not expensive when you consider that next year they will make a splendid showing, and in a few years you can divide each one into eight or ten plants.

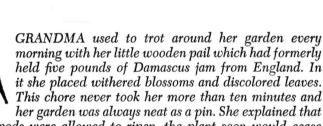

GRANDMA used to trot around her garden every morning with her little wooden pail which had formerly held five pounds of Damascus jam from England. In it she placed withered blossoms and discolored leaves. This chore never took her more than ten minutes and her garden was always neat as a pin. She explained that if seed pods were allowed to ripen, the plant soon would cease blooming because its strength went into developing seeds instead of flowers.

Phlox clumps now growing in your border which have become too crowded should be divided either in September or next spring. They can also be divided now, if you don't mind losing some of this year's bloom. If the foliage fails to revive in two days, remove all but three inches of the stems. A clump two feet wide can be divided into eight or ten small clumps. Set your new phlox plants and divisions one inch lower in the ground than they were growing previously. If you wish to divide a clump but keep part of it growing in the same spot, cut triangular pieces from opposite sides, using a sharp spade, and replant the pieces in a new spot. Fill in

178

the excavation in the old clump with rich loam, and the old plant will hardly show it has been touched.

Phlox should have shallow cultivation as they are not deep-rooted. Every spring, just as they are sprouting, they should be given a spraying with a mild Bordeaux mixture, and thereafter kept dusted with an all-purpose garden dust containing Fermate. This should be done about every two weeks and after each heavy rain. This treatment usually will prevent foliage trouble during the summer. Do not crowd your phlox. They require ample circulation around each clump and a fairly sunny location.

Cut off the top cluster of flowers as the blossom fades and seed pods begin to form, and new flower clusters will come out at the leaf axils or joints. Never allow seeds to fall from the ripened pods, because when they grow in the parent clump they probably will not be true to color. They are apt to revert to some poorly colored but huskier ancestor, and being stronger, eventually will kill their own parents. This answers the frequent question, "Why did my phlox change from beautiful flowers to plants with sickly, weak colors?"

Feed phlox clumps lightly but regularly and keep them moist. One severe drying-out of a phlox plant will often seriously reduce its blooming for the rest of the season. When you water, remove the nozzle, lay the hose on the ground, and allow the water to spread over the soil surface without wetting the foliage. If you notice the foliage beginning to change color and dry up, leaf trouble is starting. Remove all affected leaves, burn them, and wash your hands before touching healthy vegetation. Dust well with all-purpose garden dust, or with powdered sulphur or Aramite if red spiders are causing the trouble. Foliage troubles are seldom severe enough to do the phlox much damage if you dust faithfully as a preventive measure, do not sprinkle the leaves or flowers, and keep the plants uncrowded.

DAYLILIES

The new hemerocallis, better known as the daylily, is one of our thoroughly hardy garden lilies and is now blossoming in bountiful midsummer display in many northern home gardens and nurseries. This is a good time to choose some of the new varieties to add color and charm to your garden.

Perhaps you do not recognize this lily under the name "hemerocallis." It is a descendant of the lemon lily or corn lily of Grandmother's day, when its blossoms were usually a brick red or pale yellow. Hybridizers in our great universities and botanical gardens saw promising possibilities in this delicately fragrant but rather unpretentious perennial. As a result we now have truly remarkable clumps of daylilies that require little or no winter protection even in our most northerly regions and do not demand rich soil or much care.

This flower resembles the Easter lily in shape and size, but there the likeness ceases. As yet there are no white varieties, and it is not a true lily, despite its name. Lilies grow from bulbs, while the daylily grows from slightly tuberous roots. But it does come in strong red, orange, and pinks, and in delicate, elusive shades of yellow that glisten in the sunlight to medium and dark yellows and golds. It also ranges from pale pink to flashing reds, scarlets, and deep mahogany, and many blends and bicolors. The blossoms are carried on sturdy stems high above the clump of attractive, wide-bladed foliage. Each stem has clusters of up to thirty-six buds. Usually three open at a time, lasting for one day — the reason for the name.

There are many flower clusters on each mature clump. There is always a wealth of bloom, often as much as three hundred blossoms from each plant during the flowering period, which lasts several weeks. By planting early, medium, and late varieties you can have a blossoming bank of these flowers in different colors from June all through the summer and on well into the chrysanthemum season.

The lily-shaped blossoms appear to have six overlapping petals. A close examination, however, will show three sepals and three petals. The lovely six-pointed blossoms often are five inches in diameter. Many of the blossoms are fragrant, especially Hyperion, a beautiful pure yellow that is a glorified old-fashioned lemon lily.

See the list of recommended varieties at the end of the book for some favorites.

The plants are graded as to size, so you can order plants of different ultimate heights for various locations in your garden, from fifteen inches to four or five feet. The daylily is practically free from insect and fungus troubles. It will last for years without being divided, but can be divided every four or five years if you desire. It never seems to get too old to bloom. It will bloom and grow in poor soil, but flourishes in good garden soil. Many varieties are tolerant of shade and will flower with only a few hours of sun a day.

Daylilies can be planted or divided almost any time, preferably in early spring or in the late summer or early fall after they have finished blooming. To divide a clump, lift with a spading fork and pry the root mass in half with two spading forks placed back to back in the clump. For smaller divisions, repeat this operation on each half of the clump. In replanting, be sure that the crown is not covered with more than one inch of soil. Regular fertilization with rotted manure, compost, or balanced plant food will keep your daylilies growing and blooming their best year after year.

TIME TO PLANT AND DIVIDE PEONIES

From mid-August until the middle of September is the ideal time to divide and transplant old peonies and to plant new ones. This

GRANDMA knew that the odor of cedar was distasteful to many insects. So from the sawmill she got a hundred wide red cedar shingles, thick as shakes. These she placed under her ripening watermelons, muskmelons, and citrons, and these fruits never were touched by slugs, worms, or decay. Grandma counted her shingles at the end of harvest, and woe to anybody who took even one. She would have much preferred the loss of a melon to the loss of a shingle. She was of Scotch descent.

gives them a chance to become established before cold weather. When spring comes, they are ready to grow. Don't divide or transplant your peonies, however, unless they are not doing well where they are. Peony clumps will thrive in a sunny location for as long as fifty years, provided they are kept free of weeds, fed every spring and fall with well-rotted manure or bone meal in a circle around the clump, and watered well during dry weather.

If you are buying new peonies at a nursery, August is the time to plant them. You can buy relatively small, two- or three-eyed root divisions, which are inexpensive but may not bloom for several years, or you can pay more and buy an undivided field root that can be slipped into your garden with a minimum of disturbance. An undivided clump of this kind will probably bloom next summer. It must be surrounded by the original undisturbed earth. A man handy with a spade and with someone to help him can move a large peony clump with enough earth around it so that next year's bloom is not sacrificed. Be sure to have a large hole prepared to receive the transplanted clump at once.

In planting either small peony root divisions or large growing clumps, prepare the soil well in advance so the earth will have a chance to settle. Dig the holes five feet apart and at least two feet deep and two feet wide or even larger to accommodate a big clump. Throw out the earth and mix in two pounds of balanced plant food or bone meal. Cover this mixture with four or five inches of unfertilized earth. Fill up the hole with good topsoil after carefully placing the peony root in the hole. With plant food in the bottom of the hole the plant is assured of nourishment for years to come.

Plant each division or field root so the topmost bud on the roots is not more than two inches below the surface, even after settling. Too deep planting often causes peonies to fail to bloom. Even small root divisions will usually blossom the third year after planting. If they do not, they have probably been planted too deep in heavy soil and may not blossom for years, if ever. Then it is best to replant them, not so deeply. Do not purchase a root unless it is of good size, firm, shows no decay, and has at least three eyes. However, a small firm root has more promise than a large wilted root.

In spite of the longevity of most peony clumps, it is possible that old ones in your garden may need dividing. If the plants seem healthy but have a great many spindly stalks, if buds form but dry up, or if a formerly strong clump is now a ring of living vegetation with a dead center and no blossoms, lack of food is indicated. The plant has become so wide that fertilizer dug in around the clump does not reach the center roots, and of course one must never fertilize on top of peony plants or the stems and crown will be damaged.

To dig up the ailing plants, plunge a spade straight down in a circle six or eight inches away from the crown. Then gently pry up the entire plant, wash off the earth, and cut off all but two inches of each growing stem. If the clump is large, ask a neighbor to bring over his spade and help you. The two of you working on opposite sides can probably raise the plant with little harm to the roots.

Use a strong knife to divide the big root by cutting and prying. Don't use a hatchet unless necessary, and avoid bruising. Buds or eyes for next year's stalks will be found on the root. Divide so there are two to four strong buds on each healthy section. If the roots are allowed to stand in a warm breeze for several hours they become less brittle and will divide more easily. Sterilize all cut surfaces with powdered charcoal or Bordeaux powder. Discard all portions that show rot or disease. Replant, but do not expect blooms from these divisions for several years.

If you are careful, you can make a division and rejuvenate the old plant without digging up the entire clump. Remove the earth around about a third of the plant and cut off what you wish. If the center is dead, remove all the old dead roots and fill in with good rich soil.

Do not cut off the summer growth of your peonies unless they are diseased. If you do, the stubs of the hollow stems will be exposed to contamination by dogs during the winter and the peonies may cease blooming for several years. Late in the fall, gather all the dried peony stems in both hands, and with a twisting motion crush them gently down on the crown of the plant. The clump will then have ample winter protection. In the spring, cut off the old stems with a sharp knife or scissors without disturbing the plant. Never pull them loose.

Peonies are subject to botrytis blight, a fungus disease that causes shoots to turn black and wilt. This blight occurs in both early and late forms. When signs of it appear, remove all affected stalks at once, cutting them off just below the earth line. Give the clump a spraying of weak Bordeaux mixture to keep the disease from spreading.

GARDEN CARE FOR AUGUST

The perennial border is luxuriant with blooming phlox and green foliage this month, but other flowers are in bloom there too. Scattered bloom continues from veronica, campanula, and lythrum, while the scarlet beebalm and cardinal flower also add bright color. Many lilies bloom in August in northern gardens — the exotic gold-banded and Japanese lilies, the Turk's-cap lilies, and many of the shade-loving plantain lilies, which are members of the genus *Hosta* (also called funkia) and send up large, white, fragrant flowers or small lavender blooms above their symmetrical mounds of green foliage.

During this last full month of summer, it is time to take stock of your garden and make the necessary plans to keep it orderly and beautiful. It is easiest to do this now while the plants are in full leaf and have reached their maximum size.

Study your perennial border as it looks now, recall how it looked

GRANDMA would prune all her shrubs during the summer and Uncle Jerry would attend to the tree branches that had not leafed out. Grandma explained that dead wood absorbed some of the life-giving sap that should go to the living wood. As I remember, apparently dying trees and shrubs usually would make a vigorous comeback after this treatment.

earlier in the summer, and decide what changes you want to make for next year. Indicate with stakes the plants that are to be transplanted and those that should be discarded, but don't start wholesale moving and transplanting yet. Wait to make your changes late in September or next spring. Any drastic transplanting now will curtail the bloom and autumn beauty of your garden. Notable exceptions to this rule are irises, peonies, Oriental poppies, and bleeding hearts — all of which can be divided and transplanted this month.

Often border arrangements that were harmonious and beautiful a year or two ago are now too large or out of place and create a discordant note. Perhaps you have a color clash, or plants that you thought were low growers and planted in the foreground are now completely hiding the little fellows farther back. Don't allow your garden to become a jungle of rank growth. The offenders should be discarded or transplanted to another place in the garden, perhaps to the rear of the border where the large growth will be a background or foil for less vigorous but daintier plants. Tall plants can be used to advantage in screening an alley, a compost pile, or some unsightly object.

After a fair trial don't bother with perennials that do not prosper in your garden. Space and time are too valuable. Maybe a neighbor would be delighted to experiment with the difficult ones. Often such flowers will grow and bloom gloriously in another garden because of different growing conditions, or maybe just temperament. Some flowers seem almost pernickety.

It's not only a kind and neighborly act to give away plants and seeds to your fellow gardeners, but it can be a source of selfish pleasure too. Remember that your neighbors' yards are adjacent to yours — and form backgrounds for every vista around your yard. Your most carefully planned effect can fail if a poorly tended yard spoils the view. So give your neighbors encouragement and help as well as plants and seeds; don't let the beauty of your garden end at your property line.

I think all home gardeners develop an affection for flowers they have worked with, but we must be ruthless if the garden as a whole

185

is to flourish. Learn to divide, transplant, give away, and destroy for the health and beauty of the garden.

While you are at your garden analysis, pull up and destroy every weed in and around the border. Do it before they go to seed. A few hours of work now will save days of labor next summer. If August is dry, as it often is in the North, water your garden every four or five days. Lay a few flat stones in inconspicuous spots in your border on which to lay the hose, nozzle off, to allow a gentle stream to water the roots of your flowers. Do your watering in the morning, if possible, and do not wet the foliage. Continue to dust faithfully with an all-purpose garden dust and mildews and molds will not be a problem.

There may be some aster blight now on your annual asters. It seems that there always will be until we have blight-resistant seed. Around each plant sift a teaspoonful of tobacco dust — you can get this from your garden dealer. This treatment will help to repel blight. Don't plant asters in exactly the same spot next spring. Rotate your annuals and your gladioli the same way the farmer rotates his crops.

Gladioli for Flower Shows. The gladiolus is unquestionably the favorite of summer-blooming bulbs and corms, and in August it is at the zenith of its beauty. Although the gladiolus is one of the easiest flowers to grow, a little extra attention now will bring you flowers fine enough to win prizes at the state fair or a local show.

Two or three weeks before you expect your gladioli to reach full bloom, give them an extra feeding of any of the approved liquid fertilizers obtainable in the seed stores and nurseries. Keep them well watered around the stems, and keep the water off the leaves and florets. When the buds show color, dust or spray with 10 per cent DDT to protect them from thrips. Avoid getting the insecticide on the petals, however. Some gardeners apply it directly on the soil around the stalks.

Flowering of gladioli can be hastened or delayed to some degree. As closely as possible, try to have the first florets open two or three days before the flower show. If the spikes are coming along too fast and one or two florets have opened too soon, cut the spikes and place them in a pail of cold water up to the first floret. Put the pail in a cold place — 40 to 45 degrees is ideal. Remember, the longer your spikes have to remain in cold storage, the quicker they will probably fade when they are displayed in the warm exhibition hall. However, in the event that spikes are coming into bloom too slowly, allow them to remain in the garden if the weather is warm or place them in a pail of tepid water in a normal temperature. Do this a day or perhaps two or three days before the show — this will have to be determined by experimentation. This method should hurry your gladioli into the right stage of blooms for prize-winning.

GRANDMA discouraged dogs by planting annual calendulas. They are rapid growers and she grew large beds. For quick, temporary relief from dogs she would pull the plants, crush them slightly, and strew them around the yard. This was done when little cousin Willie, who was afraid of dogs, was visiting at Grandma's. The yard was then dog-free until the plants were dry. I remember I much preferred the smell of dogs to that of calendulas or of Willie, who smelled of perfumed soap and wore a Little Lord Fauntleroy suit.

More Coddling for Chrysanthemums. Continued special attention to your chrysanthemum plants will assure plenty of strong, healthy, colorful blossoms this autumn. By the first of August stop pinching off terminal buds and start building up prospective flowers by judicious feeding and by protecting them from their few troubles.

Chrysanthemum growers have discovered that timed feedings, ten days to two weeks apart, of the comparatively new liquid fertilizers work wonders with mums. This type of fertilizer usually comes in crystals or powder form. It is dissolved in water and applied on the ground around the plants. Follow carefully the

187

mixing directions given on the container. Do not use it stronger or oftener than advised. In fact, I prefer to use any of these liquid fertilizers about one quarter weaker than advocated, just to protect weak plants that perhaps could not stand the full strength.

A few sprayings of nicotine sulphate solution should keep chrysanthemum plants clean of insects. A couple of light 5 per cent DDT dustings will eliminate the tarnish bug during the bud-forming stage. Plants should be watered under the foliage every week during hot weather, but be sure to avoid getting water on the leaves. Continue to cultivate frequently but shallowly. By the end of the month your patience and hard work may be rewarded by the first blossoms of the earliest varieties.

Growing Perennials from Seed. Have you ever considered growing your own perennials from seed? This is a good time to begin. Delphiniums, columbines, gaillardias, coreopsis, Oriental poppies, and many others are dropping seeds.

It is fortunate that nature is so prodigal with seeds, because self-sown seeds usually fall in a small area close to the mother plants and on unprepared ground. Vast quantities are eaten by birds or, if they do sprout, die from overcrowding. They are often weeded out because amateur gardeners do not recognize them as flowers at this stage. A few self-sown seeds do manage to grow up into respectable perennial plants, but it is still best to remove and discard the ripening seed pods on your perennials. The seeds seldom run true in color and form to the parent plant and are more likely to resemble some nondescript ancestor.

Instead, go to your garden dealer and buy seeds of the best and latest perennial varieties. They are the recent developments of the world's foremost plant breeders. Some home gardeners sow new seed of the same kind of perennial under the shade of its leaves — every summer about this time — thus keeping the general arrangement of the border about the same but with much improved varieties. If the seedlings come up crowded, you can transplant some to other places. Don't disturb the seedlings farthest from the old plants.

A more conventional way to raise perennial seedlings in midsummer is to make a loamy bed, perhaps three by six feet, enclosed on four sides with six-inch boards. Your hotbed or cold frame would be fine for this purpose. To protect the seedbed from the hot sun and heavy rains of our northern summers, you should have a lath canopy over the bed with one-half-inch spaces between the laths. This lowers the soil temperature beneath, but admits plenty of light. The bed is thus under the complete control of the gardener. Topsoil should be filled in to raise the level of the bed several inches above the surrounding ground surface. The bed should slope slightly for drainage, and the lath canopy should be made to fit the frame.

Sow the perennial seeds in rows and label each row. Cover the seeds lightly with porous soil, peatmoss, or sand, never with clay soil. Until the seeds sprout, the surface should be kept moist.

Listed below are perennials which grow from seed sown in the summer and which will bloom either this fall or next summer. The number of days it takes these seeds to germinate is also given. Anchusa 10, achillea 10, anthemis (golden marguerite) 5, boltonia 5, campanula 5, carnation 5, columbine 5, coreopsis 5, Shasta daisy 5, delphinium 20, dianthus 5, foxglove 10, hibiscus 15, hollyhock 5, hesperis (sweet rocket) 10, gaillardia 20, linum (flax) 8, lupine 8, lychnis 10, physalis (Chinese lantern) 15, primula (primrose) 15, salvia 15, pyrethrum (painted daisy) 20, stokesia 20, trollius 50, and veronica 15.

When seedling plants have grown large enough to handle, transplant them from the seedbed to a "nursery" row in the annual bed where they can have more room and grow until time to set them in the garden border. Most varieties will be well grown by fall and can then be placed in their permanent homes. If they are moved well before October 1 and given considerable space and protection over the first winter, a number will become established and flower next year as full-grown plants.

GARDEN BOOKS

For lazy August days hammock reading is a perfect pastime, but if you want to read for profit as well as fun, try a good book or magazine about gardening. The true gardener finds as much excitement in reading about his hobby as in reading a whodunit. He knows there is always more to learn about growing the flowers he loves, and he is always eager to learn new ideas and new methods.

For up-to-date news about your favorite flowers, the journals published by organizations specializing in them are probably the best source.

GRANDMA, who was over eighty, always considered folks who had weeds growing around their houses "mighty shiftless." If a neighbor neglected his cutting, Grandma would take her sickle and go forth like a valiant soldier and cut the weeds herself. This seldom happened more than once to the same person. Sometimes a crowd would gather and cheer her on. There was a slogan in the village, "You had better cut your weeds or Grandma will do it for you." The whole village loved her in spite of her presumptuousness.

There are quarterly bulletins, for example, each devoted to news about one flower. The American Dahlia Society, 12 Warren Street, New York 7, publishes a bulletin for $3.50 a year. The American Iris Society, 417 Commerce Street, Nashville 10, Tennessee, publishes an iris bulletin for $3.50 a year; and the American Peony Society, Rapidan, Virginia, charges $5.00 a year for its bulletin. The *Hemerocallis Journal* is published quarterly, the price $2.50 annually, and the address is 7714 Fairfield Road North, Minneapolis 12, Minnesota.

The *Begonian* is a monthly magazine published by the American Begonia Society, Box 2544, Los Angeles 54, California. A subscription is $2.50 a year.

For general monthly gardening information, *Popular Gardening*, published by Gardening Publications, Inc., 90 State Street, Albany, New York, is good. The price is $3.00 a year.

And if your special interest is in trees, the National Arborist Association, Box 5607, Cleveland 1, Ohio, publishes the bimonthly magazine *Trees*, price $2.00 a year.

Of course there are books you can order from your bookstore or get from your librarian on virtually every garden problem you might encounter. For a good general treatment, try *The Gardener's Troubleshooter*, by Victor H. Reis, Ohio State University horticulturist, priced at $3.50. *Insects*, by Alfred Stefferud and obtainable for $2.50 from the Superintendent of Documents, Washington, D.C., is excellent, as is *Plant Diseases*, the 1954 Department of Agriculture yearbook, also by Alfred Stefferud and obtainable from the Superintendent of Documents for $2.50.

Another useful book is *How to Make Cut Flowers Last*, by Victoria R. Kasperski. Priced at $2.95, it tells how to cut, keep, water, press, force, dry, and even color flowers, and how to prepare and arrange flowers and foliage for decoration.

And no gardener should forget that his hobby has a glorious tradition and an interesting history. Most large libraries have old gardening books that will certainly charm you and may even offer you a hint that modern books have neglected. And you can read books by the great horticulturists of our country — try Liberty Hyde Bailey's *The Garden Lover*. Books by experimenters and innovators are fascinating, even if you can put their ideas to no practical use. Louis Bromfield's accounts of his life at Malabar Farm you will find entertaining as well as valuable.

LAST CALL TO FIGHT CRABGRASS

If August has been hot and dry, conditions were ideal for crabgrass. Even if you took all the measures we suggested against the weed during spring and early summer, you may have some mature crabgrass plants still flourishing in your lawn. Sometimes lawns that showed no signs of crabgrass in July suddenly blossom out with the pest in August. This means there must have been some seeds or small plants lying in wait deep in the turf.

Sometimes these late-sprouting clumps of crabgrass are as large as a dinner plate, often made up of just one plant or a tangled mass

191

of several plants. Usually they have scores of seed-bearing stems that will soon be scattering thousands of ripened seeds. For this condition I have found that by wetting down the lawn the day before, you can, with the aid of a putty or paring knife, remove the entire clump, usually in one piece.

This leaves a shallow hole, but you can fill it up with enriched earth and sow with a first-class grass seed mixture — not over a level teaspoonful for a 10-inch square space. Be sure to cover the seed with half an inch of fine soil or birds will get it. A light layer of loamy litter or peatmoss will help keep the soil cool and moist until the seeds sprout and are on their own. Another way to fill in the holes is to fit in pieces of sod cut to size. These soon will blend with the rest of the lawn.

If your lawn is heavily infested with crabgrass you may be able to alleviate the condition with another round of chemical warfare, unless the seeds are about to drop. In this event you had better use the mechanical method of control with the lawnmower and catch basket for the clippings. Wash the mower in the street to remove all crabgrass seeds that might otherwise be carried to parts of the lawn.

Do not expect your lawn to be free of crabgrass next summer if the infestation now is severe. It may take two or three years, but if you don't fight crabgrass your lawn will be ruined completely.

GRANDMA used to "fool" the very late-blooming chrysanthemums to make them bloom earlier to avoid frost. Beginning in August, thin black cloth was placed on frames on the two long sides of the mum beds and was kept draped over them for three or four hours after sunrise and the last three hours before sunset. Uncle Jerry said it made the mums think the days were getting shorter and winter would soon be here, so they hurried and blossomed weeks sooner. At the time I thought Uncle was fooling. But it worked, and the method is practiced by some gardeners today.

Crabgrass spreads frightfully fast. You can always count on one dependable ally, however — the sparrow. Sparrows will work for hours in your behalf, picking up the exposed crabgrass seed after it has ripened. They spread little if any seed in the process, for the seed the birds eat is practically all digested.

If you finally conclude that crabgrass has got the upper hand and your lawn is hopeless, you had better spade it all up and start a new lawn this fall. Do not begin spading it until you have scraped off at least the top inch of soil, however. If you don't do this, you may bury millions of crabgrass seeds that will be coming up for years to pester you. Fall is the best time to start or rebuild a lawn in any case, as permanent grass will sprout in the fall (crabgrass will not) and makes its best growth in the cool autumn nights. Next month we will talk more about rejuvenation for lawns that have had a hard summer.

REMINDERS

Don't feed rose plants from now on. Fertilizing after mid-August might start new growth that would not harden thoroughly before winter. Winter-killing of this growth would weaken the whole bush. Continue to dust or spray your roses against black spot, mites, and other troubles. Mulch the beds during hot August and September weather or cultivate more often and irrigate the ground surface. Don't sprinkle rose foliage.

Continue to pinch excess buds off your dahlias. Break off the two side buds in each cluster of three, leaving the center bud to bloom. Only one terminal bud should be left on each branch if you want large, perfect flowers on long stems. Go over the plants about once a week during the entire growing season.

Save all raked-up grass clippings — except crabgrass, of course — for mulching or for the compost pile. Vegetable trimmings such as cabbage leaves and carrot tops should also be composted, along with seed-free weeds, discarded cut flowers, and old leaves.

Three-foot by five-inch strips of galvanized iron, corrugated for strength, are very useful for edging flower beds, lawns, paths, or driveways. You can buy them at your garden dealer's. When thrust into the ground, flush with the surface, they will prevent vegetation like lilies of the valley and lawn grass from growing out of bounds.

If late summer storms have left a tree stump in your yard, saw it off level with the ground, drill a circle of holes four inches deep around the outer edge and fill with a strong solution of ammonium sulfamate or Ammate. This treatment is almost sure death to tree stumps and roots. It prevents them from sprouting in the lawn. Keep the solution off other vegetation.

GRANDMA *would not allow stagnant water to stand anywhere around the farm, because she knew it encouraged mosquitoes. If it could not be drained, it was treated with kerosene (Grandma called it coal oil). This was at least fifty years before this preventive was generally known, but Grandma had noticed that when the* barrels kerosene came in were used to catch rainwater under the eaves, mosquito larvae would not develop there.

One successful amateur grower of gloxinias keeps his gloxinias growing in flowerpots into September to store up food for next season, even after they have ceased blooming. Then he cuts off the tops, leaving the tubers in the pots, and stores them in a cool basement. He does not water during this dormant period. The next winter he repots them in fresh soil when the tubers show signs of life.

Mow your lawn high, at least two and a half inches, during August's hot dry weather. The grass will stay greener and healthier. Pale green lawns usually need nitrogen. Use a balanced fertilizer and keep your lawn moist to a depth of six inches.

With luck and a late fall, a sowing of annual baby's breath, poppies, mignonette, and Klondike cosmos seed will brighten your garden even after snowfall. Sow fresh new seed around delphiniums, hollyhocks, Oriental poppies, and other perennials for possible new plants next summer. Continue to clip off all dead flowers and seed pods from both annuals and perennials to encourage prolonged bloom. Delphiniums may bloom again if the stalks are cut to twelve inches; phlox, veronica, many campanulas, and lythrum will bloom repeatedly if kept from going to seed.

August is a good time to divide or transplant iris, peonies, and those plants that bloom in early summer and then go dormant — bleeding heart, Oriental poppy, and mertensia. The foliage of the last three withers and disappears in late summer. Mark their location with stakes before they vanish if you intend to move them.

Don't forget to dust both perennials and annuals every two weeks or oftener with an all-purpose garden dust. Zinnias and phlox need special attention to prevent mildew or foliage molds. If your phlox continue to have foliage blight after several dustings, remove all diseased stalks and dead leaves and plan to transplant in September or next spring to allow more ventilation between the clumps.

Never let your lawn or garden get bone dry. Water is life to flowers, grass, and trees. Try to keep the perennial border and annual beds adequately moist by thorough soakings whenever needed. Don't sprinkle; water the roots, not the foliage.

✠ SEPTEMBER ✠

Summer is fading and autumn is invading our gardens with her warm golden smile. In most of the North, September is the last full month for outdoor gardening. Warm weather and patches of brilliant color linger in the garden, but the days are noticeably shorter and the nights are chilly. Phlox, delphiniums, and petunias are now in their second — or is it their third? — blooming. Zinnias and marigolds still blossom lustily, as do many other annuals and perennials that have been faithfully watered and cut back to encourage new flowers.

Dahlias, scarlet salvia, hardy asters, and the earliest chrysanthemums make bright splashes in the border, while the last of the veronicas and campanulas add their blue and lavender tones. Killing frost will probably strike before the month is over, especially in our most northerly areas and away from the cities; but the northern gardener is alert to frost warnings, and if he can protect his flowers for a few chilly nights, they will go on blooming for several more weeks of our beautiful Indian summer.

SEPTEMBER GARDEN CHORES

In the wild flower garden black-eyed Susans, goldenrod, and the first of the Michaelmas daisies are vying with each other for attention. Under the tangle of browning leaves, where jack-in-the-pulpits ruled, are bunches of bright scarlet berries as large as cranberries. Plant these berries about an inch deep, and in a year or two you will have a whole colony of jack-in-the-pulpits. Plant the black bulbils from your tiger lilies, too.

196

This is a good time to divide some of your perennials. Many are still in bloom, or enough bloom is left so you can identify their color. This will help you to rearrange them to good advantage. Do this work soon so the roots will be well established before winter sets in. Also watch for some open areas for planting your spring-blooming bulbs in a few weeks. Move perennials that bloom in late fall — such as hardy asters and monkshood — only in the spring.

Here is a list of some of the better-known perennials with information on how often they may be divided (of course, this is somewhat governed by their size and vigor): columbine, three to four years; hardy aster, one to three years; boltonia, three years; lily of the valley, four to five years; coreopsis, two years; Shasta daisy, two years; delphinium, three to four years; helenium, three years; daylily, three years; phlox, three years; plantain lily, three to four years; iris, three to four years; peony, five to ten years; gaillardia, two to four years.

It is a good idea to label the plants you move or divide. There is considerable satisfaction and convenience in having your flowers properly identified, especially perennials. Perhaps you have several varieties of phlox in different heights and colors. If tagged or labeled when you are dividing or transplanting your clumps, they can be identified immediately. Labels to thrust in the ground cost about one cent each and an indelible ink pen with large ball, made especially for this work, about forty cents. These are obtainable in garden stores and are well worth their small cost and the little time it takes to use them.

September is also an excellent time to check the spread of weeds in the garden. Every one you get rid of now, before it scatters its seeds, will mean fewer weeds to fight next spring and summer. Get this done before autumn rains bury the seed. In the rows of the annual bed and in wide open spaces between flower clumps, a hoe can be used. Hand weeding will be necessary to pull out weeds growing close to plants and flowers. These are the most troublesome because they drop their seeds among the flower stalks. Next spring these weeds will be difficult to pull out. But every year weeds will become fewer if you do a thorough job of weeding

197

SEPTEMBER

whenever they do appear. After all visible weeds are removed, don't cultivate for a couple of weeks. This will allow birds and squirrels to eat most of the weed seeds remaining on the garden surface.

When the borders are free of weeds and the birds have cleaned up dropped weed seeds, give the loosened soil a good feeding of balanced plant food — a heaping tablespoonful around each plant — or a dressing of dried or rotted sheep or cow manure. All fertilizer and plant food should be lightly worked into the soil. Next season your plants will repay you in more and richer-colored blossoms. However, do not feed roses again this year or you will force a soft growth that will not harden in time to withstand winter.

GRANDMA told me and showed me where bees found shelter from a sudden cold fall rain when they were caught a long way from their hive. The bees would climb up into the hooded blossoms of the monkshood, a perennial garden flower and herb. If the storm lasted into the night the bees would remain protected there until morning.

In September most northern rose beds reach another period of heavy bloom if they have not been allowed to become dry. To have strong healthy roses during the heat of late summer, water is vitally important, and in most parts of the North it is risky to rely entirely on natural rainfall. Deep watering to reach well down to the roots should be repeated at least every ten days. A loose mulch, such as peatmoss, buckwheat hulls, or ground corncobs, helps to preserve moisture and to insulate the beds against the searing heat of late summer.

Pinching back or removing the small side buds that develop on the hybrid tea varieties will help to keep up continuous production of blooms even through the "dog days." Prompt removal of spent

198

flowers also helps to keep blossoming at a high level. Good north-ern-grown roses are capable of producing flowers from May into November. With intelligent handling and attention a rose garden should have color and charm without a break throughout the whole summer and up until frost.

Spraying or dusting to control fungus diseases and insects should continue during September, both for roses and the perennial bor-ders. The regular all-purpose dusting program will control black spot and mildew, the main fungus diseases, and the major insect pests, such as aphids, red spider, thrips, and rose bugs. Sprays or dusts should be applied at ten-day intervals, preferably in the early morning or late afternoon. During wet spells the frequency should be increased, as black spot and mildew increase rapidly in these periods. Remember that the spray or dust must cover the underside of the leaves as well as the top. Chores in the rose and perennial gardens are neither difficult nor time-consuming, but they do require regular attention.

This is the time of year too when annuals like asters, petunias, marigolds, and zinnias have grown tall and possibly top-heavy and inclined to flop over. Remedy this by buying a bundle of wooden support wands, one to three feet long, and a package of "quick-twist" pliable metal strips. In half an hour you can spruce up your whole garden.

Nature is dropping seeds from annuals and some perennials, and you might experiment by doing the same. Many annuals produce stronger plants when the seed is planted in the fall where the plants are to bloom. This is true of poppies, bachelor's buttons, larkspur, balsam, cosmos, cleome, nicotiana, single petunias, gaillardia, and coreopsis. Not all these fall-sown seeds will germinate next spring, but even if only a few come through, it is worth a trial in hopes of getting earlier flowers.

Your window boxes full of summer annuals will need attention in September. Give the straggly growers a haircut and they may continue blooming until frost. Most petunias when trimmed down to four inches will put forth new shoots and give another prolific display of bloom in the autumn months. Better yet, clear out the faded summer annuals from the window boxes, rock garden, and border edgings and fill these places with medium-sized chrysanthemum plants about to bloom. Your home will be festive with color until the snow comes. The medium-sized mum plants can be obtained at your local nursery in September already in bloom or almost ready.

If any of your chrysanthemums, either the tall ones in the border or the smaller ones in window boxes, are afflicted with aphids on leaves, blossoms, or buds, a spraying of Black Leaf 40 (nicotine sulphate) will usually rout the pests. Follow directions on the container for proper dilutions. Several weak sprayings are preferable to one strong one that might discolor or burn. Black Leaf 40 in the same strength as for spraying can be poured on the ground near your annual asters to prevent blight or "witch's broom" and to rout insects attacking their roots. Make a little hole about an inch from the stem and pour in about two ounces of the solution.

September is a good time to make cuttings of geraniums and other plants that you want to have in your winter window garden, or to use in your outdoor garden next spring. It is better to take slips from the geranium plants than to try to carry the old plants through the winter. After frost, however, the roots of the old plants may be dug and stored in the basement in shallow fruit crates on the floor — not hung from the rafters.

PRUNE SHRUBS NOW

Now is a good time to prune all dead wood on shrubs, hedges, and trees. Don't put off this kind of pruning until spring. In the early spring all wood looks about the same, but now, with foliage still green, you can spot every dead branch. In fact, many horticulturists advise summer pruning as a regular practice instead of pruning in early spring. Corrective pruning produces better, sturdier growth as well as more and larger blooms. It also gives the plant a better shape and keeps it healthier. Pruning should begin the second year after you have planted your shrubs.

Caragaras, bridalwreath, honeysuckle, mockorange, flowering currant, lilac, viburnum, weigela, and potentilla should be pruned now along with other early-flowering shrubbery that blooms on old wood. Remove about one third of the oldest, biggest stems at the ground level. All other canes that tend to give the bush a poor appearance should be pruned back to a strong side branch. Always avoid an unnatural, sheared appearance.

GRANDMA had no commercial fungicide for mushrooms in her lawn. When she was making soft soap for family washings, she used to pour a cupful of the lye water over the fungi, and they disappeared overnight. In a few days, Uncle Jerry would cut out the dead spot and put in a plug of green sod. It was as simple as that.

In pruning or trimming spring-flowering hedges and shrubs, you should remember that the nuclei of next year's blossoms already are set for next spring. Be careful to remove only the branches that you now can see are leafless and dead. In the future, trim soon after the blossoms have fallen in the spring.

Rambler roses and some climbers should also be pruned just after they are through blooming. Since they bloom only on year-old canes, all canes should be removed as soon as the flowers have faded. The current year's young canes, growing from the base, should be protected and trained to the trellis, since they will produce next year's blooms. On large-flowered climbers, remove several of the oldest, largest canes, cutting them off at the base of the plant. However, leave some of the older canes, removing only the side shoots that have flowered on these canes.

Prune out all sucker growth from the base of flowering plums, flowering almonds, and Cistena sand cherries. The roots are frequently more vigorous than the tops on these grafted shrubs, and suckering results. These suckers will tend to crowd out the original shrub and the plant will grow to resemble a wild plum. Shrubs grown for twig color, like the dogwood, also should be pruned now.

SEPTEMBER

Remove some of the old wood to the soil level. The new shoots have brighter colors than the old ones.

ORDER YOUR SPRING-BLOOMING BULBS

Tulips and other spring-blooming bulbs are not planted until October in most northern gardens, but September is the time to buy them in order to have the best selection. Bulbs may be ordered by mail from nursery catalogs or purchased from your local nursery or garden seed dealer. Wherever you buy them, avoid bargain lots and cut-price collections. Top quality bulbs are well worth their extra cost. Large, fully developed tulip bulbs usually blossom for several years. For good blossoms next spring, tulip bulbs should be not less than 4½ inches in circumference.

If possible, plan and prepare your spring bulb plantings a little distance from the house, so that your display can be seen from your windows, and where passers-by and neighbors can enjoy its beauty. The minor bulbs — crocuses, daffodils, scilla, and the like — should be planted earlier than tulips, even as early as September, but tulips must wait for colder weather or there is danger they may sprout this fall and be damaged.

All these minor bulbs will flourish and bloom for years to come. They may be planted in sun or dappled shade under trees or at the base of shrubbery. They are beautiful in informal groupings almost anywhere in the garden, but particularly along a walk or in a rock garden.

GRANDMA did not have the gorgeous garden chrysanthemums we have today. But what she did have she brought into beautiful bloom. She watered them when the buds were forming and until they blossomed with a weak solution — she called it garden tea — of one pound of dry cow or sheep manure dissolved in a large pail of warm water. Try it; your mums will flourish.

Then there are the larger bulbs, which are also planted a little before tulips. These include the stately hyacinths, unsurpassed for fragrance, perfection of form, and vivid colors. And narcissuses, daffodils, or jonquils — the names are often used interchangeably — are always spring favorites, with their graceful form and cheerful colors. By planting different varieties you can have them in the garden from the time the crocuses finish until early May. With many handsome varieties to choose from, it is little wonder many northern gardeners make daffodils their special hobby. There are giant trumpets, medium crowns, small cups, jonquils, poet's narcissus with its scarlet frills, and many others.

Bulbs of most of the hardy lilies that grow in the North should also be planted in the fall. This includes the Madonna lily, perhaps the most beautiful lily of all, with its tall stems bearing clusters of six to twelve huge, fragrant blossoms. Most lily bulbs are not available in the garden stores until rather late in the fall, however, so their beds must usually be prepared in advance and covered to prevent the earth from freezing until the bulbs arrive. In some areas, many lily bulbs are not available for planting until spring. In such cases, they should be planted just as early as possible. Preparing the ground this fall will help to get them started quickly.

There are many different kinds and colors of tulips to provide a rainbow garden next May. The earliest varieties, called botanical tulips, are somewhat smaller than common tulips and have shorter stems. The flowers have pointed petals. Their range of colors is making them increasingly popular. The three most popular varieties are Fosteriana, a brilliant scarlet red; Kaufmanniana hybrids, usually pink and white; and Praestans, a flaming orange scarlet. Any of these may produce a startling variation, but it is almost sure to be as beautiful as its parent stock.

The next tulips to bloom are the old reliables — Earlies, Darwins, Breeders, and Cottage tulips — which bloom in the order listed, although with some overlapping. Earlies, as the name indicates, are early bloomers, usually following or overlapping the botanicals. They come in both double and single blooms in bright, clear red, pink, yellow and orange shades on sturdy ten- to fifteen-inch stems.

Then follow the Darwins, probably the favorite among tulips, with their soft pastel blooms on stems twenty-four to thirty-two inches long. Although some are quite brilliant in color, beautiful yellows and clear whites have been developed recently. The Darwins and the Breeders bloom about the same time and have many characteristics in common, although the Breeders come in colors not found in any other kind. Their rich and unusual bi-color blendings of purple and gold, bronze and terracotta, brown and violet, buff and maroon are most attractive. Their enormous, graceful, showy blooms, many of them sweet-scented, are splendid for cutting and should be included in every garden.

Cottage tulips are not so tall or large as the Darwins and Breeders, but they are rich in the more delicate shades of orange, fawn, salmon, and old rose which are largely missing in other late varieties. Among the novelties is a black Darwin that is a dandy, and there also is a "feathered" tulip with beautiful wavy coloring on the petals. The peculiar Parrot, with bizarre, feathered blossoms in several colors, is still a favorite.

If you buy your bulbs before you are ready to plant, store them in a cool, dry place. Keep the tops of the bags open and punch a few holes in the sides for ventilation. It is a good idea to dust the bulbs with DDT powder mixed with a fungicide a few days before planting.

A GARDEN OF SMELLS

When you are planning your next year's garden, think of rearranging some of it to increase your pleasure in its fragrance. Sometimes we forget the importance of the sense of smell to life. But remember the associations you have with the smells of spring in the woods, of mint growing in a damp spot, or of thorn apples. Our ancestors were perhaps more aware of the powers of plant odors: physicians advised inhaling the perfumes of certain herbs for disease (and all their theories have not been proved wrong), ladies perfumed their wearing apparel with lavender, and the

American colonists carried to church with them nosegays of stimulating herbs to help them through the interminable sermons.

You might plan your "fragrance garden" by including in it every flower whose odor remains pleasantly in your memory. And plant them where you can smell them! Think of the pleasure to be got from the odor of nicotiana planted under the living room windows where the tired worker can enjoy its lovely night odor. And under the windows of the dining room, plant flowers with odors less sweet, for there are many flower perfumes that do not go well with the smell and taste of bacon and eggs.

GRANDMA had a tree in her orchard that bore freak apples. The upper half of the fruit was a bright yellow and tasted sweet, while the lower half was rosy red and tasted like a very tart crab apple. Today horticulturists call these apples chimeras. They result from the fruit's taking on characteristics of both stock and cion in grafting. They are not considered desirable. But this apple tree of Grandma's was quite a curiosity and folks came from miles around to see and taste the apples every autumn. Uncle Jerry always exhibited a plateful at the county fair, but never won a prize until he donated five dollars for first prize in a special class for the most curious exhibit of fruit. Then he won his own money for years. He sold cuttings from the tree for two dollars each.

A useful and fragrant addition to your yard — and one that would occupy very little space — is an herb garden. Begin with parsley and chives and mint, but go on from there to other herbs that will bring delight to your nose and new pleasure to your table. Plant sweet basil, summer savory, sage, rosemary, chervil, tarragon, lemon balm, fennel, and thyme. Experiment with growing and using these herbs and be reminded of the long, long tradition that goes back into the days before atoms and DDT to the time of stranger magic.

SEPTEMBER

There are many plants whose odors we never notice — because they are too far beneath our noses. This is true of many rock-garden plants, so build up the height of part of your rock garden and plant there thyme and lavender, rockcress and wallflowers.

REBUILDING YOUR LAWN

September is a good time to look over your lawn and do some rebuilding and seeding if necessary. The same general rules and methods we discussed in March and April apply in the fall as well. Most garden experts believe autumn is the best time to sow grass seed — even better than spring. The long, cool, dewy nights and the autumn rains, combined with the warm days, cause the seed to germinate rapidly and the seedlings to make deep roots before the ground freezes.

New grass also gets a good start at this season because most weeds have sprouted and been cultivated out. Usually the leaves have fallen from the trees before the grass becomes dormant. This is important because the newly sprouted grass gets valuable sunshine and makes deep roots in areas which are shaded heavily during spring and summer months. To guard against smothering the new grass blades, it is imperative that all fallen leaves be raked off freshly seeded new lawns every few days, as well as off old lawns.

If your lawn has been badly infested with crabgrass, however, there are probably many seeds on the surface of the soil that will sprout later if they are buried. Mow such lawns short, rake and burn the clippings, and allow a week or two for sparrows to eat as much crab seed as possible. Only then should the area be top-

GRANDMA was always disturbed when she saw bulbs blooming in straight rows. To naturalize her plantings, she filled her hands with bulbs, closed her eyes, and tossed them. Where they landed she would plant them. There was nothing diagrammatic about her bulb garden. It was natural and beautiful.

dressed and reseeded, or dug up entirely for replanting. Even so, buried crabgrass seed will no doubt keep sprouting for several years; but if in the future you mow your new grass high, fertilize well to encourage thick growth, and battle the crabgrass with every method we have discussed, you can build a really beautiful lawn.

Lawns that have a fair stand of grass but are uneven with small depressions should be raked thoroughly and the low places filled with good topsoil. Then the lawn should have a feeding of plant food at the rate prescribed on the container. Firm the filled or spaded areas with a roller, then fill in depressions made by the roller and roll in the opposite direction. Water the conditioned areas thoroughly for several days before seeding to help dissolve the plant food and to make a deep moist bed for the seed.

In most parts of the North, the best and most suitable perennial lawn grasses are Kentucky bluegrass and Merion bluegrass, bentgrass, and creeping red fescue. To these may be added white clover, although it is not considered entirely desirable because it stains more than other grasses. It does, however, add nitrogen to the soil, doesn't brown off in hot weather, and can be a salvation where the soil is sandy.

Kentucky bluegrass does not like too much heat, shade, and acid soil, although one member of the family, roughstalk bluegrass — look for it on the seed bag as "poa trivilis" — does quite nicely in shade. The two most popular fescues, red and Chewings, tolerate shade and dry soil and will take some acidity. Creeping bent grows thick and beautiful, but requires frequent mowing and persistent care. Colonial bent may be a wiser choice. Both of these bentgrasses are tolerant of shade and acidity, but need a lot of care and watering for their shallow roots. Bentgrasses are also more subject to winter-killing than the bluegrasses or fescues.

If you are seeding a brand-new lawn this fall, follow the procedures I outlined in April. If you want to spruce up an old lawn that is in fairly good condition, mow the grass short, then rake briskly to remove clippings and dead grass and to loosen the hardened soil. If the earth is very hard-packed, get from your garden dealer a foot-operated tool for aerating hard lawns.

SEPTEMBER

After raking, apply evenly a balanced commercial plant food at the rate of about thirty pounds to each thousand square feet, followed by a good soaking to dissolve the food and wash it into the ground. When the lawn is fairly dry, usually the next day, seed with a good grass mixture. After seeding, apply a light dressing of good garden soil, then water with a fine spray until the ground is soaked. The lawn must not be allowed to dry out for at least two weeks, or until the new grass is a half inch tall.

A light dressing of pulverized peat may be used instead of topsoil to cover the new seed. Several light applications of this peat over the course of a year or two will build up a springy moisture-retaining turf. Make the dressing light, however, or you may smother the grass. Spread it so sparingly that it will disappear among the grass blades overnight. Rub it in with the back of the rake. This peat is excellent also for digging in around your perennials to lighten the soil.

The grass must be kept mowed so the new grass will not be smothered. Set the stationary blade of your mower to cut at about two inches and keep the fallen leaves raked off.

SHRUBS AND EVERGREENS CAN BE PLANTED NOW

Although spring is the preferred planting time for trees and shrubs in the North, a number of varieties can also be planted successfully in September and October. The sooner planting is done the better, however, in order that the shrubs and trees may become well established before winter sets in.

A new evergreen or some flowering shrubs can add much beauty to your house, be it new or old. Walk across the street and study your house and yard from a little distance. You will almost certainly see room for improvement in landscaping. With this mental picture, visit your local nurseries and outdoor garden shops to find what you need. In many nurseries you can pick out the tree or shrub you desire actually growing in the rows or groves. The nurseryman will ball and burlap the tree while you wait, load it into the back of your car, and supply you with planting instructions. You can have it planted in your yard before sundown. If you need a number of trees, the nursery will furnish a landscaping plan and — if you don't mind the extra cost — do the planting.

There is now a variety of blue and silver spruce hardier than the expensive De Kosta blue spruce formerly imported from Germany, and just as beautiful. There is also a magnificent hardy evergreen bred from the Black Hills spruce that is suitable for groups and border plantings for medium-size yards. Arborvitae and juniper, grayish green to silver blue, also are suitable in borders and groups and can be planted fairly close to the house.

GRANDMA was making grape jelly one autumn and she told Uncle Jerry to throw out in the field, a long way from the house, a large pail of discarded grape skins and seeds. Uncle was "tired," so he put the pail behind the barn for later disposition, and then forgot it. The discarded fruit fermented, the geese and ducks ate it and became, well, just plain drunk. They hilariously hissed and quacked at each other, and then promptly went to sleep. Uncle thought it was a big joke. Grandma was indignant, and Granddad just smiled quietly — he always played safe.

Then there are the low-growing or spreading Pfitzer and Savin juniper and the Mugho pine, usually used for foundation planting. They also are excellent for a low approach to higher evergreens in corner borders and for semi-formal plantings.

FROST PROTECTION FOR YOUR GARDEN

After mid-September, frost may strike at any time in most parts of the North. In the Minneapolis–St. Paul region, we may escape a killing freeze until well into October, but you never can tell. It is always wise to be prepared to cover your flowers on a moment's notice. If we can just protect our gardens during the first few frosty nights, we may be able to keep many flowers blooming in all their autumn beauty for weeks to come, sometimes into November.

SEPTEMBER

Warm weather usually follows the first severe frosts in most areas of the North, bringing our glorious Indian summer.

Frosts tend to be unpredictable and spotty in the way they strike. They may leave your garden unharmed and freeze your neighbor's garden just a block away. Of course, there are reasons for this variance. Your garden may be more sheltered, whereas your neighbor's garden may be on lower ground. Cold currents of air descend and collect at low levels, but if there is a river or lake in the low place, nearby vegetation is relatively safe since the water rapidly absorbs the cold. City gardens generally escape frost longer than those in the suburbs and country, since nearby buildings tend to conserve the sun's heat and keep night temperatures a little higher.

GRANDMA would conduct her grandchildren to where the poisonous sumac grew — mostly in damp places — and show them how its greenish, white fruit hung down in clusters in a slinky manner. Then she would show us the staghorn or harmless sumac, which resembles its evil cousin, pointing out that it usually grew on higher ground, and how it held its plume of brown berries proudly erect. This is the sumac that should be gathered for home decoration.

A "killing frost" prediction does not necessarily mean all vegetation will be killed. It is a warning that vegetation will be frozen somewhere in the area indicated. But sometimes when there has been no frost warning, a sudden change in local weather conditions will be accompanied by frost. The familiar white hoarfrost seldom does much damage except in low or exposed gardens. But if the day has been cloudy or stormy with a northerly wind, and at sundown the weather becomes calm and clear and the thermometer is down to 40, you had better protect your garden.

Cover everything that is still blooming or will produce more flowers this season. Use sheets, newspapers, gunnysacks, hay, straw, flowerpots, cardboard boxes, or what-have-you. Metal covering is not advisable, however. The protective covering placed over vegetation acts as a tent and prevents the escape of much of the heat rising from the soil. The overhanging eaves of your house and trees in leaf also give protection. Smudges on a windless night will help because the smoke hangs over the garden and acts as a blanket. However, it is against the law to leave unprotected fires burning in cities.

One of the most important tasks when frost threatens is to bring indoors your amaryllis, Christmas cactus, and other tender house plants. If they have been left in their pots all summer, this move can be made on short notice. It is best if the change from outdoor to indoor life is made gradually, with several days on a covered porch or in an unheated room to allow the plants to adjust. Tuberous-rooted and fibrous-rooted begonias, patience plants, small geraniums, and many others, will go on blooming indoors for several weeks, or even through the entire winter in the case of everblooming begonias.

However, if frost should catch your elephant ears, dahlias, tuberous begonias, or other tubers before you get them moved, next year's growth will not be damaged. Some gardeners claim these tubers will keep all the better for having their tops slightly frozen. You can dig them up next month before the ground freezes and store them in the basement until spring.

GRANDMA would hustle out with Uncle Jerry when a killing frost threatened, and gather all the large tomatoes that were hanging on the vines. Each one would be wrapped carefully in a piece of newspaper and placed on a shelf in the cool cellar to ripen. Every week the tomatoes would be turned over. Almost all would ripen beautifully, and some years we would be eating fresh tomatoes in December. Grandma thought there was something in the printer's ink that prevented the fruit from decaying. Perhaps she was right; she usually was.

SEPTEMBER

Don't be in a hurry to dig up your gladioli. Leave them in the ground as long as possible without allowing the corms to be actually frozen. It will not harm them to have their tops frozen.

When a heavy frost threatens, dig up your large or old geraniums and four o'clocks, shake off the earth, cut off the tops, and store the roots in the coolest spot in your basement on a few boards or in a fruit crate, to keep them off the floor. Don't hang them from the rafters where it is likely to be warm. Next spring plant them outside again and you will have blossoms that are bigger and earlier than the smaller, first-year geranium or four o'clocks can produce.

GRANDMA believed, and so did a lot of other folks in her day, that a tablespoon of honey taken four times a day—before meals and at bedtime—would cure hay fever. Uncle Jerry was an enthusiastic supporter of the belief, but he insisted that the honey should be reinforced with a spoonful of whisky. Grandma was "agin" the idea, and she would hide the bottle of "spirits fermenti" —but not always successfully—during the hay fever season. She also objected to the way Uncle would smack his lips after taking his "medicine."

REMINDERS

Continue to care for your annual flowers. They may bloom through most of September and October. Water, dust, and trim them, and keep dead flowers cut. Do the same for perennial phlox, asters, chrysanthemums, and other perennials still in bloom.

There is still time this month to divide or transplant peonies, iris, Oriental poppies, and bleeding heart. Divide large bleeding-heart clumps into several plants, leaving part of the old plant without disturbance, if possible.

The tubers of mertensia, one of spring's loveliest bloomers, can also be divided now or purchased in some garden stores. Old lily of the valley beds are usually too crowded for good blooming. If this is true of yours, tear it up and replant about one tenth of the old pips.

Bone meal and wood ashes are fine peony fertilizers. Dig them in now, four inches away from and around each clump. Every few days inspect iris clumps for borers, rot, or sun scorch. Roses should not be fed again this year. New growth forced now may winter-kill and weaken the rosebushes.

Rake up acorns from your lawn. Although they seldom sprout, they may damage the grass. If stored in a cool place, they make good squirrel food during the winter.

If you are planning a new lawn for next summer, burn over the old one this fall when dry to kill weed seeds, then plow and leave it in the rough all winter. Don't burn tree leaves, however. Save them for your compost pile or dig them into the garden and along both sides of hedges.

Trim plants now that you intend to pot and move into the house later. Chrysanthemums, petunias, and many other annuals will continue blooming for weeks in pots indoors. Scrub flowerpots with soapy water, rinse with hot water, and dry in the sun to sterilize.

Mix several pails of potting mixture for winter use — one part each garden soil, clean sharp sand, loamy compost, and one quart sheep or cow manure to each bushel of mixture.

Forget-me-not and poppy seeds scattered over beds or rows of resting tulips will be beautiful next spring after the tulip blossoms.

The smaller spring-blooming bulbs, including snowdrops, grape hyacinths, crocuses, and scillas, can be planted any time after the soil is cool. Daffodils should be planted somewhat later, several weeks before the tulips. Madonna lily bulbs can also be planted any time now, three inches deep, preferably in rather sandy soil.

❧ OCTOBER ❧

Wɪᴛʜ October's bright blue weather, the beautiful northern autumn reaches its prime. Trees are ablaze in their October dress of gold, red, and maroon, and bright-colored fruits and berries ornament the shrubbery and delight the birds. Flower gardens that were kept moist during September and protected from early frosts are still beautiful. The tall blue monkshood and many late asters bloom this month, and other perennials have their second period of bloom. Roses have made an autumn come back and the later chrysanthemums are rapidly coming into blossom.

Chrysanthemums are used in fall plantings for the perennial garden, as low hedge borders, and in window boxes, replacing the exhausted summer annuals. Their high resistance to frost permits a careful gardener in the North to have flowers into November.

Chrysanthemums can still be bought this month from local nurseries, covered with blossoms and buds and ready to plant in gardens and window boxes. Practically all late autumn crysanthemums will winter well in the garden with some protection. They also do well over the winter if planted and protected in a cold frame. We will discuss the methods of winter protection in more detail next month. Meanwhile, if a very severe frost is predicted, mum plants about to bloom can be transplanted into pots and will complete their blossoming in your home with hardly a faded leaf or blossom.

TIME TO PLANT SPRING-BLOOMING BULBS

October is the ideal month to plant tulips, hyacinths, and the lesser spring bulbs, including grape hyacinths, scilla, and glory-of-the-snow (chionodoxa). Planting now will allow plenty of time for the bulbs to make good root growth before freeze-up and thus prevent frost-heaving in case of alternate freezing and thawing spells during the coming winter.

The same methods of soil preparation should be used for all these bulbs. If your garden soil is heavy, spread over the surface before spading two or three inches of compost, well-rotted cow or sheep manure, or peat. Add two to four pounds of balanced commercial plant fertilizer per 100 square feet.

In planting these bulbs, dig the hole or trench in the prepared soil a little deeper than the depth at which you intend to plant the bulbs. Then place sand or unfertilized soil in the bottom. Put in the bulbs and surround them with clean, unfertilized earth. Never allow manure or fertilizer to come in contact with the bulbs. It may rot them.

Mound the earth over the planted bulbs two or three inches above the surface of the ground. This will prevent a depression from forming when the soil settles, where water and ice might collect. When the ground is frozen solid, cover the areas where the bulbs are planted with five or six inches of leaves. This will keep the ground frozen in early spring and prevent premature sprouting. If squirrels attempt to dig up your bulbs before the ground freezes, lay old mosquito screening or small-mesh chicken netting over the planted bulbs to keep them off.

The minor bulbs, narcissuses and daffodils, and lilies should be planted earlier than the tulips. Late September through mid-October, or whenever the soil is thoroughly cool, is the best planting time for these.

Snowdrops are usually the first to appear in spring and are often found blossoming in the snow. There are single and double varieties. Plant them near evergreen foundation plantings or anywhere they are not likely to be disturbed for years.

Plant the common Dutch garden crocuses in their various shades of yellow, purple, and white in small groups in your perennial border or wild flower garden. Or they may be naturalized in quantity on banks and by paths or driveways. They will give you spring beauty for many years. The scillas, also called squills or bulbous bluebells, are universal favorites. *Scilla sibirica* and the improved Spring Beauty are Prussian blue and bloom in mid-April in most parts of the North.

Another early-blooming bulb is glory-of-the-snow, of which *Chionodoxa lucilliae* and *sardensis* are the best known. These have bright blue flowers with white centers, but there also are white and pink forms. Muscari, or grape hyacinths, are becoming more and more popular. They are at home in an average loamy soil and, like most bulbs, they seem to prefer slight shade to a full exposure to the sun. Plant in clumps. The fritillaria is less well-known but is well worth trying in a woodsy spot. It is a strange, imposing spring flower some forms of which have a curious set of double bells, one upright and the other pendant. Plant these in groups of three, six inches deep.

The large Dutch hyacinths are stately flowers of unsurpassed fragrance, perfection of form, and vivid colors. They should be planted in late September or October, before the ground freezes. They are prettiest when planted in groups of three or more. In our severe northern winters it is advisable to cover hyacinth plantings with leaves or other mulch, but not until after the ground is frozen. Remove the mulch in early spring. Hyacinths also can be grown in the house in pots or in glasses of water, using large bulbs in special

GRANDMA planted spring-blooming bulbs in the cemetery every autumn — a few of several varieties, so if one kind failed there would be others sure to bloom. She planted tulips, hyacinths, crocuses, daffodils, and anemones. There were also clumps of mertensia and Easter lilies placed there years ago. Some of these flowers she had transplanted right out of the nearby woods, and they would come up for years in the cool, moist spring without further attention. In many of our smaller cities and towns, the beautiful custom of planting flowers on graves is still permitted.

hyacinth glasses. Save a few big bulbs to start next month for indoor bloom. We will describe the proper procedure in November.

Narcissuses, daffodils, and jonquils are always spring favorites, with their varying graceful forms and cheerful colors. By planting different varieties, you can have them in the garden from the time the crocuses finish blooming till early May. Daffodils are really a type of narcissus, but jonquils, although their flowers are similar, belong to a different species. The same rules for planting apply to all these different varieties, however.

They should be planted in late September or early October, to give them plenty of time to develop a sturdy root system before the ground freezes. Bulbs planted after mid-October should be covered with a heavy mulch to prevent the ground from freezing before root growth can begin. Bulbs that are frozen in the ground before root growth starts may be prevented from growing, and lie dormant or decay during the winter. A mulch will delay this freezing and permit the necessary growth. It is well to cover daffodil and narcissus plantings the first winter with a mulch of hay or straw, applying it after the ground is frozen and removing it as soon as shoots appear next spring.

Daffodils and narcissuses require more water than most bulbs in the growing season, so incorporate considerable humus in the soil to retain moisture. These bulbs do not look well in formal rows. Mix the different colors, toss them on the garden, and plant them where they fall. Poeticus types and jonquils grow well when planted near the edge of a pool or wet spot.

Plant Madonna lilies lying slightly on their sides and with the tops of the bulbs only three inches below the surface, in soil containing plenty of humus and preferably with a gravel subsoil. A slight slope is desirable, since lilies require good drainage to do well. Madonna lilies grow their roots from the base of the bulb, but various other lilies, like the Regal, are stem-rooting, growing their roots along the stem above the bulb as well as at the base. These lilies should be planted ten to twelve inches deep, to allow plenty of room for the stem roots. All scaled lily bulbs should be planted slightly on their sides to prevent crown seepage.

217

OCTOBER

Other lilies for the northern garden include the leopard lily, the speciosum or showy Japanese lily, the candlestick lily, and the Martagon or Turk's-cap lilies. Planting instructions concerning depth and time to plant should be included when you buy your bulbs. In general, lilies should be planted in the fall if the bulbs are available before the ground freezes; otherwise, plant as early in the spring as possible. Most lilies like a rich loamy soil, good drainage, plenty of moisture, and shade at their feet but sun on their heads.

Tulips are usually the last of the spring-blooming bulbs to be planted. They should not be planted until the ground is thoroughly chilled, usually from mid-October to early November in the North. When planted too early, while the ground is warm, or if the weather should turn warm after planting, they are likely to start premature growth and actually show up above the ground before winter sets in. Tulips can be planted even after the ground is frozen if the freeze is only an inch or two thick. Just use an ax and break through the frozen ground, dig your trench and plant. Chances are good that your tulips will be almost as perfect as the ones planted earlier.

Deeper and somewhat earlier planting of tulips in the North is gaining in favor — especially if the soil is sandy. They may be later to appear in the spring, but they soon will catch up with those planted earlier. They are not so likely to have their tops eaten by rabbits and squirrels. Bulb-planting charts usually indicate a planting depth of about six inches for tulips, which means from the base of the bulb to the top of the soil. This is all right if we do not have an early spring followed by a severe frost. But here in the North I favor planting tulips ten inches deep, covered with light, loamy soil. If you plant tulips deeply, you will not have to replant them for years, provided you mix fertilizer or bone meal in the bed, deep under the bulbs. If your soil is very heavy, however, do not plant deeper than about six inches.

Plant the bulbs with a slightly twisting motion — to prevent air pockets under the bulbs — and cover them with good garden soil.

218

The bed should be raised a little, if possible, so that water and ice will not collect over the bulbs during the winter.

If the ground in which tulips are planted has been newly spaded and is quite loose, the depths should be increased another inch or so, to allow for settling, and because of the increased effect of frost heaving in newly turned soil.

The following are suggested planting depths and spacing for the bulbs. Anemones and scillas should be planted 3 inches deep and 6 inches apart; bulbous irises 4 inches deep and 4 inches apart; chionodoxa, crocuses, and snowdrops 4 inches deep and 3 inches apart; grape hyacinths 6 inches deep and 3 inches apart; tulips 6 to 10 inches deep and 6 inches apart; hyacinths and narcissuses 7 inches deep and 6 inches apart; and lilies 8 inches deep and 12 inches apart.

However, in light sandy soil, plant 50 per cent deeper, and 12 inches deep is not too deep for tulips and the narcissus family when they are planted in light soil or warm sheltered locations where bulbs tend to sprout too early in the spring. If, in spite of deep planting, your bulbs do appear prematurely, either in late fall or in early spring, cover them quickly with a mound of earth or sand.

It is a good plan to dust all bulbs lightly with DDT before planting. Mix the DDT with a fungicide obtainable from your dealer. Be sure to plant all bulbs with the pointed ends up. Keep all bulb plantings moderately moist until freeze-up. Tulips will need a covering of leaves or other mulch during the first winter but after that they will be entirely hardy and need no winter protection. The rest of these bulbs are not entirely hardy, however, and will require winter protection every year.

GRANDMA tied scaled bulbs like Madonna lilies with a strand of raveling from a potato sack. The strand, which would disintegrate in a few days, kept the scales closed until the earth was packed around the bulbs and prevented water from entering the bulbs.

OCTOBER

DIG UP GLADIOLI AND OTHER SUMMER-BLOOMING
BULBS, CORMS, AND TUBERS

Many northern gardeners wait until after a severe frost before digging up their cannas, dahlias, tuberous-rooted begonias, and gladiolus corms. This method is fine for most of these flowers, and with protection on frosty nights, many of them will go on blooming unharmed through much of October.

It is better to dig up the corms of gladioli, however, as soon as the tops have become yellow or brown, some weeks after blooming is over. You don't have to wait for a killing frost. It is much better to harvest them when the soil is dry, and there is less chance of damaging the bulbs if you use a digging fork instead of a spade.

After digging up the gladiolus plants, cut off the tops about one inch above the corms and place the corms in shallow flats, trays, or fruit boxes. If you desire, keep each variety in a separate container and label them. Do not allow the corms to lie on the garden soil where they may become infected with thrips from the nearby tops or other vegetation. The tops should be destroyed quickly, as they may be harboring insects. Do not place them on the compost pile.

To cure the gladioli corms and to destroy any thrips that may be concealed in them, keep the open boxes of corms in a warm, well-

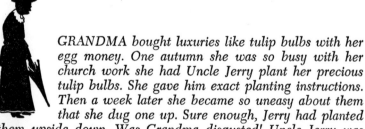

GRANDMA bought luxuries like tulip bulbs with her egg money. One autumn she was so busy with her church work she had Uncle Jerry plant her precious tulip bulbs. She gave him exact planting instructions. Then a week later she became so uneasy about them that she dug one up. Sure enough, Jerry had planted them upside down. Was Grandma disgusted! Uncle Jerry was much chagrined and took his punishment meekly when Grandma made him dig up and replant the remaining ninety-nine properly — pointed end up. Lots of new gardeners make the same mistake Uncle Jerry did.

ventilated room for a week or two. The boxes can be moved out-doors during warm fall days, but keep them out of direct sun-light and move them indoors in the evening to prevent freezing or absorption of moisture.

After this curing, store the corms for the winter in a dark, dry room at a temperature around 40 degrees. Temperatures should not go above 50 degrees nor below 35, and the humidity, if possible, should be near 75 per cent. A dusting with 5 per cent DDT should also be given to help control the thrips which feed on the corms. Thrips on corms in storage temperatures between 35 and 45 de-grees are almost certain to be killed. If such a cold storage place is not available, place the corms in paper bags — about fifty to a bag — for thirty days, with a tablespoon of napthalene flakes in a small perforated box in each bag. The box will prevent the flakes from coming in contact with the corms, but the fumes from the flakes are toxic to thrips and other insects. Punch holes in the bags for ventilation.

After treatment, remove the corms from the bags and place them in fruit boxes in a cool spot, but of course above freezing tempera-ture. Some gardeners store their bulbs in old nylon stockings and hang them in a cool basement — not near the ceiling, however, as it is usually warmer there.

When digging gladioli, you will find a number of little bulbs called cormels attached to the big corms. If you wish to propagate a given variety, save the little cormels and store them as you do the corms. Next spring plant them in boxes or pots, or in shallow fur-rows in the garden. Harvest them in the autumn and store them again, repeating the process until, after a year or two, they are of flowering size.

The wilted tops of dahlias and cannas can be cut off after a severe frost. Leave the roots or tubers in the ground to ripen for a week or two, but dig them up before the ground freezes hard. Then place them on a rack to drain and dry for a few days. Let the tubers dry in the garage, or any frostproof place, until the soil shakes off freely. If the soil is heavy, however, flush it off with the garden hose at once. Then clean the tubers and remove the dry stems.

OCTOBER

Take care in lifting dahlia tubers, because they are brittle. Cut the stems back to within three inches of the tuber and remove the fine roots and depleted roots, saving the healthy, round ones. Be careful not to break or bruise the necks or buds that show on the dahlias between the crown of the clump and the tubers. Do not break up the clumps until spring. Dahlia and canna clumps are divided just before planting in the spring.

Cut away all unsound portions of the dahlia tubers, and dust the sound parts and cut surfaces with sulphur. If dahlia tubers can be kept in a place where the temperature averages 40 degrees, they need not be covered, but in a warmer place they should be covered with sand or dry peatmoss. Be sure to label each tuber for identification next spring. Cannas are treated much the same as dahlias, but are always covered with sand, peatmoss, or vermiculite to prevent drying and shrinkage. Cannas and dahlias like some moisture, and if stored in a dry basement this may be supplied by humidifying the air or by occasionally sprinkling lightly the material that covers them. During the winter inspect all your bulbs, corms, tubers, and roots monthly to see that they are not too moist or too dry, and that no decay has started.

GRANDMA did not have DDT to destroy insects or "pests" as she called them, but she mixed up a powerful concoction all her own. It killed or drove away all insects that might be on stored bulbs or elsewhere around the cellar or house. As I remember, the awful-smelling mixture contained powdered brimstone (sulphur), camphor, slaked lime, red and black pepper, and ground cloves. About 50 per cent of the mixture was Uncle Jerry's tobacco, advertised as being excellent for both smoking and chewing. One time Uncle Jerry ran out of tobacco. He got some of Grandma's bug mixture and tried to pick out all the foreign ingredients. But I guess he missed some, because after the first pipeful he was very sick and gave up smoking for nearly six months.

Tuberous-rooted begonias should be treated very much like dahlias and cannas. After the first frost nips them, withhold water until the leaves and stems are dry. Potted tuberous begonias can be carried indoors and stored in a cool, ventilated spot. Some gardeners leave the tubers in the pots until March, when they are ready to sprout again. Begonias in beds should be forked out and set in a tray to dry and ripen. When the stems have parted cleanly from the tubers, brush off the remaining soil and store the tubers in dry vermiculite or sphagnum moss in a cool (40 to 50 degrees) temperature until spring. Tuberous begonias will also keep well in a warm basement if kept dry and covered with dry peatmoss or vermiculite.

AUTUMN LAWN CARE

October brings a double set of lawn chores. The grass must be kept mowed as long as warm weather and fall rains keep it growing, and it must also be raked free of leaves at least once a week. When chilly weather begins to predominate, the grass will no longer make new growth. It may remain green for several months or even all winter, underneath the snow, but the roots will be taking a well-earned rest.

Try to plan your October mowing so that the lawn will go into the winter with the grass about two inches high. If it is shorter, it may winter-kill, and if longer it may mat down and smother, especially if there is a heavy snow cover on the ground all winter.

Late October is the time to give your lawn a final feeding before winter arrives. Wait for chilly weather, or you may stimulate the grass into further growth this fall. You should not see the benefit of this fertilization this year, but it will give your grass a big start ahead of the weeds next spring.

Using an iron rake, give the lawn a light going-over to loosen it up, but do not tear out the natural mulch over the grass roots. This light raking will open up the sod sufficiently to allow lawn food to soak in quickly after a thorough hosing. It will dissolve into the sod where it will be available when it is needed early next spring for the old grass roots and the sprouting new grass seed.

Use any of the balanced commercial plant foods, or a special lawn food, and distribute it at the rate recommended on the container for autumn applications on old lawns, usually two pounds per 100 square feet. Some plant foods are inorganic, others are a mixture of inorganic and organic material, and some are wholly organic. However, all are good provided they are prepared by a reliable company. Cow manure is good, too, when you can get it. Get it well rotted, if possible, spread it over the lawn, and rake the area several times to work it well into the sod. Do not allow the manure to lie in piles on the grass, or even in small chunks. Big pieces that do not break up readily should be placed on the compost pile or in a covered box to decompose further.

If your lawn suffered from snow mold last spring, a treatment late this month with a grass fungicide is recommended. Snow mold may miss you entirely next spring if you act now. Heavy lasting snow on long grass seems to encourage the trouble, especially in bentgrass. Now is the time, too, to discourage winter paths across your lawn. Drive in two three-foot stakes and stretch a white rope between them, or set up snow fencing or a light fence painted white. Short-cutting on frozen sod will result in dead trails lasting well into the summer. However, leave an inconspicuous opening for the mail carrier and the paper boy.

In most parts of the North, the squirrels are very busy these days burying acorns in our lawns. Fortunately the grass will quickly cover the small holes they make, and the little oak trees will be quickly beheaded by the mower when they appear next summer. If acorns accumulate on your lawn, however, be sure to rake them off with a broom rake. They sometimes collect, especially in low places, and cause "smother spots."

Most important of all October lawn chores is keeping the lawn raked free of leaves. Most of this month and during much of November, the northern gardener must rake his lawn every few days, or at least once a week, to remove dead leaves before they become rain-soaked and packed into the grass. A thick layer of leaves pressing on the turf, especially with heavy snow on top, could smother your grass for good. Such a sodden mass also creates a fine con-

224

dition for snow mold in the spring. For these reasons leaf-raking must be done regularly and often if you want your lawn to stay beautiful and healthy. Use a broom rake when possible.

START A COMPOST HEAP

Rake you must — but don't burn those leaves! Save several bushels to use for winter protection around your shrubs and perennials. Spade some more into your garden beds and into the soil around your trees, shrubs, and along your hedges. The leaves will disintegrate into valuable plant food much faster if earth is mixed in with them as you fill the trenches and excavations, and when mixed with sand will lighten heavy clay soil.

Leaves contain nitrogen, phosphoric acid, and potash, three of the most important plant foods. Also, as they decay, they add valuable, moisture-retentive humus to the garden soil. Their acid reaction releases mineral elements into the soil that are necessary for plant life. In fact, decayed leaves are an ideal source of organic plant food. Pound for pound, tree leaves that have been properly composted are about twice as valuable as well-rotted barnyard manure.

The best way to take advantage of this valuable garden-building material is to start a compost heap. This will enable you to trans-

GRANDMA had Uncle Jerry sift hydrated lime — sometimes called garden lime — over the lawn at the end of every Indian summer. He spread it at the rate of forty pounds per thousand square feet. It was then rubbed into the sod with the back of an old wooden hay rake. All this was done early on a still evening and before the dew had formed on the grass. Next morning Uncle thoroughly soaked the lawn, washing the lime into the sod. Grandma claimed this liming was an autumn chore, that lime freshened the soil over the winter by neutralizing acidity and did not injure ripened vegetation. Grandma's lawn was always beautiful.

form the leaves you rake this fall into well-rotted crumbly humus to spread on your garden next year. All your raked leaves can go into the compost heap, as well as any grass clippings, dead flowers, and seed-free weeds that you saved from this summer's garden or will add next summer. In fact, any organic matter, including garbage, can be composted and will result in better gardens when added to your soil. Such so-called waste material as carrot tops, outer cabbage and lettuce leaves, and potato peelings must be disposed of, so why not put it to work for your garden?

To start your compost heap, dig a hole about a foot deep and four to six feet square. Pile the soil at one side for later use. A shady, inconspicuous location is best, perhaps behind a hedge or large shrub, or at the far end of the garden. The material to be composted can be enclosed with wire netting, four or more feet wide, supported on four posts. Or you can enclose it in a bottomless box made of boards, about four by six feet in size, with one of the lower boards hinged to permit easy removal of the compost. This box can be made with hooks and eyes so that it can be taken apart and quickly stored away.

Leaves and other vegetable matter will decompose slowly when piled alone in such an enclosure, but decomposition is greatly hastened by adding plant food and earth to the heap. The best method of doing this is to have a layer of plant food between each six- or eight-inch layer of vegetable material in the pile. Arrange the lay-

GRANDMA had a lawnmower in later years, but there were no leaf-chopper attachments in those days. She had Uncle Jerry rake the tree leaves into long rows; then he would rush the mower through the rows repeatedly until the leaves were well chopped and reduced about one twentieth of their original bulk, the better for compost or to be cultivated into the garden. Grandma knew well the fertilizing and soil-building value of leaves, even in those days.

ers in this fashion: (1) a six-inch or eight-inch layer of vegetable matter; (2) a generous sprinkling of complete plant food; (3) an inch of good garden loam. The loam prevents odors as well as encouraging decomposition. Repeat alternate layers of compost material, plant food, and loam until all your leaves are incorporated or the heap is as high as the netting. A few shovels of dried or rotted sheep or cow manure spread through the compost will hasten the conditioning, as will various commercially prepared products made especially for making compost. Makers of such products claim that a compost pile so treated should be ready for use in several months.

Keep the top of the compost heap concave to catch and retain rain and snow. Water the pile occasionally in summer to keep it moist. When the pile has cured for a sufficient length of time to decompose thoroughly, fork the pile through and through so as to mix all the material well. The warmer the weather the quicker the compost will form. The heap does not process in winter, but during the hot summer months it processes very rapidly. Rodents and other animals will not frequent the heap if chloride of lime is sprinkled on it occasionally. Exclude all wood, twigs, stones, and metal objects. Within a year you should be harvesting crumbly, black humus from the bottom of the heap.

Many gardeners have three compost piles — one pile that is decomposed and from which they are using the finished material; one pile which is in the process of decomposing; and the current pile which is constantly being built up with vegetable matter. Compost will not burn or harm plants as some fertilizers may. It is dandy for potting delicate house plants like African violets which enjoy a rather loose growing medium. Compost is so valuable for all garden purposes that once you have tried it, you will never again cheat yourself out of this wonderful home-made humus by burning your autumn leaves.

PREPARE YOUR ROSES FOR WINTER

One of the most important October chores is preparing roses for their long winter sleep. Even if Indian summer lingers on through the month and roses continue to bloom, the northern gardener must begin his winter protection of the rose bed. If a sudden, prolonged cold snap finds you unprepared, your roses may be seriously damaged.

The first step is to clean up all leaves and debris from the rose bed. Inspect carefully each rose plant for evidence of black spot disease, indicated by yellowing of the leaves, one or more brown or black spots, or even complete defoliation. Black spot is probably the most destructive of all rose diseases. If you find it on your plants, you should burn all the leaves on the plants and on the ground around.

The next step is tying and hilling. Gather together the branches of each plant and encircle them with a soft cord. Don't tie too tightly. Dust all the rosebushes and the earth around them with an all-purpose rose dust or spray. Now, before the ground is frozen, hill up a mound of earth at least twelve inches high around each rosebush. If the rose roots are well below the surface, you can use the surface soil around each plant and hoe it up around each shrub. Be careful not to injure or expose the rose roots, however. It is probably safer to take very little earth from between the shrubs, and to use additional earth or loam from elsewhere in the garden to complete the hilling. Hoe the soil well into the branches to prevent air spaces, but don't trim off the branches above the hill. Your roses can continue to bloom even after hilling as long as there is no killing frost.

If fairly well decomposed cattle manure is obtainable, use it to fill in the hollows between the hilled roses. The manure will help mulch the beds and will absorb surplus moisture during the winter if heavy rains or sudden thaws come. You can mix it with the soil from the hilled roses in the spring. Drainage around your roses may be improved by using the earth of the paths between the rose beds for hilling. The depressed path areas can then carry off excess water from the beds.

When you have finished hilling your roses, wait several weeks, perhaps until mid-November, before completing their winter protection. The ground must be solidly frozen before you take the final step of blanketing your roses: the purpose of this covering is not to keep the roses warm but to keep them cold, so that winter thaws will not heave the roots or start premature growth.

When the time comes, cut back the top branches of bush roses down to fourteen to eighteen inches. For bush and climbing roses, sprinkle napthalene or moth flakes on the hills and frozen ground to discourage mice and other rodents. This will also kill some hibernating insects. Wood ashes are also good.

Oak leaves are best for this insulating cover because they do not mat readily. But if you have used all your leaves in the compost heap, you can buy marsh hay as a winter covering. It costs about $1.25 a bale at nurseries, and a bale will cover two hundred square feet of garden.

Many rose growers cover this blanket of leaves or hay with a layer of building paper or other moisture repelling material, holding it down with branches and boards. Holes must be left along the sides, however, to allow for ventilation. This extra covering reduces chances of mildew or mold that might result from too much moisture in the mulch.

To protect a climbing rose, hill earth around its roots and base, take the top growth from its trellis and lay it on the ground, and cover with leaves or hay. Another simple method is to slip the entire top growth into a tube made of one or more waterproof paper sacks with the bottoms cut open. Do not tie the sacks tightly, but allow for ventilation. The bagged climbers should be laid on the ground and covered with marsh hay to protect them from moisture and the sun's heat. Still another method is to lay the climbers flat on the ground and cover them with building paper — no earth — after the ground is well frozen. All the edges of the paper are weighted down with earth to keep out mice. The mice will not eat through the building paper, nor can they burrow under it because the ground is frozen. The paper is covered with a blanket of marsh hay as with the bush roses.

Tree roses in the North should be dug up if possible, their roots packed in earth in large tubs, and placed in a root cellar or other cold storage where the temperature remains about 35 degrees.

Perhaps you can get a friendly nurseryman to store them for you till next spring. But tree roses are not generally considered hardy enough or very practical for growing in the North.

For extra protection you can scatter mouse poison under the winter covering of all types of roses.

FALL CARE FOR TREES AND SHRUBS

Your trees and shrubs need water and nourishment to give them vigor to withstand attacks of disease and insects and to send them into winter with plenty of moisture around the roots. This is very important, especially for evergreens. If this autumn has brought heavy rains, fine and dandy; but often our northern falls are dry and much watering is needed. Don't forget that your trees and shrubs need water just as much as flower borders where lack of moisture becomes visible more quickly.

During a dry September and October, water your trees and shrubs copiously but do not fertilize them. It is not advisable to feed trees and shrubbery as long as the weather is warm enough so that it might cause new, soft growth that would not harden before real cold arrived. In late October, however, when trees and shrubbery are dormant, water them for hours and fertilize them well with the root-feeding methods we outlined in April. This will place food and moisture deep in the ground where it will be available to the roots early next spring.

Most of the ground surface around many houses is covered with paving of some kind, and much of the rest of the surface is lawns and flower beds. Usually these last two areas get just enough food and water for their own requirements. Yards are kept clean and weeded, and the lawn is mowed and raked. Unlike the forest floor, your lawn has not a sufficient quantity of disintegrating vegetable and animal matter to soak down into the ground to feed the trees. Trees on small lots and crowded areas especially must be fed to keep them healthy.

By placing plant food mixed with soil in deep holes around the tree trunk, you enable the tree roots to find nourishment without coming too close to the surface. If you should strike hardpan — an

almost waterproof layer of clay and gravel several inches thick —
try to puncture it by using a crowbar or a heavy iron pipe. Starving
roots are often under this hardpan. Fertilize your shrubs in the
same way, although plant food may also be dug into the surface
soil above their roots. Give your hedges a similar feeding, with a
staggered row of holes on each side of the hedge.

Some folks use the garden hose at its strongest pressure to make
the holes. The sprinkling nozzle pressed into the soil will make
holes quickly, and will also irrigate the earth, but you will need to
put on overshoes and a raincoat to stay dry while you work.

Water all trees and shrubs either through a root-feeder attachment on your hose or by allowing the water to run slowly for hours
on the ground, with the nozzle off and a stone or shingle to spread
the flow. Be especially generous in soaking recently planted trees
and shrubs and all evergreens.

After you have soaked the soil around your evergreens, pile
leaves around them, about eight inches to a foot deep and extending out as far as the branches spread, to prevent deep freezing of
the ground. Evergreens need a great deal of water and there must
be unfrozen moisture around the roots to replace what the needles
evaporate. Broad-leaf evergreens, such as cedars and arborvitae,
that were set out this year should be protected from drying winds
and sun scald with a burlap sack placed around or over them. This
should be done late in October or in November.

*GRANDMA gathered many flowers for winter bou-
quets, including bachelor's buttons, Japanese balloon
flowers, sea-lavender, globe amaranth, baby's breath,
and grasses. She dried them in the attic, some hanging
head down and others over bowls for curved sprays.
She preserved colored autumn leaves by pressing them
with a warm — not hot — iron. To keep the leaves flexible, she
soaked them in a mixture of one part glycerine to nine parts water
and then dried them between blotters.*

OCTOBER

Remember that the second migration of the canker worm up your trees will occur this month. Repeat the spraying program you used in the spring.

If you have had to do any late pruning of your shade or fruit trees, be sure to seal the wounds where branches were removed. Ordinary orange shellac is a dandy sealer and fungicide for the ends of branches and newly-cut tree scars.

Ornamental and fruit trees planted within the last two years usually have thin bark and should be protected from winter sun scald which destroys bark on young trees. If they are not protected, next summer the bark may loosen and fall off. Light-colored building paper or heavy wrapping paper around the trees from the ground to the first branch will give satisfactory protection. You can also purchase rolls of narrow, crepe-like paper for this purpose. The roll unwinds as you spiral it around the tree trunk.

Aluminum sheets or aluminum foil will give good protection both from sun scald and from the depredations of rabbits.

Also obtainable is a liquid that can be applied on tree trunks and woody vine stems to keep away gnawing rodents both summer and winter. To protect against below-the-soil gnawers, a collar of hardware cloth — nonrusting, coarse wire netting — should encircle the trunks and extend into the ground two or more inches and as high as the estimated snow line. This also is a good protection around clematis vines — and other shrubs that mice and rabbits nibble on.

IT'S TIME FOR AN EXPEDITION

As Nature's year wanes, it's time for us to get out into the fields and woods — preferably on foot and on a weekend when we have plenty of time for just looking and meditating — and appreciate the last burst of wild beauty. Particularly now when winter is ahead, we become aware of the beauty in the form and symmetry of every plant along the roadside, and lovely as the brilliant colors of the cultivated garden are, there is loveliness also in softer, subtler tones, the pale browns and yellows of dying foliage.

You can make your expedition a productive one too by gathering autumn's abundance to carry home for winter decoration. Of

232

course you will want the colorful autumn leaves. But look too for golden bittersweet, glistening snowberry, yarrow, and dock. And even the lowly and much-maligned weeds, if you look with a fresh eye, have a charm in their autumn form that can give you much pleasure. Look for unusual ones — light, airy graceful ones and strange ones with heavy seedpods. All of these, you will find, make interesting winter bouquets.

But avoid cattails, unless you are willing to take pains to wax them. Otherwise they'll soon burst and spread a disagreeable fuzz around the house.

GRANDMA always put away in the cellar in the autumn a bushel basket of good garden earth, mixed with two quarts each of coarse sand, charcoal, and fine, dry cow or sheep manure. She carefully sifted it to remove worms. One year Uncle Jerry slipped his fishing worms into the mixture. How they did multiply and was Grandma provoked! She made him sift the whole basket whenever she wanted a potful. Earthworms are nuisances in potted plants.

REMINDERS

The first killing frost may not strike till mid-October in some parts of the North. Keep sheets, cloths, and cardboard cartons handy to cover your flowers on frosty nights. Indian summer may give you several weeks more of bloom.

In your garden are leaves that will lend themselves beautifully to lasting bouquets — red and green barberry, Japanese lantern, money flower, and Boston ivy in many autumn tones. Why not bring some of this October color indoors for many weeks' enjoyment?

When you bring in your poinsettia plant from its summer outdoors, make the transition slowly or it will drop its leaves. Before frost strikes, move it to a cool but protected place, such as a garage, for several days, then to several successively warmer rooms until

233

it reaches its permanent winter location. Keep it well watered. The poinsettia likes to go to sleep with the chickens, so keep it out of artificial light or it probably won't bloom. Feed it, stake it, don't prune any of its green stems — and you may have flowers in late winter.

Continue to dust the perennial border and annuals as long as growth and bloom continue. Insect pests and plant diseases will be active until after killing frosts. If the annuals are through blooming, pull up the exhausted plants and add them to the compost pile, unless their foliage is diseased. If so, burn them. Scatter hardy annual seeds now, including poppy, bachelor's buttons, nicotinia, coreopsis, cosmos, and columbine, and you will have extra-early seedlings next spring.

❧ NOVEMBER ❧

November brings the first snow and the beginnings of winter in most of the North, but it is not all cold and bleak. There is often one of those marvelous autumn interludes between Indian summer and winter that Grandma called "squaw winter." It usually follows stormy, snowy periods with frost. Then for several weeks there may come mild sunny days and clear frosty nights. All our flowers may be gone from the garden, and most of the autumn leaves fallen from the trees, but these last mild days before the permanent winter snow cover descends are very important ones for the garden. There are many end-of-the-season chores to attend to before the garden is ready for our long northern winter.

WINTER PREPARATIONS IN THE GARDEN

When heavy frosts have stopped all blossoming and growth in the perennial border, it is time to cut off the dead stalks and leaves. Don't be in a hurry to cut down your perennials if they are still green, however. There is a well-founded belief that the top growth, after the blossoms and seed pods are removed, keeps storing up food in the roots for next summer's growth and bloom. But when stalks and leaves are dry and brittle, or when winter seems about to close in, it's better to clean up the garden at once.

With scissors or clippers, cut off the summer growth of most perennials, leaving about five inches of the old stalks projecting above the plants. These stubs will collect drifting leaves which provide winter protection. They also will help you locate and identify the different plants next spring. Cut the leaves of iris back to about four inches, or if you prefer you can leave them as they are, most of them still green, until next spring, when the dry, dead leaves can be removed as new growth starts.

If a peony has discoloring or rotting stems, it probably is infected with botrytis rot, a disease that may spread and kill the peony plant and others near it. To curtail the rot, cut off all the top growth and burn it or put it in the garbage. Then with a trowel thrust into the ground at least an inch, remove all diseased stems. Apply a small amount of Bordeaux powder. Next spring, spray just as the new growth is poking through the ground.

Dig up all tender summer bulbs that still remain outdoors and store them for the winter in the basement. Inspect them every six weeks for mildew or decay. Avoid bruising them because bruises permit fungi to gain entrance, causing rot. Watch out for damage by rats and mice also.

Four o'clock and geranium plants may be dug up before heavy frost, their tops cut off to two inches, and their roots stored in a cool spot for replanting next spring. These old roots will produce more, bigger, and earlier blossoms next year than can be obtained from new plants. If any chrysanthemums are still blooming, you can pot them and bring them indoors to prolong the last fall blossoms for a few more weeks.

Pull up all dead annual plants and burn them. Dead roots frequently harbor hibernating insect pests that will cause endless trouble next summer unless destroyed. Also clean up weeds and rubbish. The dead stalks from the perennial garden should also be burned unless you are sure they are healthy and disease-free. Then they can go on the compost heap.

If time and weather permit, spade up your annual beds. Also cultivate fairly deeply between the perennials, if you can do so without disturbing their roots. Leave the spaded areas in the rough all winter. The exposure of the freshly turned earth to the elements will improve its condition, besides giving the birds a chance to get in some good work on insects and weed seeds.

A good time to enrich the soil is just before you spade. Spread balanced plant food over the annual beds at the rate of three pounds per hundred square feet, or well-rotted cow manure at the rate of approximately one pound on each square foot of garden area. As you spade, turn in the fertilizer. Give the spaces between your perennial clumps the same treatment, preferably using slow-acting fertilizers like dried or well-rotted cow or sheep manure or bone meal. Be careful not to disturb the perennial roots as you dig the fertilizer in. If the ground is frozen too hard to dig, just distribute the manure or plant food on the garden surface. Much of it will soak into the soil during the winter. With this treatment your garden will be ready for strong growth next spring, with food immediately available for sprouting plants.

If you have access to large quantities of well-rotted cow manure or can order a load, November is a good time to spread it on your lawn. If you buy it, it will cost a little more than a good top dressing of loamy topsoil, but it contains much more plant food, and as it breaks up it adds excellent humus to the lawn. Spread it as evenly as possible over the lawn, raking over the area several times if necessary to work it into the sod. Do not allow the manure to lie in piles, even small ones. Big pieces that do not break up easily can be placed in the flower border or on the compost pile. All winter long, during mild spells, the dressing of manure will be dissolving and working down into the soil.

Continue to keep leaves raked off the grass and mow your lawn again if necessary, to have it not more than two inches high when the heavy snows come. Long grass and the lasting heavy snows of late winter or early spring tend to encourage snow mold. If you

GRANDMA had on her farm a cave in the side of a hill with a front wall of grass sods and a double wooden tar-papered door. It was called the root house, and potatoes, other vegetables, and barrels of winter apples were stored there. It was not heated, but nothing ever froze. And all winter long we had good fresh vegetables, while the apples seemed to taste better as winter wore on.

had trouble with snow mold last spring, try an application now of a preventive fungicide, spurgeon or Semesan. Dissolve in warm water according to directions on the container and sprinkle on the grass now wherever you have had mold, or on places where the snow is usually deep and stays a long time. This is where snow mold usually occurs in the spring.

GRANDMA always attended to the chore of making the "magic circle" herself. She spread around each clump of peonies a three-inch circle about an inch deep of mixed wood and soft coal ashes, and also a small shovelful right on the top of her delphinium clump after the top had been removed. That was all there was to it and her "delphs" and "pinies" were not diseased as ours so often are today. Her neighbors all followed suit with the same result, and so do I.

If you did not get your tulips planted in October, there is still time to do it this month. Even if the ground is somewhat frozen, break the crust well with an ax and plant the bulbs ten inches deep in the soft unfrozen earth. The later they are planted, the deeper the bulbs should be placed. Toss the frozen chunks of earth on top of the planting where they will thaw in the spring. Mound the earth up a bit to allow for settling and to form more perfect drainage. Water well. Tulips can be planted as late as December if there is no snow cover and if the ground is not too deeply frozen. They will do better if planted earlier, of course, but better late planting than not at all.

If your ground is not already frozen and you do not have time to plant your tulips immediately, you can cover the place allotted for bulbs with a thick layer of leaves or manure, topped with heavy building paper or other water-shedding material. This will keep the ground unfrozen for a week or two more until you have time to plant. If you can spade it up now before covering, your chore will be easier when you do plant. After late planting of tulips, cover the bed with a mulch of leaves or hay to retard freezing of the ground and give the bulbs time to form roots before winter.

When the ground is thoroughly frozen, cover your earlier-planted bulbs with a mulch also. A heavy layer of leaves or marsh hay will keep the ground frozen as late as possible in the spring and prevent premature sprouting during an early warm spell in March or April. Such early sprouts are often destroyed by hungry rabbits, squirrels, and pheasants.

Another way to protect early tulip sprouts — and others, if need be — is to place strips of small-mesh chicken wire over the plantings now. Better yet, use strips of hardware cloth (galvanized iron netting with quarter-inch holes). Bend the strips at right angles to make tents over the bulbs about five inches high. This is excellent protection for tulips until the plants are up about four inches. By that time grasses and weeds will also be sprouting, and the animals will usually leave your garden alone. You can then remove the protective netting and store it away for another year.

As you prepare to mulch your tulip plantings, examine them to see if the ground has sunk and formed hollows. If so, add additional earth to fill the hollows and to mound up an inch or so above ground level. This will prevent water from collecting and forming an icy deep freeze around the bulbs.

Check also to see if any of your early-planted tulips or other spring bulbs have begun to sprout. In mild autumns this is not uncommon. Probably such bulbs were planted too early or not deep enough. The remedy is simple — cover them with more earth, two inches deep or more. You usually can find enough unfrozen earth along your south foundation wall to do the job, or buy some from a local nursery or greenhouse. If a bulb's folded leaves are opening, gently hold them together and press damp earth around them before covering. Earth among the leaves cause decay and loss of bulbs. If you have any doubts whether you planted your bulbs right side up — the pointed end should be up — dig up a few right now to check. If they are upside down, dig them all up and replant. It's better to be sure than to lose an entire planting.

239

NOVEMBER

If Madonna lilies are now sprouting in your border, don't worry. These bulbs usually send up shoots in the fall and remain somewhat green all winter. Just cover them with some light mulch and a moisture-repellent, ventilated box, such as a fruit crate. If you planted Easter lily bulbs in your garden last spring, give them the same protection. They probably will come up next summer and give you beautiful blooms.

When the old stalks are cut down in the perennial border and the ground is frozen hard, then it's time to cover the border with its winter blanket of insulating mulch. Most perennials in our northern gardens are winter-hardy, and in many gardens they need and get no winter protection other than the leaves that drift in around them. However, a few of the more tender plants would be safer with a mulch around and over them after the soil starts really to freeze. Young plants and those transplanted or divided this year are also more susceptible to winter killing than old established specimens and should be given some protection.

A winter mulch pays real dividends during mid-winter and early spring thaws by keeping the soil shaded and frozen. It will lessen soil heaving and also prevent the deadly freezing of water on the crowns of plants where drainage is poor.

Tree leaves, marsh hay, excelsior, evergreen boughs, and loose material from the compost heap make good mulches. Oak leaves make excellent insulation against thawing and freezing. Contrary to an old belief, oak leaves do not contain enough acid to harm most vegetation, and they do not pack down like other leaves. Mulches for winter protection should be of material that does not compress easily. If you are using leaves, let them drift in among the border plants during most of the fall; then for somewhat tender perennials, add enough more after the ground is frozen to make a four- to six-inch layer. Marsh hay should be spread from six to ten inches deep. Dead branches or chicken wire can be placed on top of either leaves or hay to hold them in place. Shallow fruit crates or seed flats can be placed upside down, slanted to shed water, over plants needing special protection.

Established iris clumps need little or no winter mulching, but

240

new iris plants that haven't had time to develop an ample root system are likely to be lost unless protected. A covering of leaves, marsh hay, or straw, plus two pieces of roofing material laid criss-cross on top to shed water, is sufficient.

Most garden variety chrysanthemums are hardy if given the ordinary winter protection for the perennial border outlined above. However, if you are doubtful about the hardiness of some of the new varieties you planted this spring, you would be wise to take further precautions, even though reliable northern nurseries do not sell outdoor mums unless they are reasonably hardy in our climate.

One good way to give chrysanthemums extra protection over winter is to plant them in a cold frame as soon as the bloom has been destroyed by frost. Cut off the tops, water well, and cover the transplanted mums with a dry mulch. Cover the cold frame with glass sash or boards to keep out snow and rain. Lacking a cold frame, I transplant — for the winter — new mum varieties along the outside south foundation wall of my house where the earth is somewhat warmer. These I mulch with two feet of leaves and protect from snow and rain with steeply slanted sheets of wallboard painted white. The ends are left open for ventilation.

GRANDMA kept a sharp lookout for the destructive, parasitic dodderweed that occasionally appeared in her garden. It is a weird, almost colorless, leafless growth, not much larger than a cotton thread. It grows from tiny seeds around garden flowers, breaks away from the earth and subsists entirely on the sap of its host, drinking from its victim with needle-like sucking organs. It twists itself around garden plants as large as dahlias or chrysanthemums, usually strangling them. Grandma called it strangleweed or gold thread or love vine. Uncle Jerry called it devil's hair or hell-bind. Grandma always burned the weed and its victims. A garden infected should be all burned over to destroy the seeds.

Another method is to cut down the chrysanthemum tops after they have been killed by frost, dig up the clumps, and plant them close together in a protected spot. Water the plants well to settle the dirt around the roots. Next, build a temporary board frame around the plants and cover with old storm windows or boards. Straw or a canvas covering over the boards will give additional protection and prevent sudden temperature changes. For gardeners who have only a few chrysanthemums, a simpler but perhaps not quite so effective method is suggested. Cut off the tops, tuck hay, straw, or leaves under the branches and over the plants, and cover with inverted, open-sided boxes, such as peach crates, to shed water. You may also want to scatter poisoned grain to protect plants from small animal pests.

In all these methods, the object is not to keep the plants warm but to keep them dry and at an even temperature, and also to prevent frost heaving. In the spring many new mum plants can be propagated from shoots or suckers that start from the old plants. These can be cut off from the old clumps and replanted in the border or chrysanthemum bed. The old clumps can also be pulled apart, making several divisions that will develop into blooming plants.

Clematis also requires some special winter protection even if it is growing in a protected spot close to your house. After the leaves are dry and mostly fallen and the ground is frozen, cut the top growth down to four feet. Sprinkle garden lime on the clump at the earth line and on the soil around the plant. Place collars of wire mosquito netting or hardware cloth around each clump, extending from one inch into the soil up to the height of the estimated snow cover, to protect stems from mice, rabbits, and squirrels. Then heap around the plant a two- or three-foot layer of leaves held in place by branches or by the old vines that you have cut off.

For additional protection from mice, which sometimes dig under the wire collars and girdle the stems at the ground line, drop poisoned grain or mothballs into the collars where birds can't reach. Never place poison on the open ground, and keep it out of children's reach. Better yet, destroy what you don't use. If you prefer, you do not have to cut off the clematis' top growth now. You can wait until spring and then prune about half of the previous year's growth. Clematis blooms on the current year's branches, not on the old canes.

GRANDMA hilled the earth around her roses about ten inches high, and when the ground was well frozen she covered the rose beds with short evergreen boughs to keep the ground frozen and the roses reasonably dry. But as the country settled up, evergreens, shrubbery, and trees on public lands became scarce, so Grandma had Uncle Jerry cover the entire rose garden with upright corn shocks instead. They resembled little Indian tepees when covered with snow in the moonlight.

Toward the end of November, when the ground is well frozen, it is time to complete the winter protection of your roses. Cut off the tops of the rosebushes above the hilling. Hills and the ground between them should be well covered with a good insulating blanket of marsh hay, straw, excelsior, or dry leaves. Oak leaves are best because they don't mat readily. Many rosarians believe the entire rose bed should then be covered further with light-colored waterproof paper or other moisture-repelling material, held down with boards or branches. I find the low wire fencing used around peony clumps and borders is good for holding down the winter covering. Holes should be left at the sides of the covering for ventilation. Whatever covering you use, remember that the purpose in covering roses, shrubs, and most flowers is to keep them frozen and dry, and at as even a temperature as possible all winter.

One final garden chore before winter sets in — bring into the basement a pail or two of sifted loamy garden earth and a pail or two of compost for repotting plants during the winter, and also for starting seeds, bulbs, and tubers that require a very early start next spring. Get in a supply of sharp builder's sand also, to add to your potting earth mixtures, and small bags of bone meal and dried sheep or cow manure for fertilizer. With these supplies your gardening pleasures can continue all winter indoors.

LAST WATERING BEFORE FREEZE-UP

Late autumn in the North sometimes brings drought, dry winds, and prolonged sunny weather that combine to cause a large deficit of moisture for our trees, shrubs, and gardens. If October and November have been even moderately dry, don't put your hose away before giving all trees and shrubs — except roses — a thorough soaking. Roses should not be watered after their summer growth is killed by frost. Dryness will not harm them in their present dormant condition, and watering might start next year's buds into premature growth.

If the perennial border is dry more than an inch or so below the surface, it too should be watered as thoroughly as possible before freeze-up. It is not good for perennials to go into the winter with dry roots. You should also water your spring-blossoming bulbs, but not heavily — just enough to moisten the ground so that it will cover the planting with a frozen-earth protection. This watering of the border should be done, if possible, before the ground is frozen, but even if the ground is partly frozen, there will be days before the permanent winter freeze-up when the ground will soften sufficiently to absorb moisture. Water before applying the winter mulch of hay or leaves, if possible, but even if the mulch is already in place, the border should be watered, mulch and all, if the drought is severe.

Trees and shrubs should be watered through a root feeder, through one- to two-foot holes around the trunk, or by allowing the hose to run for hours, nozzle off, on the ground beneath the spread of branches. Use a shingle or flat stone to spread the flow of water and move the hose frequently. Thorough watering before freeze-up is especially important for recently planted trees and shrubs and for evergreens of all ages and varieties.

Even if your evergreens are already mulched for the winter, soak the ground thoroughly if dry weather has been prolonged.

244

Wind and late fall sunlight cause a great loss of water by evaporation. If this happens at a time when the soil is deeply frozen, the roots cannot absorb enough water to replace that lost by evaporation. Three-year-old needles drop from evergreens every year, but one- and two-year-old needles should remain. If these begin to drop, it is probably due to lack of moisture in the soil. Make sure, therefore, that evergreens go into the winter season with plenty of moisture around their roots.

The foliage of evergreens should also be sprayed with the garden hose now and once or twice during the winter. Pick a day when the temperature is above freezing, and thoroughly soak the foliage. This will cleanse dust and soot particles from the pores of the needles and supply moisture which will be taken into the tissues of the plant. If the evergreens are wrapped in burlap for the winter, spray foliage, burlap, and all, to provide all possible protection against excess evaporation.

Don't neglect any of your garden plantings — evergreens, shade trees, shrubs, or perennials — in a long fall dry spell. One rain or one melted snowfall will not make up for an extensive moisture shortage, so water generously for as long as your plants can absorb it.

STORING GARDEN TOOLS

When late fall garden chores are finished, gather up your garden tools for winter storage. Now is a good time to clean and sharpen them and condition them against rust. You will do a better job on the tools if you work in the warm basement. Scrape off all mud (steel wool will help), and rub and polish them first with a coarse and then with a fine grade of sandpaper.

If you have time, sharpen the trowels, hoes, spades, and other edged tools. A grindstone is best and quickest, but a sharp, rather coarse file will do a good job. Then rub all metal surfaces with an oily rust inhibitor — a mixture of kerosene and old crankcase oil will do — or you can spray them with liquid wax or the plastic used during the winter on the chrome of your car. This material is also fine for coating snow shovels to keep snow from sticking.

Clean and oil your lawnmower. If you have a power mower,

treat it as carefully as you would an outboard motor, and if you are in doubt, let your dealer do the servicing. It is your most valuable garden tool. Oil all bearings of tools with wheels.

Your spraying and dusting equipment should be cleaned thoroughly of old spray materials. Take the nozzles of sprayers apart and clean them. Ammonia is good for cleaning any sprayers that have been used for 2, 4-D or other weed killers. Even a little residue could be disastrous for the garden if the sprayer is later used for other purposes. Oil the pumps of sprayers and set them away without screwing down the tank caps, so the rubber gaskets are not compressed. Dusters should be cleaned and the outside metal parts oiled. Instead of oil, powdered graphite should be used on the inside.

Fertilizer and seed spreaders require special care. Don't put them away with just a dusting. Take out the brushes or space gauges and give them a special cleaning because plant food residue can cause corrosion. Wash and dry well, oil the moving parts, and paint or spray with plastic any exposed places that might rust.

If you own one of the combined plant-food spreaders and seeders on wheels, it represents quite an investment and should be given special care. Otherwise corrosion may make it useless before spring. Wire-brush it thoroughly to remove plant food and rust, then turn the hose on the spreader and rinse it out thoroughly. Dry it and brush all surfaces with powdered graphite. Spread graphite on the shut-off mechanism on the bottom of the spreader, oil the wheel axles, and paint all bare spots.

GRANDMA had three low wide pots of parsley, mint, and chives growing all winter long in her window. These she lifted from her garden in November, cut off most of the top growth, and potted them in ordinary garden soil. They supplied her with fresh seasoning until spring.

Drain and coil your hose, but don't attempt to do this if it is cold and filled with ice. Wait for a warmer day or allow it to thaw in the basement. Coil it up neatly, on a reel, preferably, or hang it up on at least two flat pegs or hooks. Don't just throw the hose in a tangled heap on the floor where it might be damaged. Another storage method is to coil it in a bushel basket. Don't forget to turn off your outdoor water supply and drain the pipes.

During the winter, sandpaper smooth the wooden parts of your garden tools, especially the handles, and paint them a bright yellow or red. This will enable you to spot them easily when they are misplaced in the garden. And while you are at it, give the wheelbarrow a paint job. It will last much longer. If it is made of wood, a galvanized iron liner — costing about $3 — will add years to its usefulness. Give the inside measurements of your barrow to your tinsmith or hardware dealer and he will cut the metal to fit the wheelbarrow. You can attach it yourself using large-headed, galvanized roofing nails.

POT SPRING BULBS NOW FOR INDOOR BLOOM

What could be more cheering in midwinter, when the landscape is covered with snow, than a potful of gay, blossoming tulips, daffodils, or hyacinths in your window? You can have these lovely spring flowers months ahead of time by planting them now in pots for bloom indoors in January and February. You can still buy spring bulbs in most of the garden stores, and by starting a potful every two weeks or so from now until Christmastime, you can have continuous spring color when our northern land is buried in snow.

Tulips. The best tulips to buy for indoor forcing are the single, early varieties, as they have comparatively short stems and do not bend and lean over as would the tall varieties. The earlies come in yellow, red, purple, and orange, and in bicolors of yellow and red. Sometimes you can find other low-growing varieties in the garden stores, but avoid the tall types for winter forcing.

If possible, use the wide, low flowerpots called bulb pans, similar to the large African violet pans, and place in them as many bulbs as the pot will comfortably hold, about an inch apart. Place the flat side of the bulbs toward the side of the pot — that's the side where the broad lower leaf always grows — with the pointed tips of the bulbs about half an inch below the earth's surface. Use rather sandy, good garden earth for potting. If your earth is heavy and not porous, mix in about one part sphagnum moss or compost and one part coarse sand to two parts earth. Suitable tulip-potting earth can be had from your garden dealer or local greenhouse. It is not expensive and you will not require much.

For many years it was thought that to force tulips, the potted bulbs had to root for a couple of months in a dark, cool greenhouse, a cold frame, or in a two-foot-deep pit out of doors, first covered with a layer of straw or hay, and then mounded with earth. The whole mound was then covered with mulch or leaves. A much easier method, however, is to place the potted bulbs on or close to the floor of a moist, cool fruit closet or vegetable room in your cellar or basement. A temperature of 40 to 50 degrees is desirable. A two-inch layer of moss or loamy peat on top of the pots will help hold moisture, but don't water too much. Keep the earth just pleasantly moist.

Occasionally examine the bulbs for root growth. Spread one hand over the top of the pot, with the sprouts, if any, extending up between your fingers. Invert the pot and jar the edge to loosen the pot from the mass of soil and roots. The pot can then be lifted off, leaving the roots and earth exposed. When properly rooted, the roots should cover the lower part of the soil with a thick network. Usually the leaves will then be up two or three inches and the blossom bud can be plainly felt or seen. If only a few roots are to be seen, the plant is not rooted enough to flower satisfactorily, and the rooting period must be continued.

When the bulbs are well rooted, take them out of the dark, cool forcing room and place the pot in a shady, cool window — a north window is fine — until the leaves and buds have become quite green. Then they can be placed in a bright window, but should not get too much sunshine. Cool temperatures will produce the best flowers. Too much warmth makes the stems tall and weak, so that they require support. The pots should be watered regularly to keep the soil moist but not flooded. Tulips should be in full bloom in twelve to fourteen weeks from the time they were potted.

If you do not have a place in your basement or garage cool enough for rooting bulbs, a cold frame or outdoor pit in the earth near the house foundation can be used, provided the temperature can be kept above freezing. Some home gardeners use the light well just outside their basement window for forcing bulbs. You can bury the pots in the earth floor of the light well or bank them heavily with a mulch of earth, hay, or leaves. The top of the well must be covered with storm sash or boards to retain the heat of the house, but these should be opened slightly if the well becomes too warm.

GRANDMA always replaced her garden tools on or in their special hooks or bins in the toolhouse. Uncle Jerry was not so careful. Usually he would open the door and throw them in, much to Grandma's distress. One day he stepped on a prostrate rake and the handle flew up and hit him on the nose. The names he called that rake you won't find in the dictionary. Grandma ran into the house with her hands over her ears, but I think she was laughing.

Daffodils, crocuses, and hyacinths can be potted and rooted in the same way as tulips.

Hyacinths. Hyacinths can also be grown in water alone, in special hyacinth glasses. These vases have a flared top above a narrow opening, to hold the hyacinth bulbs just above the water. You can also use ordinary glass jars with openings just big enough for a large hyacinth bulb to sit securely on top. It is a good idea to place stones in the jars to keep them from tipping and to help prevent the bulbs from actually touching the water; and a few pieces of charcoal will keep the water sweet.

Hyacinth bulbs come in white, pink, blue, red, and cream. Choose large, healthy-looking bulbs and plan to start several a week or two apart for a continuous series of bloom this winter. The bulbs should be brushed clean of old roots, loose skin, and earth. Place them on the jars and pour in clean water until the water is a quarter of an inch below the base of the bulb. The tighter the bulb corks the jar, the better. It will prevent evaporation. Add a little water from time to time, as needed to maintain the original level. The evaporation will soon start the roots growing downward into the water.

Keep the jars in the coldest part of the basement and keep them dark. Cover with cardboard boxes or paper bags to keep out light. When the roots reach the bottom of the jar, top growth will commence and a big bud will appear. Now you must exercise your patience. Wait until the bud is four inches above the bulb — pay no attention to the leaves — before bringing the jar into a warm place and shaded light for a few days.

You can then watch the bud slowly turn green and then to its appointed color, opening in a few days and filling the whole room with an alluring fragrance. Keep the blooming hyacinth in a bright, cool window, not too sunny, and the flower will last for two or three weeks. When bloom is finished, keep the bulb watered until spring, when it can be planted outdoors, where after a year of vegetating it will begin to bloom again each spring.

GRANDMA was always thoughtful of her friends the birds. In the late autumn when the ponds and brooks are frozen over and there is no snow for the birds to consume as a substitute for water, most birds suffer terribly from thirst. But not so on Grandma's little farm. Until snow fell, one of Uncle Jerry's chores every morning was to pour hot water on the ice in the bird bath. I think Uncle enjoyed it as much as the birds. They would flock around him, lighting on his head and shoulders. Sometimes when he was tardy and someone else watered the birds he would grumble like all get-out, remarking, "This ain't right, strangers only frighten the birds."

Other bulbs. Daffodils and narcissuses — the golden Soleil d'Or and the Paper White narcissus — can also be grown in water alone for indoor bloom rather than in pots of earth. Usually as many bulbs of one variety as possible are set out in a shallow bowl, pebbles are added to hold the bulbs in place and, water is kept just below the bottoms of the bulbs. Like the hyacinth, the narcissus must be rooted in a dark, cool place, but it usually roots more quickly. Blooming begins within six to eight weeks after planting and lasts for several weeks. By starting several bowlsful now and throughout the early winter, you can have continuous, fragrant bloom from these delightful flowers. See the January chapter for more instructions.

Other bulbs may also be started for indoor bloom at any time from November through January or February. These include the beautiful calla lily, with its white, yellow, or pink waxy flowers; anemones and oxalis, small bulbs with attractive flowers; and the giant amaryllis, especially the Royal Dutch hybrids, with their spectacular, large blossoms in many brilliant color combinations. All of these may be started whenever the bulbs are available at your garden dealer's, or whenever you need them to provide a succession of indoor bloom. Remember that only the very best bulbs are suitable for forcing indoors. Inferior ones that might do outdoors will not thrive as pot plants, each of which should be a nearly perfect specimen.

Two books should be very helpful to the northern gardener who is starting bulbs. *Bulb Magic in Your Window,* by Ruth Marie Peters (M. Barrows & Co., New York, $3.95), tells you how to grow bulbs in your window garden all year around. The book is packed with bulb lore and more than sixty pictures, some in color. For both indoor and outdoor bulb growing, be sure to get *The American Gardener's Book of Bulbs,* by T. H. Everett (Random House, New York, $5.95). This is the most complete and up-to-date book on bulbs ever published. It contains all information that a bulb grower, amateur or professional, requires. It provides an illustrated manual on bulbs rare and common, on planting inside and outdoors, and on all aspects of propagation and culture.

251

NOVEMBER

Trees are precious assets to all home grounds, both for their appearance and in sound financial terms. Real estate people estimate that beautiful trees can increase the value of a property by as much as 20 per cent. Besides, trees around the house can reduce the temperature inside by many degrees, and they serve to insulate the house against street noises.

But trees require some care — not constant attention, except for watering and feeding, but occasional action. With the passing of the years, trees inevitably become diseased in part or are injured.

If large, high trees suffer damage from one of these causes, you will probably have to hire professional tree surgeons. Without proper equipment and training an amateur can endanger both himself and the tree.

But if the injuries are minor, the homeowner can give valuable aid to his trees. Proper treatment, particularly taking pains to remove branches flush with the trunk, will usually save the tree. Such cuts should leave only smooth-surfaced, streamlined oval wounds, tapering vertically, with an open groove in the lower end to allow rain and sap to drain away.

Before making these cuts it is frequently necessary to take certain preliminary steps to prevent stripping the bark below the saw cut. This is especially true if the limbs to be removed are more than five inches thick.

One of the most common ways of preventing stripping is to remove the limb by means of two preliminary cuts, leaving only a stub for the final cut. The first of the preliminary cuts is made about ten inches beyond the point where the final cut is to be made. This is done by sawing upwards from the lower side of the branch until the saw begins to pinch or the limb has been sawed about a third through. Then the second preliminary cut is made from above, about six inches closer to the final cut. Sawing is continued until the branch splits off.

By supporting the weight of small branches with one hand while sawing with the other, it may be possible for you to eliminate the preliminary cuts in some cases.

252

After this preliminary work is done, proceed with the final cut. This is made by sawing off the stub flush with the trunk. There should be no definite protruding stub left by a correctly made saw cut. On the other hand, the handyman should not carry the idea of flatness to an extreme: this would increase the size of the resulting wound unnecessarily.

GRANDMA'S Thanksgiving dinner was always served on a spotless white Irish linen tablecloth with a bright red border. It was one of Grandma's cherished wedding gifts. All the substantial food was raised on the farm, from the huge twenty-five-pound turkey to the filling in the pumpkin pies. There was always a large bowl of California oranges and bananas festooned with bunches of silvery Sultana raisins for a centerpiece both ornamental and edible.

After Grandfather's somewhat lengthy Thanksgiving grace he would stand, and looking over the relatives exclaim, "Who wants a drumstick?"

All the little folks would shout "ME!"

Grandfather would reply, as he always did, "This turkey would have to be a centipede to satisfy all you children," and we, as we always did, would laugh uproariously. Thanksgiving was indeed a glorious day!

Sometimes it requires the exercise of some judgment to determine just where the final cut should be made to ensure rapid healing. Generally the inexperienced worker errs on the side of leaving too much rather than too little shoulder.

The shape of the wound has an important effect on the speed of its healing. Other things being equal, smooth regular wounds heal more quickly than rough irregular wounds. Movement of the healing callous is largely downward through the inner bark. Sidewise movement is restricted, so areas cut off from the natural lines of sap flow heal slowly or not at all.

Jagged extensions of bark at the margin of the wound or protruding branch stubs are often cut off from the tree's food supply. And even if the food remains available, the callous will not cover such projections as quickly and efficiently as it will cover similar areas of smooth surface.

Paint wounds with tree paint or shellac. Do not paint the edges of the wound within a quarter inch of the outer bark, because a layer of cambium cells form the bark elements toward the inside layer, and if the cambium is painted the wound may never be covered, and the tree will rot.

After surgery, trees must be given ample water and fertilizer.

NATURE IN THE CITY

Now that another gardening season is over, those of us who do our gardening in towns and cities can look back and be especially grateful for the natural beauty we created and enjoyed during the past summer. City gardeners sometimes seem to forget that they *are* in the city, and that the "balance of nature" is quite different in the city from what it is in country woods and fields. City-dwellers must recognize that their plants and trees are living under different conditions.

There are many trees that grow easily in the rich moist leafmold of the forest but survive hardly or not at all when they are transplanted to the city.

The animal population is different, too. For example, the "natural" enemies of the squirrels, such as hawks, are not present in the city, and squirrels multiply. And many birds cannot live in city conditions. That is why we should learn to appreciate those that do. There is something unreasonable and thoughtless in the hatred many "nature-lovers" feel for the sparrow, that happy urbanite. The sparrow without doubt eats as many harmful weed seeds and insects as would a rarer and more colorful bird. So let's learn to be more tolerant of our fellow city-dwellers.

REMINDERS

If you feel really adventurous, try sowing sweet peas in November instead of early next spring. Plant in a deeply prepared trench just as you would in spring and mound the soil above ground level. If the seeds are winter-killed, you lose only the price of the seed and a little labor. If the seeds sprout next spring, they can make their most important growth in the cool weather of April and May, which they like, and be in bloom weeks early.

Keep the leaves raked off the lawn. Leaves pressed into the turf by heavy all-winter snows result in "kill spots," sometimes over the whole lawn if brown spot or snow mold takes over in the spring. But don't disturb the leaves that drift under and protect the shrubbery.

Never light a fire on good earth in the garden because the heat may destroy as much as two inches of good topsoil.

Clean the leaves out of your gutters and down spouts. Often melting snow falling from eave troughs and freezing on climbers or shrubbery will crush them. Place over these plants a temporary board roof to protect them.

Plant a few petunia and ageratum seeds in pots, and pot some mint plants for your indoor winter garden.

To protect shrubbery and trees, especially evergreen seedlings, from rabbits, try painting the trunks with a special rabbit repellent paint obtainable in seed stores. When shrubbery grows too thick and close to be painted, the paint can be thinned with alcohol and sprayed on in two coats.

✠ DECEMBER ✠

By the beginning of December, the first layer of the winter-long snow cover has already blanketed most of the North. It is likely to be March or even April before the northern gardener sees bare ground in his garden again. The winter ahead may seem long and bleak to the eager gardener, but there are compensations. The beauty of fresh snowfalls, the patterns of bare branches against the winter sky, the pleasures of winter sports, and the Christmas festivities all help to make a northern December exciting. Best of all, the northern gardener can go on growing flowers and greenery indoors, with new methods and new plants to be experimented with each year.

GROWING HOUSE PLANTS UNDER ARTIFICIAL LIGHT

One of the newest methods indoor gardeners should try is growing house plants under artificial light. Nearly every northern gardener has dreamed at one time or another of owning a small home greenhouse, where he could garden all winter to his heart's content under controlled conditions of heat and with the abundant natural light that so many plants need. But building and maintaining a greenhouse, even a small glass lean-to on the south side of the house, is expensive and requires more time and skill than the average gardener may have.

The most practical and interesting substitute for growing flowers in a greenhouse of your own is to grow flowers under controlled artificial light. Both incandescent and fluorescent bulbs can be used, and plants will flourish as if they were in natural sunlight.

256

A dark basement, attic, or any unused corner of your home can become a blooming indoor garden with only a moderate expenditure — around $20 — for equipment.

For a detailed introduction to this exciting method of indoor gardening, get *Growing Plants under Artificial Light,* by Peggie Schulz (M. Barrows and Co., $3.50). Step by step the author takes you — with illustrations and ample instructions — through all the processes, from building the equipment to growing the tubers, bulbs, and seeds into perfect blossoming plants. All this actually can be accomplished in rooms where there is no daylight or sunlight, and the results are usually for more satisfactory than can be obtained with window-sill gardening.

As you learn these new techniques, you will find that because you can control the exact amount of light your plants receive, they grow and flower much more quickly than on most window sills. The leaves appear healthier, colors are brighter, and the danger of sun damage to African violet and gloxinia leaves is avoided. Plants develop with perfect symmetry, since the set-up ensures equal illumination from all sides.

White fluorescent lamps, daylight fluorescent lamps, incandescent bulbs, or a combination of two of these can be used. Fluorescent tubes have the advantage of providing a wide extent of light and little heat, and are economical to operate for long periods of time. The incandescent bulbs furnish red rays that are lacking in fluorescent light and make a closer approximation to sunlight.

An ideal setup — except for plants that cannot stand the heat of incandescent lamps — combines two 40-watt daylight fluorescent tubes and two 25-watt incandescent bulbs, or a multiple of this arrangement. Or all white or all daylight fluorescent tubes, or one of each, will also give satisfactory results. The tubes are mounted on wrought-iron legs (bought at your furniture store), or more permanently, on plywood and suspended over the bench or table that holds your plants. Two such tubes will provide enough light for an area 2½ by 4 feet.

Reflectors, homemade or purchased, are essential, and pulleys and chains can be used to adjust the distance between light and plants. An automatic timing device to turn the lights off and on costs about $7 and is a great help. Most plants require between fourteen and eighteen hours of artificial light each day, but with two 40-watt tubes the cost is only about ¼ cent per hour. With an initial investment of not much more than $20, the cost of this new approach to indoor flower growing is modest enough to tempt many a northern gardener.

You can start experimenting with artificial light more conservatively if you wish, by growing ivy, pothos, and other foliage plants in planter lamps or under any reading light that is in use from four to six hours a day. This light will supplement the weak winter daylight and will produce healthier leaves than on foliage plants grown in most north windows. African violets also benefit by supplementary exposure to light from table lamps, and professional growers often use 100-watt incandescent floodlights to force amaryllis and gloxinias into bloom. Once you begin to discover the possibilities you will want to explore them further, so get Mrs. Schulz's book and start experimenting.

INDOOR FOLIAGE PLANTS

As the long northern winter begins to close in, we appreciate more than ever the pleasure of having green plants growing about

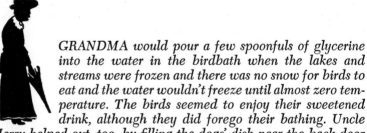

GRANDMA would pour a few spoonfuls of glycerine into the water in the birdbath when the lakes and streams were frozen and there was no snow for birds to eat and the water wouldn't freeze until almost zero temperature. The birds seemed to enjoy their sweetened drink, although they did forego their bathing. Uncle Jerry helped out, too, by filling the dogs' dish near the back door with fresh warm milk after each milking. How the birds would swarm around that dish! Even after the blue jays and magpies had drunk their fill, they would savagely go after the two dogs, pecking and chasing them away from the coveted dish of milk.

us indoors. Foliage plants are among the easiest house plants to grow as most of them do not require direct sunlight as many flowering plants do. A north window or even a coffee table or mantelpiece far from direct light will suit some of the handsomest varieties of foliage plants.

Ivy. English ivy is the parent type of most of the ivies grown indoors and is one of the most popular of all house plants. It grows best in bright light but not direct sunshine and in a cool temperature — not over 70 degrees. Most varieties of English ivy can be trained to climb on a support or around a window frame, though some, like Japanese ivy, grows upright on a woody stem. All ivies like a well-drained soil rich in organic matter and regular fertilization. The soil should be kept constantly moist and the leaves sprayed or sponged frequently to reduce the likelihood of scale insects or spider mites, the worst enemies of ivy. Ivy cuttings can be rooted and grown for a long period in water alone, but soil-grown plants are best as permanent specimens.

Philodendrons and Other Broad-Leaved Plants. In recent years the larger varieties of philodendron, dieffenbachia, and other tropical-looking plants have become tremendously popular as indoor house plants. The dramatic appearance of the large handsome leaves and the adaptability of these plants to average home conditions make them especially valuable for decorative purposes. The cut-leaf philodendron, spade-leaf philodendron, Swiss cheese plant *(Monstera deliciosa),* and other large varieties are usually grown in large pots or tubs and trained around a thick central support wrapped with moss that can be kept moist.

Both the large varieties of philodendron and the smaller ones — the familiar heart-leaf philodendron, for example — do best in a moist, rich, porous soil and in bright light but not sunlight. Warm temperatures do not bother them, but a minimum of 65 degrees is recommended. Most varieties are climbers or trailers and can be trimmed when growing tips become too long. The trimmings can be rooted in moist sand, vermiculite, or water to start new plants.

Philodendrons are subject to very few plant troubles, but their

259

leaves may turn yellow and drop off if they are kept too dry, if the pot is too small or the soil poorly drained, or if they are chilled. They will tolerate even darker spots than most foliage plants, but for large leaves and the healthiest appearance give them plenty of light.

Dieffenbachia, also called dumb cane, is another large, jungle-like plant that grows on a woody stem and generally has spotted or variegated green and ivory leaves. Among the best varieties are spotted dumb cane and Roehrs dumb cane. Like philodendron, dieffenbachia will tolerate poor light but does best in bright light, and requires a minimum temperature of 60 degrees. It should be kept a little dry, however, rather than constantly moist.

The ficus varieties, which include the rubber and fig plants, are also large-leaved plants that grow upright on woody stems and make dramatic accents for indoor decoration. They also like bright light but not sun, temperatures above 60, and a moist soil. The dracaenas are also upright growers but somewhat smaller in ulti-mate size. There are many varieties, some with spotted or varie-gated leaves, all requiring bright light, warm temperature, and a moist, well-drained soil.

Pothos is a smaller, trailing plant, very similar to the heart-leaf philodendron in appearance — except for a ridged instead of a smooth stem — and in culture, except that it should not be watered so freely. Sansevieria, the familiar snake plant, is another upright type with stiff sword-like leaves edged with lighter green or yel-low. It is a succulent and can go for long periods without water, making it one of the most tolerant house plants known. It will withstand almost any adverse condition except low temperature, but grows best when partially shaded, in moist soil, and at 65 to 70 degrees.

Chinese evergreen is another tough house plant, with attractive variegated or deep green leaves. It prefers good light and plenty of water but can survive in poor light, high temperatures, and dry soil — or grow in water alone. Peperomias are also tough, generally smaller in growth, and very attractive where a lower-growing foli-age plant is needed. They like bright light but not sun, tolerate darkness, and should not be kept wet or their leaves will rot off. Coleus is one of the few foliage plants that requires full sun — to bring out the bright red and green leaf colors. Keep it moist and pinch it back frequently to induce branching and sturdy growth. It can be planted outdoors in summer.

GRANDMA did not water her house plants with spring water from the stone milk house or water from the well. She said both were so hard they killed her flowers. She used soft water from the rain barrel and in winter melted snow. When she couldn't get these, Uncle Jerry would tote in a couple of pailsful from Lynn Brook, a mile away — and how he would growl. But his bark was worse than his bite. He would do anything for Grandma.

Ferns. Ferns are no longer so popular as house plants as they were in past years, but they still have much to recommend them. Their natural habitat is a dimly lighted location and it is mainly the hot dry atmosphere of most modern houses that makes ferns somewhat difficult to keep healthy indoors. Nearly all varieties like a moist atmosphere, good drainage, and a moist soil consisting of at least 50 per cent organic material. The maidenhair fern is one of the fussiest in requiring high humidity and is not well adapted to the ordinary home.

Other varieties — the familiar Boston fern, birdsnest fern, leatherleaf fern, holly fern, and the small table ferns — all will do well in bright light but not strong sunshine and at a minimum temperature of 65 degrees. The staghorn fern is usually grown on a fiber-covered piece of wood or bark which is immersed in water as often as necessary to keep it from drying out. This fern will survive temperatures as low as 40 degrees on a porch or shaded patio.

The chief enemies of fern are aphids and fern scale insects. The latter appear as flat, round, or oval brown or white scales on the

261

underside of the fronds and on the leaf stalks. Don't confuse them with the natural spore cases found on the backs of fern fronds. These occur in a fairly regular pattern and on the undersides only; scale insects are scattered irregularly and appear on leaf stalks as well. Spraying with nicotine sulphate (Black Leaf 40) is the best control for fern scale.

Cactus. Many varieties of cactus are suitable for indoor growing. Cacti are distinguished by their numerous spines and the absence of leaves and are classified as succulents — fleshy plants adapted to storing water. Cacti are slow growing, sometimes small in size, and excellent for dish gardens or planters. They like a sandy, well-drained soil, full sunlight if possible, and only enough water to keep the stems from shriveling. In periods of active growth and flowering and during the summer, however, water more frequently.

Plant food may be given two or three times a year to improve growth if the plants are in a sunny location. Temperature should go no lower than 65 degrees. The chief exception to these rules is the Christmas cactus, which is an epiphytic cactus and requires entirely different culture. We will discuss it later in this chapter.

FLOWERING INDOOR PLANTS FOR GIFTS

One of the pleasantest aspects of December for the northern gardener is the appearance of hundreds of different flowering plants for sale in the florists' shops and greenhouses. There is no finer Christmas gift for a gardener, either to give or to receive, than a potted plant in bloom and bearing the promise of weeks' more flowers to come.

With proper care most flowering gift plants will continue to be beautiful until the last bud has opened. Almost all these plants were raised in cool, moist greenhouses, however, and some of them do not take kindly to the sudden change into the hot, dry atmosphere found in most homes. However, by placing the plants in windows best suited to them you can enjoy many of them for weeks after the holidays.

If possible, keep your plants cool at night, even though you have to move them to another room. The night temperature should be about 60 degrees or less. Most plants can be watered by standing them for twenty minutes in a large pot of tepid water that comes nearly to the top of the pot. Do this about twice every week — oftener for some — and at the same time spray the leaves of smooth-leaved plants with tepid water, using a rubber hand spray. Never spray or water plants with cold water as it comes from the faucet.

Do not water plants with hard water if it can be avoided. Use rain water or melted snow. Don't use water from a water softener device, as it may harm your plants seriously. Turn plants frequently to keep them shapely. Many gift plants come in pots covered with aluminum foil. Loosen the foil to prevent mildew and puncture the bottom to allow ample drainage.

If you are delivering gift plants or flowers, be sure your car is warm. Just one chilling on a cold December day and the gift may be ruined.

Azalea. The azalea is one of our best house plants. It will blossom for weeks, and with proper care will repeat its blooming for many years to come. Two kinds are sold by florists: the indoor species, which looks like a little tree with a rounded top, and the hardy outdoor sort which has been forced to bloom in winter. The latter has low branches. Both kinds like moderate sunlight, a relatively cool temperature, and a great deal of water — the best method of watering is to immerse the plant in a pail of water when the soil looks dry, probably about once a week.

The average azalea plant in a six-inch pot is three and a half or four years old when it is sold. Many of them have been grafted onto a hardier root system, which adds to the life and beauty of the plant. The azalea can be kept for many years.

After your azalea has finished flowering, continue to keep it moist and in a light window. Fertilize every four weeks, using a special acid fertilizer — magnesium sulphate or Epsom salts — which is obtainable from your dealer. Use a teaspoonful dissolved in water to a six-inch pot. Start fertilizing at the end of the flowering season and continue until the following October. Apply fertilizer when the soil is moist, then water with plain water.

DECEMBER

Prune the soft green foliage back about an inch or two in May, to keep the plant shapely. In June set the plant outside in a semi-shaded spot, burying it up to the rim. Keep moist with frequent sprayings. Take it inside the first week of September before the first frost, and place it in a cool bright room until it flowers. The second year, repot it in fresh peatmoss and a slightly larger pot after it flowers in the spring. Occasional feedings of sheep manure or balanced plant food should be made throughout the year.

GRANDMA would be making "pomanders," or clove apples, every year about this time. She made them for her closest friends to place in their linen chests and clothes closets and also to hang on Christmas trees. This is her recipe: Press whole cloves into a medium-size, uncooked apple, continuing until the entire fruit is a mass of clove heads. Allow it to dry for a couple of weeks — it won't spoil or decay — then roll it in powdered cinnamon and, if you can get it, orris root. Tie a bow of ribbon to the stem or hang it by a double loop of ribbon or tinsel cord. These enchanting spicy balls will last for years. I have one that Grandma made over sixty years ago, and it is still delightfully fragrant.

Begonia. Fibrous-rooted begonias are among the easiest to grow and most popular of all house plants. These are several varieties, including the Melior or Christmas begonia, with bright green leaves almost covered with large pink or red blossoms; the ever-blooming type sometimes called wax begonias, which are hardy, cooperative plants that bloom all winter indoors and most of the summer outdoors; and several other varieties that are grown less for their flowers than for their handsome foliage.

The Christmas begonia is a little fussier than the everblooming varieties and blooms for a shorter period, but bears larger and more profuse blossoms. It prefers a moist atmosphere, some sunlight every day, and moderate watering. When the plant has ceased blooming, cut off top growth to within two inches of the soil and place in a semishady spot to rest with a minimum of watering. If you are lucky it may bloom again.

Everblooming begonias, like the Christmas begonia, enjoy a fairly sunny window, but cool night temperatures. They are free bloomers, and should be pinched back if they become "leggy." The cuttings root easily in water or sand and can provide a constant supply of new plants. Water regularly and do not allow the soil to become entirely dry. Begonias of all kinds thrive on a light misting or spraying with water every day during the indoor season. Feed them regularly with a balanced plant food and move the plants to larger pots whenever the roots become matted and the foliage is extending beyond the circumference of the pot. Begonias bloom best when slightly pot-bound, however, so shift them only to the next largest pot size.

Christmas Cactus. This old-fashioned favorite differs markedly from other cacti grown indoors. It is a large, long-lived plant, often surviving for several generations, and is covered with beautiful large cerise flowers for two to three months during the winter. It grows best in a sunny window, constantly moist, porous soil, and cool temperatures. Flower buds will not form unless night temperatures drop at least to 65 degrees. Even after buds are formed, they may drop before flowering if temperatures are too high or if they get too little light.

Fertilize once a week with a balanced plant food or sheep manure while buds are forming and water thoroughly when the soil is nearly dry. In the summer the Christmas cactus should be placed outdoors in a semishady, protected spot and watered as needed until late summer. Some gardeners then reduce watering drastically for four to six weeks and bring the plant into a dark basement to induce the setting of buds. Other gardeners have equally good luck with a normal regimen of water and sunlight after the plant is brought indoors. You might try both methods alternately if your Christmas cactus has not bloomed well, but if it blooms on its present schedule, don't change.

Cyclamen. The cyclamen is one of the most beautiful of greenhouse-raised house plants. When given proper care, which includes a cool location, especially at night, it may blossom for weeks. Then, after a short rest period, it may start another blossoming in early spring.

The cyclamen prefers cool, moist conditions. Keep it in a good light but not in sunshine — a north or east window is fine — and as cool as possible. You can lengthen the blooming period by placing the plant in a cool (50 degrees) hall or basement each night. Avoid pouring water on the center or crown. It is better to water it by placing the pot in a deep pan of water for an hour every two or three days, whenever the soil begins to dry. When your plant has finished flowering, gradually decrease the watering so it will go into a rest period. The pot, with the bulb somewhat exposed, can be placed in the basement or any cool (not freezing), dry place until June or July, when it can be started into growth again. Water sparingly until foliage begins to appear.

A teaspoonful of complete balanced fertilizer should be given in water about every four weeks. Turn the plant occasionally, so that all sides receive proper light. Your plant should then flower again next December, if not before. Water your cyclamen with cool water, about 50 to 60 degrees. Do not use water that has been treated with a water softener, but natural soft water, such as rain water, is ideal.

If a leaf or flower stem wilts or dries up, remove it with a quick pull from the plant's crown.

Fuchsia. The fuchsia is rapidly coming into favor again. It is a beautiful house plant that was popular years ago and was one of the house plants that Grandma grew in tin cans on her kitchen window sills. They thrived in the steam-laden atmosphere originating from the spout of the singing teakettle. Fuchsia then carried the old-fashioned name of Lady's Eardrops because of its odd blossoms. For some reason it practically disappeared from the window garden for long years, but it can be purchased now in most greenhouses.

The fuchsia prefers an east window or a cool south window if shaded from an excess of sunshine. The pale rays of the January or

February sun will not injure it, however. After blooming ceases the fuchsia requires a rest period. The soil is allowed to dry gradually, and the pot is removed to a dark basement for two or three months. After this rest, the plant is repotted in soil with a high humus content. A complete plant food should be added to the potting soil to furnish needed nourishment. The plant is then brought to the light and allowed to start new growth. Keep it moist and feed every three to four weeks after growth starts, and before long it should be blooming again.

GRANDMA'S Christmas cactus always came into glorious bloom before Christmas and continued into March. The beautiful red blossoms grew on the ends of the flat leaves and hung in a cascade of color over the side of the pot. Grandma had brought the plant up to Canada from the South. She got her cuttings for it from her grandmother, from a plant over a hundred years old.

Geranium. Geraniums are a little more humble and proletarian than some flowering gift plants, but few others have remained so consistently popular. It can be grown either indoors or outdoors, but if your plants bloom indoors in winter you cannot expect outdoor bloom as well — and vice versa.

The geranium is an ideal plant for overheated modern houses and apartments. It will prosper in a dry atmosphere that would kill African violets, but it will also do well in a reasonably moist atmosphere. When grown indoors, it needs full and constant sunshine. Ordinary house temperatures and humidity are satisfactory, but a temperature of 70 to 75 degrees by day and 60 degrees by night is ideal. Pinch back if it becomes leggy.

Water geraniums thoroughly when they need it, but avoid overwatering. Do not sprinkle the foliage, but dust the leaves once a week with a clean paintbrush and turn the plant frequently so all

267

sides may receive the full light from the window. Set the plants outdoors in spring when the weather is warm, let them continue blooming as long as they will, and then take cuttings in August for new plants for next winter's bloom. Geraniums bloom best when their roots are crowded, so do not repot too often.

Hydrangea. A potted hydrangea requires plenty of water while blooming. If the soil dries out it will wilt. Water daily — twice a day if the room is dry and hot — by setting the pot in a large pan of water until the soil is thoroughly soaked. It likes a lot of light — full sunlight if possible — and a cool temperature at night will enlarge the flowers and lengthen their life. Keep it out of drafts.

In the spring, after the hydrangea is through flowering, cut it back to three inches and plant it in the garden. Repot in late summer but leave the plant outdoors until after the first light frost. Then store it in a cool dark corner of your basement, keeping it moist until January, when it will start to grow and bloom again in a sunny window.

Poinsettia. Poinsettias, the traditional Christmas plant, come in three colors, red, white, and pink. The bracts are commonly called blossoms, but they are really colorful leaves. The poinsettia must be kept moist but not flooded. It requires a warm, even temperature — not over 75 degrees — and direct sunlight. If it becomes dry, the leaves drop off. A sudden change in temperature, strong sunshine, a draft, or excessive dryness will all cause a loss of foliage almost immediately. Do not allow the temperature to drop below 60 degrees at night.

After blooming cut the stalks back to a few inches and store in a cool, shady place until spring, when it can be planted in partial shade in the garden, pot and all. In the fall before frost, repot the plant in a larger container and bring it into the house — first to a cool porch or garage, then to a north room, and then to a sunny window. If you keep night temperatures cool and keep the poinsettia out of artificial light after October, it may bloom again even more beautifully than it did the year before.

Miniature Rosebush. A potted rosebush with miniature blossoms is a delightful gift. Treat it kindly and you can transplant to your garden in the spring where it will bloom again. Indoors it needs moderate watering, even, warm temperatures, and some sunshine. Avoid sudden temperature changes.

When the plant is through blooming it should be pruned back, removing the top six to eight inches of each stem. Never prune away the old growth that was made the previous year. In May, remove it from its pot and plant it in the garden. If given adequate winter protection it will become a permanent resident and will bloom outdoors next year.

Other Gift Plants. Some gift plants, such as cineraria, Jerusalem cherry, and calceolaria, are greenhouse-grown annuals and just can't stand overheated homes. So enjoy them while you may and discard them without regret when bloom is over. Cineraria and calceolaria require an abundance of water but can be given too much. If kept in a cool room with a humid atmosphere, they should last from two to three weeks. Do not place them in direct sunshine but try to give them plenty of light. Remove faded flowers and discard when through blooming.

Jerusalem cherry is a cheerful little holiday bush with scarlet berries — not really cherries, however. Keep it cool or it will lose its berries and leaves. Water moderately and set it in a window where it will receive all sunlight possible. Avoid drafts and sudden changes in temperature around the plant. These plants are usually short-lived in our overheated homes.

Primulas or primroses require constant moisture and need a cool, humid atmosphere for best development. Water them by setting the pots in a tub. Keep moisture from the crown, give them good light, keep old blooms cut off, and the plants should bloom through spring. Then they should be discarded.

OTHER CHRISTMAS GIFTS FOR GARDENERS

Whether you are looking for a Christmas gift for a dyed-in-the-wool home gardener, for a friend who is only mildly interested in gardening, or for yourself, the task is easy. Just look around in the garden stores, flower shops, and nurseries, and you will discover many things to delight a gardener's heart. A new spade, an insect duster, a power lawnmower, a bale of peatmoss, a fertilizer spreader, or a sack of lawn food would not look out of place beside a gardener's Christmas tree.

There are garden soil-testing kits any gardener can use. With one of these, you can learn from the soil itself just what foods are needed and how much to apply in every plot to suit the requirements of different plants. A good kit costs less than $5. All gardeners can use plant labels. Many now are made of dull-finish plastic that will retain pencil markings until they are removed with kitchen cleansing powder. They come in many sizes and shapes.

GRANDMA made little suet plum puddings for the birds. When she was making our Christmas puddings, she always saved generous pieces of suet with which she mixed nuts, raisins, currants, and cracked corn. She rolled them all into balls about the size of crab apples. Through the balls she threaded a three-strand braid woven from the short ends of bright red yarn she used when knitting mittens for her grandchildren. On Christmas morning the little puddings were hung for the birds on the evergreen trees on each side of the road that ran from the farmhouse to the pike.

Bulbs for the indoor garden are always a good choice, and you can still buy calla lilies, narcissuses, hyacinths, and crocuses. Amaryllis bulbs are just coming in at most garden stores. All are dandy gifts for shut-ins, especially if a pot and potting earth are included. Get a folder of planting instructions from the dealer. In some cases it may be better for you to do the potting.

The huge Warehoven strain of Royal Dutch amaryllis bulbs should be in the stores about now. It is unquestionably among the finest of all amaryllis. The huge blossoms come in white, pink, brilliant and dark red, and also variegated colors. The giant bulbs are developed in Holland and weigh up to two pounds each. With proper care after blooming the bulbs will last for years. There is also the beautiful Roman hyacinth for growing in earth. These bulbs are about tulip size and can be planted three or more to a pot. Like the amaryllis, they require no long rooting treatment as tulips do.

A Christmas box of fresh English holly with red berries, or of heather, will always be appreciated. Another very acceptable present is a gift certificate for a tree — shade, fruit, or flowering — or for shrubbery or a new rose. Any of these can be delivered next spring when planting conditions are right. Any member of your local nurserymen's association or the American Association of Nurserymen can take your order and make delivery almost anywhere in the United States. You can send a gift card to the recipient at Christmas time.

Elderly people who can't get out, children, and all nature lovers would enjoy a bird-feeding station (with a sack of bird food) that could be hung just outside the window where a constant parade of feeding birds could be watched. There is a new bird food, saffron seed, which is so hard that sparrows pass it up, but it is thoroughly enjoyed by cardinals and bluejays. It is obtainable in some garden stores.

For women gardeners there are smart kneeling aprons made of waterproof khaki. These have pockets for notebooks, seeds, and small tools. Other gifts that will be appreciated are imported chrome-plated, rustproof pruning shears. They are light but practical. There is also a powerful stainless steel insecticide sprayer that is rustproof and will last for years.

Another lasting gift for a flower enthusiast would be a membership for next year in the state horticultural society. In Minnesota this includes a subscription to the *Horticulturist,* a magazine tailored for the home and professional gardeners of the Upper Midwest. Send $2 and the name and address to Editor E. M. Hunt, University Farm, St. Paul 1, Minnesota. A special Christmas letter will be sent to the recipient.

Specialized garden books are always an excellent choice for gifts, provided that you choose with a gardener's particular interests and abilities in mind.

271

DECEMBER

For an avid flower gardener, you might buy *The Concise Encyclopedia of Favorite Flowers,* by Marjorie P. Johnson, edited by Montague Free (American Garden Guild and Doubleday, $3.95). This is a convenient 250-page book which carefully describes each of 106 most popular garden flowers.

GRANDMA never had trouble with her Christmas trees drying and losing their needles. They were always fresh and green. A day or two before Christmas Uncle Jerry and we children would plow through the snow to the nearby balsam woods where we would choose the tree carefully and Uncle would cut it. The tree was set up at once in the parlor. It stood in a large bucket surrounded by stones. The bucket was covered with a pillow slip and encircled by a wide red or green ribbon tied in a bow. Grandma filled the bucket with hot water sweetened with maple syrup. Often the tree would grow new needles before the end of the holidays.

Gardening for Color, by William H. Clark (who must be an artist as well as a gardener) is published by Little, Brown and costs $2.95. It tells how to achieve a harmony of color in blossoms, vines, shrubs, and trees, and for further convenience lists plants by size as well as color. This book would be a great aid to planning a garden.

Specialists in daylilies — and their number is growing — would find *Daylilies,* by Ben Arthur Davis (Tupper and Love, $3.50) of great value. It is a comprehensive work on the culture of hemerocallis, including regional chapters by specialists from those areas.

Gardeners who are fascinated by the tuberous begonia would like to have *Tuberous Begonias,* by Worth Brown (M. Barrows and Co., $3.50). Gloxinia specialists would enjoy *Gloxinias and How to Grow Them,* by Peggie Schulz. Indoor gardeners should have *Plants in Pots,* by William H. Clark (Little Brown, Boston, $2.95), an alphabetically arranged guidebook that tells of the re-

272

quirements of heat, light, humidity, water, food, and air for each of many house plants.

YOUR CHRISTMAS TREE

Choosing a Christmas tree is one of the pleasantest tasks of the holiday season. If you live in a wooded area, perhaps you can go into your own woodlot and choose a fine, big tree — with the children's help, of course. Most of us who live in big cities have to buy our trees at a service station, grocery store, or one of the neighborhood Christmas tree lots, surrounded by noisy buses, cars, and jostling crowds. But it is fun anyway and with the children's help you tie the tree onto your car where everybody can see it and drive triumphantly home.

Be careful not to tie the tree too tightly or crush it with the trunk cover, as its branches are brittle in frosty weather. A couple of burlap sacks or an old quilt will help to cushion it.

The American Association of Nurserymen suggests that the best all-round Christmas tree is the balsam fir. It is native to Minnesota and Wisconsin. The shiny bright green foliage is whitish underneath and aromatic. The needles are three fourths of an inch long, remain on the tree a long time, and are very fragrant. The spruce is also a good tree, but tends to shed its needles more freely. It is symmetrical, thickly branched, and can be bought from three to twenty feet high. Pick out a tree that is fresh and green — not one that looks dry and is dropping its needles.

Don't feel disturbed or guilty about cutting or buying evergreens for Christmas trees. Today most Christmas trees are "harvested" as a crop or to give living room to regular plantings. Evergreens grow far too slowly on the poorer forest soils and wet bog areas to produce lumber or pulpwood crops. Thus Christmas trees are the only profitable harvest that can be produced on such inferior land.

Another Christmas tree source is "thinnings." In growing trees as a lumber crop, frequent thinning is essential to allow the larger trees room to live and grow. The thinnings can be sold as Christmas trees — and fill several needs: first, as bringers-of-joy into many homes; second, as an income source to northern foresters; third, as "life insurance" for upcoming timber crops.

Once you have got your tree home, the first procedure is to make it as fireproof as possible. A tree that is green and pliable will absorb moisture before and after it is placed in the house, and will present little fire hazard. If the weather is mild and above freezing, keep the tree outside — first standing it in hot water — for several days. Otherwise keep it in the cool basement. Cut a few inches off the base — a diagonal cut is best — to assure free absorption of water. Then lay the tree on the ground or basement floor and sprinkle it with warm, not hot, water and keep it covered with wet sacks or damp paper for several days.

GRANDMA always had Uncle Jerry shovel a 36-inch path from the farmhouse to the turnpike road — a good eighth of a mile — after a snowstorm. One Christmas when the snow was almost five feet deep Uncle Jerry had a bright idea and made the path half width. Aunt Mina, who weighed over two hundred pounds and wasn't liked by Uncle Jerry, drove ten miles to the farm and then couldn't get through to the house. She went home very angry. Uncle tried to escape Grandma's wrath by saying, "She could have come through sideways." Grandma retorted, "You know perfectly well Mina hasn't got any sideways."

If your tree holder allows the tree to stand in water, keep it well filled with a plant-food solution. If you do not have a water-well stand, put your tree in an eight- to sixteen-quart bucket. Fill in around the tree with rocks and then fill the bucket with plant-food solution, one cup of commercial plant food per gallon of water. Keep adding water during the holidays as it is absorbed by the tree. This treatment will help keep the tree green and fire resistant. Trees often will grow needles on the ends of branches during the holidays, and may absorb half a pail of water in twenty-four hours.

Another method to make your tree fire-resistant and needle-retentive is to spray it with a solution of 30 per cent water glass (sodium silicate) mixed with 70 per cent water, in which has been dissolved a teaspoonful of soap flakes (not detergent) to each quart of water. After the first coat dries, apply two more coats a day apart. You can get water glass at your drug store.

Another fire retardant is an almost saturated solution of ammonium sulphamate, one or more pounds dissolved in a gallon of warm water. Sprinkle all needles and branches of the tree several times, using a watering can and allowing it to dry between applications. This chemical can be obtained at seed stores and is not expensive. The tree can then stand in the solution. Remember there is no known method that will make an evergreen absolutely fireproof, but a moist green tree is much slower to ignite than a dry one.

Place the tree in the coolest corner, away from doorways, registers, and fireplaces. Don't smoke or strike a match near the tree, and of course, don't use wax or paraffin candles for decorations. Don't use old, worn electric light strings, or strings that are at all questionable, and never leave the lights burning when you leave the house. Don't use inflammable decorations of any kind. Fireproof cotton for snow effects is obtainable in the stores.

You can make safe, beautiful snow by dissolving one cup of soap flakes in one cup of warm water. Then whip with an egg beater. Apply the stiff white froth on the tree with your fingers, working from the top downward. Allow the children the fun of helping. The "snow" tree will still be beautiful at the end of the holidays, but this treatment does not fireproof the tree. Just as soon as it becomes dry or begins to drop its needles, it should be discarded. A dry Christmas tree is so inflammable it is almost explosive. Don't take any chances — there will be another Christmas and another lovely tree next year.

REMINDERS

If your gladiolus bulbs have been in paper bags with naphthalene flakes for over a month, remove them from the bags, give them a dusting with 10 per cent DDT powder, and store them on shallow trays in a cool, dark, dry place until spring.

In the event of a heavy, clinging snowfall — quite likely to occur at this season — do not brush the snow downward off the laden evergreen branches or you might break a branch. Lift the branches with the flat side of a broom and gently toss off the snow.

GRANDMA'S house was a very busy place during the week before Christmas. In the evenings the grandchildren made decorations for two Christmas trees, identical in size. One was for us and the other for the children who lived in the orphans' home in town. The big dining room table was pulled out and we sat around it stringing cranberries on linen thread, and popcorn tinted pink with cochineal. Jacob's ladders were made of stiff colored paper and angels were cut out of silver paper. Bright red snow apples were polished, and there were oranges and a lot of popcorn balls covered with taffy to hang on each tree.

If you have a large level lot, why not make a home skating rink for the children? If the lawn has considerable slope, you may have to set up a few boards as a retaining wall but usually a bank of snow a few inches high around the rink area will do the trick. Wet the snow slightly with a watering can, or with a light spray from the garden hose. When the snowbank freezes it will hold in the water for the rink. With the hose, give the enclosure a light flooding on the snow. When this freezes, the ground should be watertight and you can go ahead and flood the area.

Do not try to form the rink with one flooding. Make several shallow applications of water, allowing thorough freezing after each flooding. Later, as the ice becomes chipped and rough from use, sweep it clean, and give it another light flooding, just enough to resurface the ice. On very cold days when the water might freeze in the hose, you can resurface the ice with a sprinkling can and hot water. Walk backward as you sprinkle so you will not step in the freshly applied water.

The rink may injure your lawn a bit, but a little work and grass seed will remedy the damage, if any, in a few weeks next spring.

Heat your snow shovel and polish it with floor wax or paraffin. The snow will not stick to the shovel and your labor will be greatly reduced.

Merry Christmas to all and the happiest New Year ever in your garden!

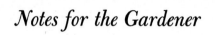
Notes for the Gardener

TABLE 1. SELECTED ANNUALS AND BIENNIALS FOR GROWING IN THE NORTH

Name	Height	Germ. Time in Days	Final Distance Apart	Bloom	Remarks on Culture
Ageratum	4–24″	5–10	7–10″	May–frost; blue, lavender, white	Used for edging.
Alyssum (sweet) Compact Spreading	2–4″ 10″	5–10	5″ 10″	White, purple	Will tolerate shade. Self-seeding. Blooms all summer. When sheared back will bloom again. Can be potted for winter growth. Sow ¼ inch deep.
Amaranthus (summer poinsettia)	48–72″		18″	Red, bronze	Colored foliage. Large, coarse, shrub-like.
Anagallis (pimpernel)	2–18″		6″	Summer, early fall; red, blue	Full sun. Rock garden and borders.
Anchusa (bugloss, capensis)	to 18″		12″	True blue	Full sun.
Arctotis (African daisy)	to 36″	12	12″	White	Sandy soil. Full sun.
Aster (China)	12–18″	8	1″	Midsummer–frost; purple, white	Rich soil. Full sun. Clean, neat. Shallow-rooted. Keep some distance from calendulas. Support tall exposed ones. Self-seeding. Put in different spot each year.
Baby's breath (gyphsophila)	18″	8	12″	White	Can be dried for winter bouquets. Use in rock gardens. Sow often.
Bachelor's button (cornflower)	30″			Pink, red, white, blue	Full sun or part shade. Will bloom all summer if dead ones are removed.

TABLE 1–Continued

Name	Height	Germ. Time in Days	Final Distance Apart	Bloom	Remarks on Culture
Balsam	24–36"	10		Pink, white	Rich, moist soil. Full sun.
Begonia (semperflorens)	12–18"		1"	White, pink, red until frost	Sun or shade.
Castor-oil plant	4–8'		4–6'		Background plant.
Bellflower (Canterbury bell, campanula)	2–2½'	8	1"	White, lavender, blue, rose, pink	Annual and biennial.
Brachycome (swan river daisy)	12"		6"	All summer; blue, white, pink	Edging, rock gardens. Full sun. Short-lived flowers.
Browallia	1–2'	5–10	9"	Blue	Moist soil. Long blooming.
Calendula	12–24"	10		Yellow, buff, cream apricot, orange	Full sun, cool moist soil.
California poppy (eschscholtzia)	12"	8	6"	June–frost; white, red, yellow	Sandy, poor soil. Very hardy.
Calliopsis	1–36"	15		Yellow, gold	Self-seeds. Full sun. Used in mixed borders and waste places.
Carnation	15–18"			White, red, yellow	Biennial also.
Clarkia	to 2'		9"	Rose, purple	
Cockscomb (celosia)	2–3'	5–10	1'	Red, purple, yellow, gold	Full sun or part shade. Can be dried for winter bouquets.
Coleus	8–18"	9			Colored foliage.

TABLE 1—Continued

Name	Height	Germ. Time in Days	Final Distance Apart	Bloom	Remarks on Culture
Cosmos	36–72"	5	3'	Scarlet, rose, white, yellow, orange	Full sun. Use for background.
Dahlia (dwarf)	to 24"	5	18" or more	All but blue	Rich loamy soil. Full sun.
English daisy	6"	5–10		Fall; white, pink, rose	Really biennial. Semishade. Moist soil. Rock gardens.
Everlasting flower	15"	15		Pink, white	Dry soil.
Forget-me-not	9"	9		Blue	Hot, dry, sunny.
Four o'clock	24"	6	18"	Yellow, pink, red, white	Plant anywhere.
Foxglove	to 6'		6–8"	June–July; white, purple	Really biennial. Sun or half shade. Self-seeding.
Gaillardia	24"	15	9"	June–October; red, yellow, petal-tips	Full sun.
Geranium	to 18"		8–12"	Red shades; May–June	Full sun.
Gerbera	1–2'	10–20		Red, white, orange	Plant indoors in January. Rich sandy soil.
Godetia	9–36"	6	1'	Summer–fall; white, red, pink	Poor soil, moist, half shade.

283

TABLE 1—Continued

Name	Height	Germ. Time in Days	Final Distance Apart	Bloom	Remarks on Culture
Heliotrope	12–24"	14	12"	Lavender	Full sun, good soil.
Hibiscus	2–10'		1'	July–frost; yellow, blue	Shrub-like.
Euphorbia (Snow-on-the-mountain)	3–4'		1'		Causes eczema. Foliage plant. Dry, sandy soil.
Hollyhock	5–8'	5	18"	Red, white, pink	Really biennial. Annual varieties must be planted very early. Esp. Indian spring.
Kochia	to 5'	10–20	24"		Temporary hedge. Brilliant red fall foliage.
Larkspur	12–48"	7–14	6–7"	Red, white, blue, pink	Sow shallowly ⅛ inch deep.
Lavatera (annual mallow)	6–10'		18–24"	Rose, red, white	Temporary hedge. Full sun. Dry soil.
Lobelia	4–18"	14		Blue, white	Full sun or part shade. Pinch after seedlings are well started.
Lupine	12–36"	5–10		Late summer, early autumn; blue, white, yellow, rose	Sandy soil, endure drought. Annual and perennial variety.
Marguerite	18"	6		White, yellow	
Marigold	1–4'	4–5	12–24"	Yellow, orange	Sun, low nitrogen soil. Easily grown.
Mignonette	6–18"	5–10	12"	All summer; red, white, yellow	Moist soil, part shade.
Nasturtium	9"–9'	9	8"–6'	Yellow, red, mahogany	Poor soil, full sun. Don't transplant. Subject to aphids.

284

TABLE 1–Continued

Name	Height	Germ. Time in Days	Final Distance Apart	Bloom	Remarks on Culture
Nicotiana	18–48"	6	9–12"	White, red, salmon, cream	Dry upside down. Moist, part shade.
Nigella (Love-in-a-mist) . .	18–24"	10–20	6"	Blue, white	Self-sows. Short blooming season.
Pansy	1'	8–20	6"	Spring–June; all but red	Cool growing conditions.
Petunia					
Balcony	18–24"	10–20	10"	Summer–frost; all but blue and orange	Fancy double varieties should be started indoors.
Dwarf bedding . . .	12–18"	6–10	12"		
Giant ruffled . . .	12–15"	10–20	6"		
Phlox drummondi . . .	to 15"	9–14	6–9"	Early; white through purple	Grow anywhere. Full sun.
Pinks	6–24"			Late spring, another burst in fall	Full sun. Slightly alkaline soil.
Poppy	to 36"	7	12–18"	Scarlet, white, pink, salmon, apricot	Dust seeds with ant powder. Full sun. Sandy loam. Short-lived flowers. Burn tips of stems after picking.
Portulaca	6"	10–20	6–10"	Spring; white, yellow, salmon, pink, rose, red	Ground cover, mix seed with sand. Grow in sand, among rocks. Full sun. Self-sow, but revert to pink.
Salpiglossis	30"	10–20		July–frost; yellow, crimson	
Salvia	18"	15		Early summer–frost; blue	

285

TABLE 1–Concluded

Name	Height	Germ. Time in Days	Final Distance Apart	Bloom	Remarks on Culture
Scabiosa	15"	7	1'	Lavender, white, rose, cream, purple	Full sun.
Snapdragon	15–36"	10–20	10–12"	White, yellow, pink, crimson, lavender	Sun or semishade, rich alkaline soil. Support tall ones.
Spider flower (cleome spinosa)	5'		15"	Pink, white	Good screen. Weed out rose-purple ones. Full sun, very light shade.
Stock	to 30"		15"	White, lilac, yellow, blush, red, purple	Requires cool growing conditions.
Strawflower	36"	6	12–18"	Fall; yellow, red, orange, white	Full sun. Grown mostly for drying. Pick just as they open, hang upside down.
Sweet pea	8"–6'	12–20	12"	Late summer; pastel colors	Cool moist soil. Plant 12–18 inches deep in trench with compost or peatmoss. Pick often. Mulch.
Tithonia (Mexican sunflower)	36–72"		3'	Fall; red, orange	
Torenia	12"		6"	Summer, fall; pink, blue	Sun or semishade. Foliage turns red.
Verbena	6–12"	10–20	6–12"	Midsummer–fall; white, pink, rose, scarlet, lavender	Thin, pinch. For carpet, peg down trailers.
Viola	8"	5–10	9"		Really biennial.
Wallflower	1–2'		1'		Needs cool, moist soil.
Zinnia	12–48"	4–5	12"	Late summer–fall; all except blue	

TABLE 2. SELECTED PERENNIALS FOR GROWING IN THE NORTH

Name	Height	Space Between	Bloom	Remarks on Culture
Achillea (milfoil, yarrow) .	1½–5'	8–10"	June–July; small double white flowers	Full sun, good soil, divide every 3 years. Cut shoots back after flowering.
Agrostemma (mullein) . .	2½–6'	4–8"	June–July; purple	Sun, light soil. Self-seeding.
Alyssum	12"	12"	June–Sept.; yellow	Saxatile blooms in May.
Anchusa (Dropmore) . .	15–18"	18"	April–May; clear blue	Full sun.
Anthemis (golden marguerite, St. John's daisy) . . .	2–3'	12"	May–Sept.; yellow	Full sun, moderately rich soil.
Arabis (white rockcress) .	12"	6"	April–May	Shade or sun, dry soil. Good for edging, rockery.
Armeria (thrift, sea-pink) .	6–9"	10"	May–June; pink to red	Full sun, sandy soil.
Artemisia (wormwood) . .	1½–5'	18"	May–October	Full sun, poor, dry soil. White and silver foliage. Pollen bad for hay fever.
Aster	2–4'	2'	Fall; white, pink, blue, lavender	Full sun, soil moist during growing season, dry when dormant. Divide every 2 or 3 years.
Astilbe (florists' spirea) .	2–3'	18"	June–July; pink	Partial shade; rich moist soil.
Aubrietia (purple rockcress)	3–6"	12"	May; purple	
Baby's breath	2–3'	24"	June–Sept.; white, pink	
Balloon flower (platycodon grandiflorum)	1–3'	12"	June–Aug.; white, blue, lavender, pink	Full sun or light shade. Self sows.
Beebalm (bergamot, monarda) . .	3–4'	12"	July–Aug.; scarlet	

TABLE 2—Continued

Name	Height	Space Between	Bloom	Remarks on Culture
Bleeding heart	2–3′	7–24″	Early spring; rose, pink	Light shade, rich soil. Large, spreading plant. Move in early spring or after flowering.
Blue flax (linum perenne)	1½–2′	12″	June–July; blue	Flowers drop after noon. Can be grown from seed.
Boltonia	4–8′	36″	Aug.–Sept.; pink, purple	Will naturalize.
Brunnera macrophylla (dwarf anchusa)	9–15″	12″	April–May; blue	
Bugleweed (ajuga)	to 10″	9–12″	May–June; blue	Sun, light shade, full shade. Rich soil. Excellent for edging.
Catananche caerulea (cupid's dart)	1½–2″		June–Aug.; blue	Requires some winter protection.
Cerastium tomentosum (snow-in-summer)	6″		June; white	Creeps, white foliage.
Chrysanthemum	10–36″	12–18″	Late summer, fall; gold, bronze, yellow, pink, magenta, white	Full sun, very rich soil. Pinch back. Divide every spring.
Cimifuga (bugbane, fairy candle, black snakeroot)	to 6′		Midsummer; white	Light shade, rich moist soil. Good for woodland planting.
Columbine (aquilegia)	1–4′	8–12″	Late spring–early summer; blue, yellow, red, white	Full sun, light shade. Can be grown from seed. Subject to leaf miner.
Coral bells (heuchera)	18″	9″	June–July; white, coral, red, pink	Sun, part shade, rich soil.
Coreopsis (tickseed)	2–2½′	18″	June–Oct.; yellow	Can be grown from seed. Prune faded flowers.

TABLE 2-Continued

Name	Height	Space Between	Bloom	Remarks on Culture
Daisy, painted (pyrethrum roseum, chrysanthemum coccineum)	18–24"	1'	May–July; red, pink	
Daylily (hemerocallis) . .	1½–5'	2'	May–Aug.; pale yellow to maroon	Sun or light shade. Rich soil.
Cornflower (centaurea montana)	1½–2'	12"	June–Sept.; blue	
Delphinium				
Dwarf (Chinese) . . .	12–18"	8–12"	Late spring–early summer; blue, white, purple	Full sun, moderately fertile soil.
Pacific hybrids	4–6'	1½–2'		Subject to crown rot and cyclamen mites. Can be grown from seed.
Forget-me-not	6–12"	6–9"	April–June; blue	Can be grown from seed.
Gaillardia	2–3'	12"	June–frost; red, yellow	Full sun, dry, sandy soil. Can be grown from seed. Divide in spring.
Gas plant (dictamnus albus, rubra)	2–3'	24"	May–June; white, purple	Exceedingly permanent.
Geum	1½–2'	12"	June–Aug.; orange, scarlet	Good soil. Requires careful winter protection.
Golden glow	5–9'	12"	Aug.–Sept.; yellow	Full sun, part shade. Subject to aphids and red lice.
Harebell (campanula carpatica)	9–15"	12"	July–Sept.; white, blue	Full sun, part shade.
Helenium (sneezeweed) .	2–6'	12–18"	Late summer–early fall; gold, yellow	

TABLE 2—Continued

Name	Height	Space Between	Bloom	Remarks on Culture
Heliotrope	4–5'	12"	June–July; white	Very tender. Light, rich soil. Bedding plant.
Hosta (plantain lily, funkia)	1½–3'	24"	July–Sept.; lilac, white	Shade essential, wet soil. Fragrant.
Iberis (candytuft)	9–12"	2'	May–June; pale lilac	Trim off excess growth.
Lathyrus latifolius (perennial pea)	6–8'	12"	July–Sept.; deep rose	Can be grown from seed.
Lupine	3–5'	12"	Early summer; purple, blue, red, yellow	
Lychnis	1–1½'	6–12"	June–July; red, orange	*Chalcedonica* fairly permanent.
Lythrum	3–4'	18"	July–Sept.; rose, purple	Likes wet soil.
Mertensia virginica (Virginia bluebell)	1–2'	9"	April–May; blue	Transplant in autumn.
Monkshood	2–7'	6–9"	Aug.–Sept.; blue, white	Light shade, deep rich soil. Poisonous.
Myrtle (vinca minor, trailing periwinkle)		12"	Late spring–Sept.; blue	Ground cover. Sun or light shade. Requires winter protection.
Nepeta (ground ivy, catmint)	15"	12"	June–frost; lavender	Blooms intermittently. Cut off early in spring.
Oenothera (evening primrose)	1–2'	1–2'	June–Aug.; yellow	
Oriental poppy	3–4'	12–18"	Late spring–early summer; pink, salmon, red, white	Full sun, part shade, very rich soil. Pest-free.
Penstemon (beard-tongue)	2–5'	1"	June–frost; white, pink, scarlet	Full sun. Requires winter protection.

TABLE 2–Concluded

Name	Height	Space Between	Bloom	Remarks on Culture
Peony	2½–3½'	2½–3'	Late spring–early summer; white, pink, red, yellow	Full sun. Not too deep. Use wood ashes in spring.
Phlox	2–4'	12–18"	Summer; red, pink, white, purple	Full sun or light shade, moist rich soil. Clip off fading flowers. Subject to red spider, mildew.
Physostegia	3–5'	1–2'	July–Sept.; pink to purple	Some varieties are invading.
Pink	6–13"	8–10"	Late spring–fall; salmon, pink, rose, crimson, maroon, white	Needs well-drained soil to survive winter. Can be grown from seed.
Primrose (English primrose, primula vulgaris)	4–6"	12"	April–May; blue, white, pink	Light shade, deep rich moist soil. Needs winter protection.
Scutellario	1'	9"	July–Aug.; blue	Dry soil.
Sedum	1–2'	1'	Late summer; pink	
Shasta daisy (chrysanthemum maximum)	2–3'	1'	Early to mid summer; white	Full sun, rich soil. Needs winter protection.
Sidalcea	3'	1'	June–July; white, rose	
Sweet william (dianthus barbarus)	1–18"	9"	Early summer; white, red, salmon, pink	Full sun, moderately rich soil, can be grown from seed.
Trollius (globeflower)	2'	1'	May–July; orange, yellow	Prefer moist soil.
Verbena	1'	1'	June–Sept.; red, purple	
Veronica	to 2½'	6–9"	July–Sept.; blue	Cut off stalks after blooming.
Viola	6–8"	9"	June–Aug.; all colors	Good for borders. Will naturalize.

TABLE 3. TENDER BULBS, CORMS, AND TUBERS FOR GROWING IN THE NORTH

Name	Height	Space Between	Depth to Plant	Bloom	Remarks on Culture
Acidanthera (Murieleae) . .	12–20"	6–9"	4–6"	Late summer–fall; cream, white with purple	Store at 55–65°. Requires long growing season, plant early.
Anemone (Coronaria) . . .	6"–1'	7–8"	3"	May–June; blue, rose, scarlet, white	Sandy, loam-enriched soil, sunny location. Plant as early as possible, since cool growing is preferred.
Begonia (tuberous)	9–24"	10–12" if not set out in pots	1–2" when rooted	Summer; pink, red	Rich, moist. Start indoors, hollow side up. Pinch side buds.
Caladium	9–24"	Set out in pots	2"		Grown for red, pink, green, white foliage. Rich, moist loose soil, semishade, sheltered location. Water foliage well. Store dry, 60–65°.
Calla	9–36"	6–12"	2"	Summer; white	Rich, coarse loamy soil. Sunny. Plant with top 1" above ground.
Canna	12–18"	18–24"		Summer; pink, yellow, red	Deep fertile moist soil. Sunny. Store dry, 40–50°.
Cooperia	4–9"	2"	1–2"	Summer; pink, white	Sandy soil. Full sun. Store 35–45°.
Crinum	1–3'	18–36"	6"	Summer; white, pink, purple	Rich, humusy soil. Sun or light shade.
Dahlia	2–6'	2–3'	2–3"	Fall; all colors except blue	Plant tuberous root horizontally. Pinch at 12". Stake tall ones.

TABLE 3—Concluded

Name	Height	Space Between	Depth to Plant	Bloom	Remarks on Culture
Galtonia (summer hyacinth)	2–4'	18–24"	5–6"	Summer; white	Easily grown; treat like gladiolus.
Gladiolus	1–5'	6–9"	4–6"	Late summer; all colors	Avoid planting in rows. Full sun. Subject to thrips. Store 40–50°.
Gloriosa	36–120"		2"	Summer, fall; red, yellow, orange	Light soil. Water freely. Sun with light shade. Twines.
Gloxinia	6–12"		1"	Summer; white, purple	Pots or window boxes.
Ismene	24"	8–12"		Summer; white	Rich deep soil. Store dry, 60°.
Montbretia	24–48"	2–3"		Summer, fall; gold, yellow with red	Fertile sandy soil.
Oxalis	6–12"	2–4"	2–3"	Spring, summer; pink, red, purple	Sandy. Sun or light shade.
Ranunculus	3–18"	3–4"		Yellow, white, scarlet	Woodsy moist soil, part shade. Plant as early as possible like anemone coronaria.
Tigridia	12–24"	5–6"	3"	Summer; red, yellow, white	Fertile. Full sun.
Tuberose	30–48"	6"	3" deep top half out	White	Buy new ones every year. Sheltered sunny. Requires long growing season. Plant early but not while frost is still evident.
Zephyranthes	2–8"	2–3"	2"	Spring, summer; white, yellow, purple	Light loam.

TABLE 4. HARDY BULBS, CORMS, AND TUBERS FOR GROWING IN THE NORTH

Name	Height	Space Between	Depth to Plant	Bloom	Remarks on Culture
Amaryllis (lycoris)	2–3′	10″	5″	Late summer–fall; lavender-pink	Sun or light shade, deep sandy soil.
Colchicum	4–12″	6–9″	2–3″	Late summer; white, lavender, pink	No foliage at time of bloom. Plant in fall. Deep sandy soil. Protect in winter.
Chiondoxa (glory-of-the-snow)	3–6″	2–3″	2″	Spring; blue, pink, white	Plant in fall. Fertile sunny soil. Self-sows.
Crocus	2–4″	3–4″	2–3″	Spring; white, lavender	Plant in early fall. Sun or light shade. Light, rich soil. Will naturalize.
Daffodil (narcissus, jonquil) .	4–18″	2–9″	3–6″	Spring; yellow	Plant early in fall. Moist, sheltered spot, sun or light shade. Protect in winter.
Fritillaria	8–16″	4–8″	3–5″	Spring; purple, white, red, yellow, orange	Deep rich sandy soil. Moisture essential. Difficult to grow.
Grape hyacinth	6–12″	2–3″	2″	Spring; dark blue	Plant in fall in fertile, sunny soil.
Hyacinth	6–8″	2–9″	5–6″	Spring; white	Plant in fall in full sun.

TABLE 4 – Concluded

Name	Height	Space Between	Depth to Plant	Bloom	Remarks on Culture
Iris					
Bearded	3–5'		½" deeper than rhizome is thick	Spring; all colors	Plant before frost, mulch. Moist soil with much organic matter. Water Japanese daily. Keep all kinds dry during dormant period. Use DDT for iris borer.
Dwarf bearded .	4–12"				
Siberian . . .	to 48"				
Lily of the valley	6–8"	6–8"		Spring; white, pink	Deep humusy soil. Plant spring or early fall.
Madonna lily	3–4'	1'	1½"	June; white	Plant very early in autumn after dusting with fungicide.
Lily speciosum (show lily) .	3–4'	3'	10"	Aug.–Sept.; white, rose, crimson, pink	Bloom looks like orchid.
Scilla (squill)	6–12"	3–5"	4–5"	Spring; white	Moist, deep soil. Dappled shade. For rock gardens and naturalizing.
Snowdrop	5–9"	2–4"	2–3"	Early spring; white	Plant in fall; will naturalize.
Tiger lily	50–60"	2–3'	10"	August; orange	Very easy to grow.
Tulip	6–26"	4–5"	6–10"	Spring; many colors	Plant in November, full sun or part shade. Subject to tulip fire.
Turk's cap lily	48"	2–3'	10"	July; yellow	Best as cut flower, stem soft.

Trees, Shrubs, and Vines for Growing in the North

TREES

Basswood (American linden), 60'.

Birch, cutleaf European, 30'. White bark, requires moist site, subject to birch borer.

Birch, paper, 30'. White bark, requires moist site, subject to bronze birch borer.

Black walnut, 50'. Large, wide, handsome tree.

Boxelder, 50'. Irregular form, brittle branches. Male tree has no bugs.

Butternut, 50'. Moist, sheltered site. Edible nut.

Cottonwood, 80'. Not for small grounds. To avoid "cotton," plant only male trees.

Elm, Siberian, 40'. Not often used on lawns. Medium sized.

Gingko, 30'. Narrow, upright, fern-like leaves. Plant only males.

Green ash, 50'. Drought resistant.

Hackberry, 50'. Subject to witch's broom, insect galls.

Hickory, 60'. Shaggy bark. Hardy only in southern Minnesota.

Honeylocust, 50'. Open, spreading. White flowers in June. Good for lawns.

Horsechestnut, 30'. White flowers in early June. Not completely hardy.

Kentucky coffeetree, 50'. Open, spreading, needs moist site.

Littleleaf linden, 50'.

Locust, black, 30'. White, fragrant flowers in early June. Subject to borer, and therefore short-lived.

Magnolia (cucumber tree magnolia), 50'. Upright, round top. Greenish-yellow flowers in late May and June.

Maple, Crimson King.

Maple, cutleaf.

Maple, Norway, 50'. Makes dense shade.

Maple, red, 50'. Narrow, upright, needs moist site. Red flowers, red leaves and fruits in fall.

Maple, silver, 75'. Large, brittle, not recommended for lawns.

Oak, 40–60'. Hard to transplant.

Ohio Buckeye, 30'. Small round tree, yellow flowers. Very hardy, insect-free. Foliage yellow in fall. Transplant only when very small.

Poplar, Bolleana, 40'. Upright growth, silvery leaves. Short-lived in dry sites because of fungus growth in trunk.

Poplar, Lombardy, 50'. Tall, upright. Dark colored bark. Subject to fungus trunk canker, winter injury.

Poplar, white, 50'. Suckering habit. Maple-shaped leaves.

Willow, golden, 40'. Yellow twigs.

Willow, Niobe weeping, 40'. Hardiest of weeping trees. Branches annoying in old trees.

Willow, white, 50'. Not for lawns.

SHRUBS

Almond, flowering, 3–5'. Low, compact. Pink blossoms, April and May. Reasonably hardy.

Althea, 12'. White, red, lavender, blue and pink blossoms, late August, September. Oval-shaped flowers, look like hollyhocks. Recommended only for trial in most sheltered areas, not dependably hardy.

Amur maple, 15'. Red fruit in early fall. Showy red autumn leaves.

Barberry, Japanese, 4'. Low, compact. Yellow blossoms, late May. Buy rust-free varieties. Elongated red berries fall and winter. Redleaf variety has red foliage all season.

Beautybush, 5'. Upright, spreading. Pinkish white blossoms, May. Purple-black fruit. Red foliage in fall. Prefers wet soil. Slow to attain flowering state.

Boxwood, Korean, 2'. Compact. Will tolerate shade. Needs winter protection. For the specialist.

Buddleia (butterfly bush), 5'. Spreading. Purple, white, pink, red blossoms, August, September. Cut back annually; winter-kills to ground. Will blossom first year from seed if started early.

Bush cinquefoil, 3'. Compact. Yellow and white blossoms, June–frost. Full sun, needs lime in soil.

Chokeberry, black, 3'. Low, branching. White blossoms, May. Round purple fruits, red foliage in fall.

Chokeberry, red, 5'. Small, spreading. Pink blossoms, late May. Red fruit and foliage in fall.

Chokecherry, 15–20'. Large. White blossoms, May. Edible dark purple fruits good for jelly. Subject to X virus.

Coralberry, Chenault, 2'. Small compact. Pink blossoms, mid-July. Red berries; kills back in winter.

Coralberry (Indian currant), 4'. Branching. Purple-red fruits, inferior to Chenault.

Cotoneaster, 6–8'. Compact. White blossoms, late May. Peking hardy here. Protect for winter. Blue-black fruit.

Crab, Bechtel, 20'. Double pink blossoms, late May. No fruit.

Crab, Eley, 20'. Reddish-pink blossoms, mid-May. Purplish foliage, fruit-bearing.

Crab, flowering, 15–20'. Branching. Pink, white blossoms, May–June. Colorful apples in fall.

Crab, prairie, 25'. Blossoms late May, June. Grows in thickets in moist spots, fruit in fall.

Currant, 4–6'. Low, dense. Scarlet fruit in fall. Use male plant for rust resistance.

Daphne, 1'. Prostrate. Pink, white blossoms, April–May. Evergreen. Needs winter protection. Moist, well-drained limed soil.

Deutzia, 3–4'. Upright. White blossoms, May–June.

Dogwood, 20–25'. White, pink, yellow blossoms, May–June. Scarlet foliage and berries in fall.

NOTES

Elder, American, 8'. Coarse. White blossoms, late June. Dark blue fruits, good for pies, wine, birds.

Golden, 8'. Coarse. Yellow foliage. Blue fruit. Needs full sun.

Euonymus (burning bush), 3–8'. Compact, well formed. Red foliage in fall, fruits in fall for birds.

Forsythia, 4–5'. Open. Yellow blossoms, April. Border shrub. Needs winter protection except Korean Forsythia ovata.

Garden snowberry, 5'. Compact. Pink blossoms, mid-June. Scarlet fruit in fall.

Hawthorn, 10–20'. Compact. White, pink blossoms, May–June. Scarlet fruit in fall.

Highbush cranberry, American, 8'. Branching. White blossoms. Tolerates wet soil. Edible (European variety not edible).

Honeysuckle, 6–10'. Large, spreading. White, yellow, coral blossoms, May–June. Red fruits, June–fall.

Hoptree, 12'. Large. Picturesque winged fruits.

Hydrangea, 4–6'. Compact. White, pink blossoms, July–August. Prune in spring. Used in sheltered, moist spot.

Ilex (holly) verticillata, 8'. Need plants of both sexes to get berries. Bright red berries used for Christmas decorations. Plant in moist, sheltered spot, acid soil.

Indigobush, 6'. Dark purple blossoms, May. Grows in wet places.

Juneberry (Allegheny serviceberry), 15'. White blossoms, early May. Excellent purple fruit for pies, etc., in July.

Leadplant, 3'. Deep purple blossoms, June–July. Silvery foliage. Dry soil.

Lilac, Amur, 10'. Large, spreading. White blossoms, late June.

Lilac, Chinese, 8'. Large, compact. Purple, white, red-purple blossoms, late May. Does not sucker.

Lilac, common, 15'. Large, coarse. White, purple blossoms, late May. Use only on large grounds.

Lilac, French, 5–7'. Single and double flowers.

Lilac, Japanese tree, 20'. White blossoms, mid-June.

Lilac, late, 10'. Large, coarse. Rose, white blossoms.

Lilac, Persian, 5'. Pale purple blossoms, late May.

Macrantha, 4'. Blossoms April, May.

Mayday tree, 25'. White blossoms, May 1. Looks like chokecherry.

Mockorange, 15–20'. White blossoms, May–June. Varieties: Virginalis, Snowflake, Frosty Morn.

Mountain ash, American, 20'. White blossoms, June–July. Grow in moist site, protect from sun scald. Red autumn fruit much loved by robins.

Mulberry, red, 20'. Resists adverse city conditions. Fruit like blackberry in June–July.

Mulberry, Russian, 20'. Fruit white, poor.

Ninebark, 4–6'. Large, coarse. Pink, white blossoms.

Peashrub, Pygmy, 4'. Small, spreading. Yellow blossoms, May–June.

Peashrub, Russian, 6'. Upright, spreading. Pink blossoms, June.

Plum, flowering, 8'. Large, coarse. Pink blossoms, early May. Suckers.

Quince, flowering, 5–6'. White, pink, red blossoms, May–June.

Redbud, eastern, 15'. Heart-shaped leaves.

Russian olive, 30'. Yellow blossoms, mid-June. Drought resistant.

Salix (blueleaf Arctic), 4'. Grows north of Arctic Circle. Blue-green leaves.

Saskatoon, 6'. White blossoms, late May–June. Delicious black fruits in fall.

Serviceberry, 15'. White blossoms, early May. Edible black fruits in July.

Smoketree, 8'. Not fully hardy. Yellow-orange foliage in fall.
Snowball, 8'. White blossoms.
Spirea, Anthony Waterer, 2'. Low, compact. Semi-hardy.
Spirea, Billiard, 4'. Upright, open. Pink blossoms, June–July.
Spirea, Blue, 3'. Blue blossoms, July–August. Winter-kills to ground.
Spirea, Bridalwreath, 5'. Dense. Double white flowers like tiny roses, late May.
    Not hardy in Minnesota. Foliage turns red-orange in fall.
Spirea, Froebel, 2'. Low, compact. Similar to Anthony Waterer, but more
    vigorous.
Spirea, Garland, 5'. Upright, spread. White blossoms, early May.
Spirea, Japanese, 2'. Low, compact. White blossoms, July.
Spirea, Vanhouttei, 6'. Dense. White blossoms, late May. Hardy.
Sumac, cutleaf staghorn, 12'. Beautiful orange autumn foliage.
Sumac, fragrant, 3'. Spreading. Yellow blossoms, May.
Tamarisk, fivestamen, 10'. Tall, open. Pink blossoms, mid-July.
Tamarisk, Odessa, 6'. Pink blossoms, mid-July.
Weigela, 5'. White, pink, red blossoms, early June. Kills back in winter.
Willow, purpleosier, 4–8'. Upright. Use purple twigs for basketweaving.

VINES

Bittersweet, 20'. Yellow fruit, scarlet interior.
Boston ivy, 30'. Foliage red in fall. Kills back in winter.
Chinese wolfberry, 8'. Creeping, purple-violet flowers, July–September, red
    berries in fall. Ground cover in poor soils.
Cinnamon vine, 10–20'. White flowers, heart-shaped leaves. Needs sheltered
    location.
Clematis jackmanni, 20'. Purple flowers, hardy.
Clematis paniculata, 30'. White flowers, September, vigorous but not too
    hardy.
Clematis tangutica, 20'. Yellow flowers.
Clematis virginiana, 18'. White flowers, July. Purple foliage in autumn. Hardy.
Cobaea scandens (cup and saucer vine). Blue and white bell-shaped flowers,
    annual.
Dutchman's pipe, 30'. Green pipe-shaped flowers, heart-shaped leaves.
English ivy. Sheltered spot, sun or shade. Not hardy.
Honeysuckle, 20'. Flowers orange to scarlet, mid-June to August, red berries
    in fall. Subject to aphids.
Linaria (Kenilworth ivy). Annual, for rockeries.
Moonflower, 20–30'. Pink, white flowers, scented at night. Start early in sunny,
    sheltered location.
Moonseed, 12'. Twining, ivy-like. Black, grape-like fruit.
Morning-glory, 10–20'. White, crimson, pink, blue flowers. Heat-loving, resist-
    ant to transplanting.
Trumpet creeper (bignonia), 30'. Orange to scarlet flowers. Full sun, sheltered
    location.
Wintercreeper (euonymus radicans). Sun or shade, sheltered location.
Wistaria, 12'. Violet flowers, late May and June. Not very hardy.
Woodbine (Virginia creeper), 50'. Red foliage in fall.

Recommended Varieties

AFRICAN VIOLET

Azure Beauty
Innocence
Pink Delight
Navy Bouquet
Alma Wright
Double White Madonna
Fleur Petite
Star Sapphire
Kay's Quilted
Ruffled Queen
Pink Ideal
Chaska
Pot O' Gold
Blushing

ALYSSUM

Little Gem: white
Royal Carpet: deep
    violet, long-blooming
White Carpet of Snow:
    dwarf
Violet Queen

ASTER

Powder Puff: early
    flowering
Burpeeana
Rose Marie: rose-colored

BACHELOR'S BUTTON

Blue Boy

CALIFORNIA POPPY

Geisha

CELOSIA (COCKS-COMB)

Empress: deep red
Golden Fleece: pure gold

Pampas Plume: 3' tall,
    easily grown
Toreador: dwarf, red,
    often 12" across

CHRYSANTHEMUM

Alert: purple
Avalanche: white
Adorable: lavender pink
Autumn Beauty: bronze
Apache: red
Bronze Giant
Chippewa: purple
Chiquita: yellow,
    button pompon
Crowning Glory: bronze
Dr. L. E. Longley:
    lavender
Dark Red Gold
Delight: yellow
Evelyn Devaney:
    lavender
Early Crimson
Early Gold: yellow
Early Kathleen: bronze
Football Bronze
George Luxton: bronze
Golden Mound: cushion
    type
Lee Powell: yellow
Lemon Drop: button
    pompon
Loveliness: spoon type
Lipstick: cushion type
Myrtle Walgreen: purple
Muriel Rice: yellow
Major: cushion type
Orchid Helen
Old Lavender
Paper White

Purple Waters
Prairie Sunset: lavender
Purple: spoon type
Royal Robe: purple
Ruthann Lehman
Redglow
Remembrance
Reflection
Rouge
Snowspoon
Talisman: apricot button
    pompon
Violet
White Cloud

COLUMBINE

McKana's Giant hybrid
Clematiflora:
    clematis-like flowers

COSMOS

Fiesta: 30" high, scarlet,
    gold
Orange Flare
Orange Ruffles

DAHLIA (MINIATURE)

Cardinal
Little Marvel: red
Little Edith: yellow
Ida: white dwarf
Ike: red dwarf

DAHLIA (PERENNIAL)

Avalon: yellow
Deep Velvet: dark red
Royal Pennant: purple
White Wonder: white

DAYLILY

Evelyn Claar
High Noon
Painted Lady
Colonial Dame
Pink Prelude
Revolute
Prima Donna
Cibola
Pink Damask
Potentate
Dauntless
Ruffled Pinafore
Salmon Sheen
Pink Dream
Georgia
Garnet Rose
Naranja
Caballero
Orange Beauty
Midwest Majesty
Crimson Glory
Lady Bountiful
Athlone
Pink Charm
Colonel Joe
North Star

DELPHINIUM

Chinensis Blue Mirrow
Imperial
Pacific Giants

FORGET-ME-NOT

Cynoglossum Bluebird:
blooms all summer

GAILLARDIA

Tetra Fiesta: red with
yellow
Burgundy: wine-red

GLADIOLUS

Appleblossom:
mid-season bloomer
Eisenhower: salmon
Red Charm
Royal Stewart
Vagabond Prince:
brown-red

IRIS

Aladdin's Wish: plicata
Aldura: plicata
Amandine: white
Amigo: violet
Black Forest: violet
Cherie: pink
Chivalry: blue
Confetti: plicata
Danube Wave: blue
Firecracker: plicata
Garden Flame: violet
Golden Eagle: yellow
Golden Treasure: white
Great Lakes: blue
Gudrun: white
Harriet Thoreau: pink
Helen McGregor: blue
Lady Mohr: yellow
Master Charles: violet
Mattie Gates: yellow
Mulberry Rose: violet
New Snow: white
Ola Kala: yellow
Pierre Menard: blue
Pink Cameo
Pink Sensation
Pinnacle: white
Ranger: violet
Raspberry Ribbon:
plicata
Red Valor: violet
Rocket: yellow
Tiffany: plicata
Winter Carnival: white
Zantha: yellow

MARIGOLD

Glitters: early bright
yellow
Man in the Moon: 3' tall,
3", pale yellow
Butterball
Rusty Red: 18" high,
yellow-edged
Mammoth
Tangerine: 15" tall,
2" wide
Fluffy Ruffles

MORNING-GLORY

Blue Star: earlier than
Heavenly Blue
Scarlett O'Hara:
climbing, burgundy red
Candy Pink: rose-pink

NASTURTIUM

Golden Gleam
Golden Glow: bush
variety

PEONY

Karl Rosenfield: red,
inexpensive
Felix Crousse: red, older
variety
Monsieur M. Cahuzac:
red
Cherry Hill: red
Mary Brand: red
Lora Dexheimer: red
Departing Sun
Mikado
Sarah Bernhardt: pink
Therese
Walter Faxon
Lady Alexander Duff
Albert Crousse: pink
Monsieur Jules Elie
Baroness Schroder
Le Cygne
Alice Harding: white
Primivere: white
Solange: white
Duchesse de Nemours
Myrtle Gentry: pink
Katharine Havenmeyer:
pink
Edwin C. Shaw: pink
Lillian Gumm: pink
Ama-no-sode: pink

PETUNIA

Ballerina: dwarf, salmon
pink, large, ruffled
floriferous
Comanche: F_1 Hybrid,
multiflora, red
Popcorn: white, dwarf,
ruffled

NOTES

Radiance: pink
Lipstick
Crusader: white
Fire Chief: dwarf, 12″ tall, scarlet
Pink Frills
Prima Donna: rose-pink, ruffled, fringed grandiflora, AAS 1955, F_1 Hybrid
Fire Dance: salmon-scarlet grandiflora, F_1 Hybrid
Paleface: multiflora, F_1 Hybrid
Black Prince: mahogany-red balcony

PHLOX (ANNUAL)

Globe: red, white, pink, low mounds of bloom

PHLOX (PERENNIAL)

Sir John Falstaff: salmon pink
Cinderella: rose pink
Violet Beauty: purple
Mary Louise: white
World Peace: white
Daily Sketch: pink
Leo Schlageter: scarlet
Harvest Fire: crimson
Rokoko: lavender

POPPY

Sweet Brier Shirley: double

ROSE, CLIMBING

Blaze
Brownell #122: light yellow
Brownell #126: dark pink
Gladiator: carmine
White Dawn: white double

ROSE, FLORIBUNDA

Baby Blaze
Circus: small, low, 1956 AARS winner; changing colors, yellow-red
Fashion: pink, AARS, 1952
Floradora: red
Jiminy Cricket: vermilion changing to coral, AARS, 1955
Lilibet: red changing to pink, AARS, 1954
Ma Perkins: coral pink, AARS, 1935
Pinocchio: salmon pink
Red Pinocchio: carmine
Spartan: orange-scarlet
Vogue: cherry-coral
World's Fair: black-scarlet

ROSE, GRANDIFLORA

Carrousel: dark red
Queen Elizabeth: pink, first grandiflora

ROSE, HYBRID TEA

Chrysler Imperial: stiff red, 1953 AARS winner
Crimson Glory: dark red
Eclipse: deep gold
Forty-niner: red and yellow
Fred Howard: buff-yellow, orange pink, AARS, 1952
Helen Traubel: porcelain pink
Katherine T. Marshall: medium pink
Love Song: bicolor salmon-pink and yellow
Lowell Thomas: yellow, AARS, 1944
Mirandy: dark red, AARS, 1945
Mission Bells: salmon-pink, AARS, 1950
Mojave: orange blend, AARS, 1954
New Yorker: scarlet
Nocturne: dark red, AARS, 1946
Peace: golden
President Hoover: cream, yellow, pink
Rubaiyat: light red, AARS, 1947
Show Girl: pink, AARS, 1950
Sutter's Gold: yellow-orange-red, AARS, 1950
Tallyho: pink, AARS, 1950
The Doctor: pink, AARS, 1950
Tiffany: pink, yellow at base, AARS, 1955
White Swan

SNAPDRAGON

Alaska: white
Giant tetra
Velvet Giant: red

STOCK

Trysomic

SWEET PEA

Cuthbertson: heat-tolerant

TITHONIA

Torch: red

TULIP

Triumph
Mrs. Agnes Kennedy Ridder
Red Emperor

WEIGELA

Eva Rathke
Bristol Ruby
Vaniceki

ZINNIA

Giant Fantasy
Peppermint stick: striped dwarf
Persian Carpet: small double, orange, purple, gold, brown
Blaze: flame-color giant
Eskimo
Sunny Boy
Floradale: scarlet
Pure Gold

302

Index

✿ INDEX ✿

305

INDEX

watering, 153; digging up, 220, 223; mentioned, 34, 48–49, 211
Begonia Society, American, 190
Begonian, The, 190
Bergamot. *See* Beebalm
Bethlehem star, as houseplant, 14
Biennials, 33
Birch tree, 125; weeping, 47
Bird baths, 126–27, 151
Bird house, 97–98
Birds, care and feeding, 3, 4, 94, 142, 150, 250, 258, 270
Bittersweet, 46, 233
Black spot, on roses, 136
Black-eyed Susan, 196
Bleeding heart, 32, 36, 102, 106, 113, 185, 195, 212. *See also* Perennials
Blight: on peonies, 184, 236; on asters, 186
Bloodroot, 32, 100, 101
Blue lace flower, 117
Blue squill. *See* Scilla
Bluebell, 101, 171
Boltonia, 189, 197. *See also* Perennials
Books, garden, 191, 271–73
Bordeaux mixture, for perennials, 82, 102, 179
Botrytis blight, on peonies, 184, 236
Boxelder tree, 125
Bridalwreath: aphids on, 130; pruning, 131, 200–1; mentioned, 128
Bromfield, Louis, 191
Brown, Worth, 272
Buckthorn, 143–44
Buckwheat hulls, as mulch, 198
Bulb Magic in Your Window, 251
Bulbs: indoor planting, 12, 247–51; storage of, 25, 26–27, 55, 60, 275–76; summer-blooming described, 34; removing protection from, 82; spring-blooming described, 202–4; planting spring-blooming, 213–20; digging up, 236
Burning bush, Grandma's, 33. *See also* Dictamnus

Cactus, 11–12, 262; Christmas, 12, 211, 265, 267
Caladium, as house plant, 12, 62
Calceolaria, 269
Calendula, as dog repellent, 187

Calla lily: indoor planting, 12; forcing, 251
Calliopsis, 117. *See also* Annuals
Campanula (Canterbury bells), 33, 36, 152, 171, 184–96 *passim. See also* Annuals
Canadian peatmoss, 154
Canker worm, 69, 232
Canna lily: storing tubers, 26–27; described, 34; digging up, 220–22; mentioned, 99
Canterbury bells. *See* Campanula
Caragaras, pruning, 200–1
Cardinal flower, 101, 170, 184
Carnation, 189. *See also* Annuals
Catalogs, seed, 28–30
Catalpa tree, 85
Cedar shingles, as insect repellent, 181
Celosia, 117
Charcoal: for house plants, 9–23 *passim*; as insect repellent, 60; in window box, 61
Cherry, Jerusalem, 269
Chickweed, 67, 129, 143
Chimera apple tree, 205
Chinese evergreen, 260
Chionodoxa, depth of planting, 219
Chokecherry, as hedge, 46
Christmas cactus, 12, 211, 265, 267
Christmas tree, 3–4, 272, 273–74
Chrysanthemum: Shasta daisy, 35, 170–71, 189, 197; varieties of, 111–13; summer care of, 171–72; fertilizing, 187–88; forcing, 192; spraying, 200; potting, 213; fall care of, 236; winter protection of, 241–42; mentioned, 34, 36, 196. *See also* Perennials
Cineraria, 269
Cistena sand cherry, pruning, 201
Clark, William H., 272
Clarkia, 117. *See also* Annuals
Clematis: planting, 91–93; winter protection for, 242–43; mentioned, 46
Cleome (spider plant), 39, 117. *See also* Annuals
Climbing Roses, 138
Clove apple. *See* Pomander
Cold frame: building, 51–54; ventilating, 126; chrysanthemums in, 214
Coleus, 195, 261. *See also* Annuals
Columbine: described, 32, 36; wild flower garden, 101; growing from

306

INDEX

Elm tree: roots of, 42; Chinese hedging, 45–46; American, 47, 85, 125
Epsom salts, as fertilizer for azalea, 263
Euonymus, 45, 46
Everett, T. H., 251
Evergreens: hosing in winter, 27; watering, 80; pruning, 84; planting, 86–87, 208–9; red spider mite on, 161; making new spire branch on, 161–62; fall care of, 230–32; mentioned, 48. *See also* Shrubbery; Trees
Exhibiting: preparing entries, 147–49; length of stems, 149–50; preparing gladioli, 186–87

Ferns: as house plants, 8, 261–62; in garden, 36; in window box, 62
Fertilizing: house plants, 10; African violets, 20; window box, 62; lawn, 64, 95, 224, 237–38; sweet peas, 70–71; fruit trees, 79; shrubbery, 84; clematis, 92; perennials, 103, 129; roses, 105, 193; before vacation, 157–58; trees, 160–61; irises, 165; chrysanthemums, 171, 187–88; peonies, 213, 238; in fall, 236–37
Ficus, 260
Fig plant, 260
Fireproofing Christmas tree, 275
Flower Show Guide, The, 150
Flowerpots, 16, 21
Fluorescent light, for growing plants. *See* Artificial light
"Fooling" chrysanthemums, 192
Forcing: spring-blooming bulbs, 60, 247–51; chrysanthemums, 192
Forget-me-not, 102, 170, 213. *See also* Perennials
Forsythia (golden bell), 43, 59
Four o'clock, 117, 236. *See also* Annuals
Foxglove, 33, 189. *See also* Annuals
Fragrance, garden, 204–5
Free, Montague, 272
Fritillaria, 216
Frost protection, 103–4, 209–12. *See also* Protection, winter
Fuchsia, 266–67
Fungicides. *See* Dusting; Spraying
Funkia as ground cover, 47

Gaillardia: described, 35; growing from

seed, 188; dividing, 197; mentioned, 117, 170, 189
Garden clubs, 147
Garden Lover, The, 191
Gardener's Troubleshooter, The, 191
Gardening for Color, 272
Gas plant. *See* Dictamnus
Gentian, 101
Geranium: sunlight for, 8; cuttings from, 49–50, 200; Grandma's, 62; taking indoors, 211–12, 236; mentioned, 131–32, 195, 267–68. *See also* Annuals
Ginger, wild, as ground cover, 47
Ginger root, 101
Gingko tree, 146
Gladiolus: storing corms, 26–27, 275–76; planting, 115–16, 151; thrips on, 116, 130; for shows, 186–87; digging up, 211, 220–23; mentioned, 34, 275–76
Glory-of-the-snow, 214–16
Gloxinia: as house plant, 16–17, 19, 60; starting tubers, 17–18; from seed, 18; from cuttings, 18–19; mentioned, 132, 194
Gloxinias and How to Grow Them, 17, 272
Godetia, 174. *See also* Annuals
Golden bell (forsythia), 43, 59
Golden marguerite (anthemis), 35, 189. *See also* Perennials
Goldenrod, 196
Grandma: on birds, 4, 94, 98, 126, 142, 150, 250, 258, 270; on trees and shrubbery, 7, 26, 46, 68, 101, 146, 184, 205; on insect pests, 8, 56, 76, 135, 168, 173, 181, 194, 222; on house plants, 11, 14, 16, 22, 52, 59, 62, 161, 233, 246, 261, 267; on fertilizers, 19, 40, 43, 202, 225, 226, 238; on flower garden care, 30, 33, 38, 49, 86, 89, 96, 104, 109, 117, 139, 149, 154, 157, 158, 167, 178, 190, 192, 198, 206, 219, 241, 243; on lawn care, 65, 125, 145, 187, 201, 249; manners, remedies, and recipes, 114, 120, 123, 130, 138–40, 164, 170, 209, 210, 211, 212, 216, 231, 237, 253, 264, 272, 274, 276
Grape hyacinth, 174
Grapevine, 5, 99

308

INDEX

INDEX